OTHER BOOKS BY DAVID WISE

NONFICTION

The U-2 Affair (with Thomas B. Ross)

The Invisible Government (with Thomas B. Ross)

The Espionage Establishment (with Thomas B. Ross)

The Politics of Lying

The American Police State

The Spy Who Got Away

Molehunt

Nightmover

FICTION

Spectrum

The Children's Game

The Samarkand Dimension

CASSIDY'S RUN

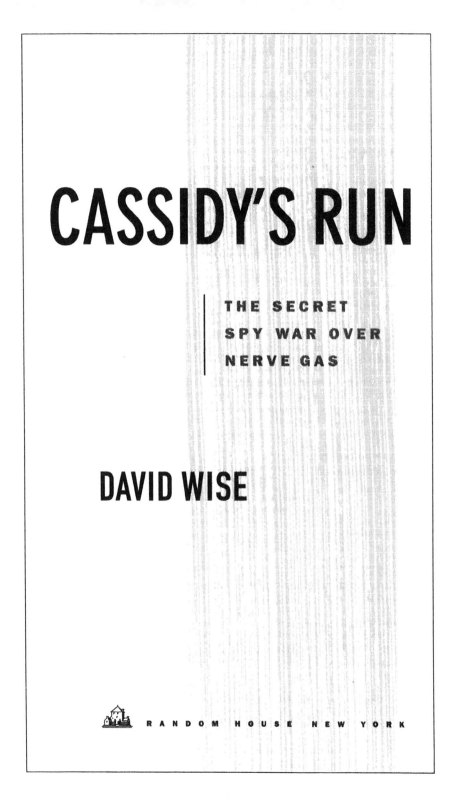

CASSIDY'S RUN

THE SECRET
SPY WAR OVER
NERVE GAS

DAVID WISE

RANDOM HOUSE NEW YORK

ISBN 0-812-99263-6
Library of Congress Cataloging-in-Publication Data

Wise, David.
    Cassidy's run: the secret spy war over nerve gas / David
    Wise.
        p.   cm.
    Includes index.

    1. Espionage, Soviet—United States—History.
    2. Cassidy, Joseph Edward. 3. Chemical weapons—United
    States. 4. Biological weapons—United States.
    5. Intelligence service—United States. 6. United States.
    Federal Bureau of Investigation. I. Title.
    E839.8.W55   2000   327.1247'073—
    dc21   99-15802

Random House website address: www.atrandom.com

Printed in the United States of America

TO ROBERT D. LOOMIS

CONTENTS

CASSIDY'S RUN

"LIKE A POLE THROUGH MY GUT"

The Cessna 172 seaplane had run into a sudden, dangerous summer storm. Flying low above the lake country in northern Minnesota, the light craft, with the pilot and one passenger aboard, was being buffeted by strong winds and torrential rain.

The pilot called the tower in Hibbing. He said he had to make an emergency landing. In the brief, terse conversation, he indicated he would try to set the plane down in Sturgeon Lake, northwest of Chisholm. But at the last moment, tossed about in the howling wind and rain, the pilot apparently changed his mind and attempted to land in Dewey Lake, which was much smaller but nearer to his position. The Cessna approached the north end of the lake, close to the shoreline. It was 5 P.M., Thursday, August 25, 1977.

Certain officials of the United States government were keenly aware of the flight and its secret purpose. The two men aboard were not vacationers looking for a fishing camp, nor were they businessmen returning home. The pilot, Trenwith S. Basford, and his younger passenger, Mark A. Kirkland, were both special agents of the FBI.

Only two weeks earlier, Mark Kirkland had turned thirty-three. His wife, Julie, decided to throw a surprise birthday party.

"There was Mexican food, I hired a flamenco dancer. A lot of friends came, Boy Scouts, people from the neighborhood, and a few from the office." The couple's two little boys had a great time at the party. "Kenneth was two months shy of being three, Christopher was one year old."

The Kirklands had a good life together. They lived in Minnetonka, near Minneapolis, in an old, three-story farmhouse they were renovating. A devout Mormon, Mark was the leader of the local Boy Scout troop. Five years before, he had realized his lifelong ambition of becoming an FBI agent.

Normally clean-cut and clean shaven, Kirkland was a striking figure at his birthday party in long, shaggy hair and a full beard. Julie knew why; her husband was undercover on a case. He had not told her a lot of details, but she knew he was trying to pass as a college student. "People at church, the Mormon church, questioned him about it," Julie said. "It wasn't common to have shaggy hair."

Julie was concerned about the case. It seemed to involve a lot more than college students. At twenty-five, with two small children, she worried that her husband's work might put him at risk. This was not an idle fear. Two years earlier, Mark's best friend and fellow FBI agent, Ron Williams, had been killed on the Pine Ridge Indian Reservation near the tiny village of Wounded Knee, South Dakota.[1] Mark and Ron had

---

[1] Williams and Jack Coler, another FBI agent, had both been killed in a June 1975 shootout at the Oglala Sioux reservation, the scene of a seventy-one-day siege in 1973 by supporters of the American Indian Movement (AIM). Dozens of AIM activists shot at the agents' car; one, Leonard Peltier, was convicted and sentenced to life. His conviction became a cause célèbre for Robert Redford and other supporters, including the Dalai Lama, who argued that Peltier deserved a new trial.

served in Army intelligence together, joined the bureau around the same time, and went through training together at the FBI academy in Quantico, Virginia. Both were assigned to Los Angeles and then to Minneapolis. "Mark was best man at Ron's wedding," Julie recalled. "And he was out at the Oglala Sioux reservation when Ron was killed."

Then there was all the flying Mark was doing. Lately, he had been up on several aerial surveillances with Tren Basford. Julie deduced it was connected to the same case.

When he left on another surveillance two weeks after the surprise flamenco party, she admonished him gently. "I knew he was going up in the plane. I said, 'Don't be a kamikaze, don't push the plane to the limit.' He had a pat answer. He kissed me on the forehead and said, 'You worry too much.' "

That was on Tuesday. Now it was two days later. Julie Kirkland remembered every detail of that day. "In the late afternoon I had gone with friends, John and Geri Christianson, to the Farmer's Market to buy peaches and tomatoes. We were going to make some baskets for shut-ins at church. At the market it was a beautiful late summer afternoon, with a few rain showers, then sunshine and very pleasant, but I got this sensation of freezing cold and a sense of panic. Through my head the words were echoing, *Go home.* The Christiansons could see the panic in my face. I said, 'I have to go home.' I got home, and the baby-sitter was there. And Kenny had been crying. I put Kenny on my knee and said, 'What's the matter?' And he said, 'Daddy's crying, Mom.'"

Tren Basford's wife, Letitia, was also uneasy. As a pilot's wife, she paid close attention to the weather, and she knew her husband was flying that day. Despite the sunshine, the wind had come up. Gray, fast-moving clouds occasionally darkened the sky. "I was concerned that day because it was a very strange day with strong and conflicting winds. I was at the State Fair outside Saint Paul, and I didn't like the weather." The wind seemed to keep changing directions, whipping across the open fairgrounds.

Still, she knew her husband was a good and careful pilot. "He had held his pilot's license for ten years and owned his own plane for seven. He was experienced with floatplanes. I would stay up at our lake place in Canada all summer and he would fly up weekends." In fact, he planned to fly there when the surveillance was over; Letitia was to drive up, take their boat in, and meet him at the cabin, on Jackfish Lake.

Tren Basford was a straight arrow. A tall, quiet man, he was looking forward to his retirement in four months after serving thirty-five years in the FBI, mostly during the era of J. Edgar Hoover. Born in Red Lodge, Montana, he had been raised in Minnesota; his father was a dentist, his mother an English teacher.

When he was only thirteen, while on his paper route, he saved a man's life. The *Minneapolis Evening Tribune* ran his picture, and the headline told it all: BOY SCOUT SAVES VICTIM OF GAS POISONING, SLIPS AWAY AFTER "GOOD TURN." The man, A. H. Warner, had been working on his car in his garage when he had been overcome by carbon monoxide. Young Tren heard Warner's wife cry for help, and he performed artificial respiration on the unconscious man for ten minutes before an ambulance arrived; then, quietly, he left.

He met his future wife at the University of Minnesota, where her father, August Charles Krey, was head of the history department. They dated for five years, then married in 1941, after Tren had graduated from the university's law school. He joined the FBI in 1942, working in Newark, Baltimore, and New York during World War II. He handled everything from espionage and sabotage to criminal work. In one of his first cases, Basford joined the search for the eight Nazi saboteurs who landed at Amagansett, on Long Island, and at Saint Augustine, Florida, by submarine during the war; all were captured, and six were executed. Basford was transferred to Minnesota in 1957, where he investigated bank robberies and other criminal cases.

Coming home was a happy assignment for Basford, who loved hunting, fishing, and flying. Every year when the walleye season opened on May 15—probably the biggest holiday of the year for Minnesota fishing enthusiasts—Basford was in the lake country. During hunting season, he brought back venison, wild duck, and pheasant.

Letitia, whom everyone called Tish, knew little about her husband's work. She did not know why he was flying that day. "I simply assumed he was working on an important case. It was none of my business. I go back to Hoover's day, when if you were asked what your husband's business is, you said, 'He works for the government.' During the war, I couldn't get a library card because I wouldn't tell them where he worked. Tren never told me very much about what he was doing."

In the days before Basford got his plane, he and Tish traveled by car and canoe "around the Gaspé and Cape Breton Island, all though Maine and the Maritimes, up to Yellowknife and across Canada to Alaska. We portaged into wild lakes and watched the northern lights. We always took the small roads and the unfrequented ones."

As the years went by, Tish Basford had more reason to admire the quiet, handsome man she had married. "He helped to rehabilitate some of the people he had arrested. We had ex-felons using the band saw in the basement and calling him when they had troubles. He was a kind, thoughtful, and compassionate man."

Julie Kirkland still had the odd, cold sensation when she returned from the Farmer's Market. She felt growing apprehension that something had happened to Mark. She cleaned the house, made dinner for the kids, gave them baths, and put them to bed around 8 P.M.

Then she made her first call to the bureau. Most often, on an aerial surveillance, the plane would put down for the night wherever the target stopped, and the agents would go to a hotel.

"Usually when they got into a hotel, they could patch me through," Julie said. "I called the bureau operator, and she was shaken. I asked, 'Can you patch me through?' She was very nervous and said, 'I don't believe they're back to their room yet. I'll have them call you.' I waited another hour and called again. The feeling of coldness returned. The operator again said they are not at the hotel. She said, 'I'll have to have someone call you.'

"I waited and called the bureau again. This time I was aggressive. I said, 'Give me an FBI agent *now.*' She blurted, 'I think someone's on their way to talk to you.'

"Sometime between eleven and midnight, there was a knock on the door. John Shimota, an agent and a dear friend, and Dave Flanders, the assistant agent in charge, were there.

"I believe it was John Shimota who told me. But I knew. When they were banging on the door, I said, 'I've got to answer that door.' I just couldn't bring myself to answer the door. Then I heard one of the agents talking about breaking a window. So I had to go to the door. When I opened it, I said, 'I know, you guys.' They looked kinda surprised. They asked me to sit down. I said I wanted to know what happened to Mark. They kept asking me to sit down.

"They said, 'There's been an accident. Honey, you've got to sit down.' I said, 'He's gone, isn't he?' And John said, 'Yes, he's gone.' And he held me in his arms.

"I'd been living with it for hours. I kept saying, 'This cannot be happening to me. This can't be true. What about my boys? They'll never know their father.' I was very upset. I didn't cry for about an hour. I felt like someone had rammed a pole through my gut. I can't explain the physical pain I felt."

The first call to the Saint Louis County sheriff's department had come in at 5:05 P.M. from Fred McLeod, who lived on the west side of Dewey Lake. He had heard something and believed a plane might have crashed in the lake. A moment later, a woman who lived at the lake called in with a similar report. Deputy Sheriff John Anderson and Nick Milkovich, the twenty-four-year-old township police chief, jumped in Anderson's squad car and headed north for the lake. On the way, the Hibbing police department radioed that an eyewitness had reported a plane upside down in the northeast side of the lake, with only its tail above water.

By 5:25 P.M., the officers were at the scene. The yellow and white Cessna, with the aircraft number N84260 clearly visible at the rear of the fuselage, was resting upside down in about twelve feet of water. In the laconic language of the sheriff department's report, there was "no visible sign of life."

The plane had crashed directly in front of the lakeside home of George Pajunen. According to the official report, "Pajunen stated he heard a plane flying low, then a loud noise and then silence." Several residents went out in small boats to try to rescue the plane's occupants, but there was nothing they could do. One eyewitness thought the plane had tried to land twice and on the third attempt had lost power and plunged into the lake. Other residents reported it had been raining hard and that there had been fog in the area when the Cessna crashed.[2] Deputy Anderson also noted the fog.

To Nick Milkovich, the most telling evidence that the plane had had engine trouble was that it had gone down so close to shore. Milkovich had flown a lot in floatplanes, and he knew that normally a pilot tried to land into the wind and to stay well clear of trees, which meant that the plane ordinarily touched down toward the center of a lake, not near the shore.

Milkovich also had reports from residents in Chisholm, to the south, who said the plane, its engine sputtering, had a few minutes earlier flown low over the town, as though it might try to land in Longyear Lake right in Chisholm.[3]

---

[2] Minnesota was experiencing freak weather conditions that week. The day after the fatal crash, tornadoes ripped through Crow Wing, Wadena, and Otter Tail counties in central Minnesota, injuring seventeen persons. Some of the worst damage occurred in Brainerd, about a hundred miles from the crash site.

[3] The exact cause of the crash may never be known. The National Transportation Safety Board, which investigates most aviation accidents, has no record of the crash. Betty Scott, an NTSB spokesperson, said that in 1977 the NTSB did not investigate crashes of planes flying on government business, although it sometimes does today. "Even though the plane was owned by an individual, if it was on official business, it would not be in our system."

More deputies arrived. The county medical examiner and divers were summoned. The plane's floats seemed to have exploded, and the fuselage was twisted, indicating that the plane had gone into the water nose down and flipped over. The pilot and his passenger had died on impact, still strapped in by their seat belts.

Tish Basford was sorting laundry when they came up the walk. John Otto, the special agent in charge in Minneapolis, and his wife, and Basford's partner, Frank Grady, and his wife, arrived around 10:30 P.M.[4]

"When I saw them," Mrs. Basford said, "I knew. I think every law-enforcement wife knows it might happen at some time. John Otto was unbelievable, I will never forget his great kindness.

"I do not blame the bureau, it was an act of nature. Tren never had to face the ravages of old age, disease, and futility. He died in his prime, being useful and doing what he most liked to do."

The FBI, the Minneapolis *Star* reported the next day, said that the two agents were "on routine investigations" at the time of the crash. The FBI spokesman in Minneapolis, Arthur Sullivan, professed not to know "where they were flying from or their destination." Sullivan seemed to go out of his way to assure reporters that Basford had "worked his entire career in what we call criminal matters, not security cases." The Minneapolis *Tribune* similarly reported that FBI officials said the agents "were on routine business at the time, helping Duluth authorities in a number of cases."[5] The St. Paul *Dispatch* said the FBI explained that the two men "had been in Duluth assisting agents there for several days." These stories and others did not indicate that anyone in the news media had questioned why, if the agents were working in

---

[4] Otto later rose to associate director of the FBI, then the number-two position in the bureau, and for nearly six months in 1987 he served as acting director after FBI chief William H. Webster left to head the CIA.
[5] FBI agents are rarely killed in the line of duty. The *Tribune* story noted that the last two agents to die on duty had also been stationed in Minneapolis—Ron Williams and Jack Coler, killed in 1975 at Wounded Knee.

Duluth, their plane had crashed some seventy miles northwest of that city.

The FBI's statements were a cover story. In fact, Kirkland and Basford at the time of their deaths had been conducting airborne surveillance of a University of Minnesota professor. The professor had been driving north, toward the Canadian border, with his wife and two children. Other FBI agents in cars had been trailing the target on the ground.

The FBI made a calculated decision to mislead the press and the public about the circumstances of the deaths of the two agents. For years, even the agents' wives and families were told nothing. Until now, the secret has been kept.

The bureau could not afford to divulge the truth, for the crash of the Cessna threatened to unravel the longest-running espionage case of its kind in the history of the cold war, an extraordinary drama that had begun two decades earlier.

The University of Minnesota professor was a Soviet spy, a trained agent of the GRU, the Glavnoye Razvedyvatelnoye Upravlenie, the Soviet military-intelligence agency.

The existence of the case was known only to the president of the United States, his national-security adviser, and a handful of federal officials.

At the highest levels of the United States government, it was code-named Operation SHOCKER.

2

THE DANGLE

On a warm night in August 1959, Commander Boris M. Polikarpov, who was listed as the assistant naval attaché at the Soviet embassy in Washington, left the YMCA on G Street, two blocks from the White House, after a game of volleyball.

The Y was only a few minutes' walk from the Soviet embassy on Sixteenth Street, a beaux-arts mansion built by the widow of George M. Pullman, the inventor who designed the railroad sleeping cars that bear his name.[1]

Polikarpov was a short, tough-looking Slav, with slicked-back straight hair and coarse features. His official position was a cover job. He

---

[1] Mrs. Pullman never lived in the house. She sold the ornate mansion in 1913 soon after it was completed; a few months later it was sold again, this time to the czarist government. It did not become an embassy until the United States recognized the Soviet Union in 1933.

was in reality a spy, an officer of the GRU. Muscular and physically fit, he had been selected for the YMCA volleyball team that traveled around the Washington area to play other clubs in competition. He had been posted to Washington more than a year earlier.

On this night, Commander Polikarpov noticed an American army sergeant, in uniform, sitting on the steps of the Y and enjoying the summer evening. He was one of the Thursday-night regulars. They had played together in pickup games for several months, sometimes on the same team, sometimes on opposing teams. They did not really know each other, however.

"Hi, have you had dinner yet?" the Russian asked.

The sergeant said he had not. He fell into step with his occasional teammate, and they walked together to a little Italian restaurant nearby.

A big, strapping man of thirty-nine, Sergeant Joseph Edward Cassidy, at six foot one, towered over Polikarpov. Born in Erie, Pennsylvania, Cassidy had spent five years in an orphanage, dropped out of high school, and gotten a job at the local steel plant. He had worked in the intense heat of the open-hearth furnace, turning scrap metal into molten steel. He entered the army in 1943, during World War II, and decided to stay after the war ended. At the moment, he was a first sergeant assigned to the army's nuclear power field office at Fort Belvoir, Virginia.

At the restaurant, although Polikarpov did not give his name, it was clear to Cassidy that his new friend was a foreigner. His English was imperfect, and he spoke with an accent. Over chicken cacciatore, the two men chatted about volleyball. The Russian asked how long Cassidy had been playing at the Y. Five months, the sergeant replied. There was more small talk, and they parted.

For Polikarpov, a trained intelligence officer, the familiar espionage dance had begun. The casual encounter, a friendly dinner, and the Russian, with luck, might gradually be able to develop the American sergeant into a paid source, a spy for Moscow. Polikarpov had already known how long Cassidy had been playing at the Y. He had watched him since he had first showed up in March and had noticed him in uniform before. Although Cassidy was only a noncommissioned officer, there was no telling what information he might have access to or might be able to obtain in the future. It was entirely possible that the big, amiable sergeant, if handled carefully, might be recruited as an agent in place—a mole inside the United States Army.

The thought was surely exciting to the GRU officer, for a good recruitment might bring a medal; it would certainly be a giant step toward a promotion. His superiors would be pleased.

Above all, this recruitment would be safe. Cassidy was no walk-in, a volunteer spy who had showed up unannounced at the embassy or the consulate, offering his services in return for money. The GRU was well aware that the United States military and the FBI often sent such would-be double agents. The Russians were always extremely wary of these bogus volunteers, suspecting, often rightly, that they were really working for American intelligence.

But here the shoe was on the other foot. It was Polikarpov who had spotted Cassidy as a possible developmental. The big sergeant seemed a simple man who enjoyed sports and a good meal. The GRU officer could hardly wait until next Thursday; he would invite the sergeant to dinner again.

The next morning, Cassidy drove alone to a fried-chicken restaurant on U.S. Route 1 and Kings Highway, a few miles north of Fort Belvoir. He met there with two agents of the FBI. He reported the approach by the volleyball player and their dinner together. Those were the words that, for many months, the FBI agents had been hoping they would hear.

Inside the intelligence division of the FBI, the news was electric. Polikarpov had made contact. WALLFLOWER was operational.[2]

The genial sergeant was, in the jargon of the spy world, a dangle. He had been carefully selected by the bureau and army intelligence and put in the way of Boris Polikarpov. Much like a metal lure flashed to a bluefish

---

[2] Cassidy would have preferred a more exciting code name, but he had no choice; WALL-FLOWER it was. Most FBI code names for individuals are chosen at random and have no special meaning.

in the surf or a delicately tied mayfly presented to a trout in a mountain stream, Joe Cassidy had been sent to play volleyball at the YMCA, where, from its surveillance, the FBI knew that Polikarpov played on Thursday evenings. Now, after five months, Polikarpov had taken the bait.

The following Thursday, Cassidy lounged on the steps outside the Y again. Years later, he remembered those first contacts with clarity. "I always made a point to get out front of the Y ahead of him," he said, "so he'd see me in uniform when he came out." On this second Thursday, Polikarpov greeted Cassidy and asked if he had a car.

Cassidy's blue Buick was parked nearby, and he offered his friend a ride. "We went in my car to a different restaurant," Cassidy recalled. Dinners with Polikarpov soon became a regular Thursday-night event. "A number of times we went to the Old English Raw Bar along the Potomac. He liked oysters on the half shell." During their second dinner together, Polikarpov introduced himself simply as "Mike." He did not reveal that he was a Russian or that he worked at the embassy. Cassidy did not press him.

In the course of their early conversations, Polikarpov asked Cassidy casually whether he was married, where he lived, how long he had been in the army, and where he was assigned. At the time, Cassidy and his wife lived in Alexandria, not far from his job at Fort Belvoir. Cassidy explained that he worked in the nuclear power area; his job was to help train operators for the army's nuclear power plants at Belvoir, Idaho Falls, and in Alaska.[3]

Occasionally, Cassidy asked a question, but "Mike" seldom answered. "When I would ask questions he would answer with a question."

Russians like to drink, and Cassidy felt he had to keep up. "Polikarpov was drinking vodka on the rocks. I was drinking bourbon and ginger ale.

---

[3] Although the public was generally unaware of it, the army in those years operated its own nuclear power plants, including a plant at Fort Belvoir, used for research and training as well as to generate electricity. The Army Corps of Engineers built the plants in the early 1950s, mostly to provide power to military bases in remote areas. In addition to the plants at Belvoir, Idaho Falls, and Fort Greeley, Alaska, the army also ran a nuclear plant for the air force in Sundance, Wyoming, and one in Greenland, nine hundred miles from the North Pole. By 1973, the army was out of the nuclear power business, and the plants had been shut down.

Some nights we would not break up until around two A.M. Although I watched my drinking, I felt I had to play the game.

"Sometimes with a glow on, he would have me drop him off in locations in Washington that I was not familiar with, like Walter Reed Army Medical Center. I would have a job trying to find the Fourteenth Street bridge. I would get home, grab a few hours sleep, then go off to work."

Polikarpov, like a skilled spy, was proceeding slowly. He knew it was important to cultivate a source gradually. But after several dinners, it was time for the first move.

"One night we were eating, and he said, 'Joe, can you do me a favor?' I said, 'If I can.' "

Polikarpov took the plunge. "We're interested in some nuclear power information," he said.

"I don't know what country you're from," Cassidy replied, "but I'm loyal to my country. I would never do anything to hurt my country."

"No, this is peaceful," Polikarpov protested. "We in Russia have some—"

"Oh, you're from Russia?"

Polikarpov nodded. "We have some desolate areas," he continued, "where we would like to get power. I'll pay you for the information." Polikarpov paused. "Joe, I don't want you to do anything improper." But it was terrible, the Russian went on, that there were people in his country who had no electricity. All he was asking Cassidy to do was to help him help his people obtain basic necessities.[4]

Cassidy waited a long moment, as though he were turning the matter over in his mind. "OK," he finally replied. "Since I consider you my friend, I will try to help you, within limits. As long as it's peaceful, I'll see what I can do."

---

[4] Polikarpov, in this first request, asked for information about nuclear power, a much less sensitive topic than, for example, nuclear weapons. Often, an officer of the GRU or the KGB made an initial request for something even more innocuous—perhaps an unclassified telephone book or manual. If the potential recruit provided it, the officer would ratchet up a notch and ask for a more important document. From there, the officer might ask for secret information and offer to pay for it. Polikarpov was more or less following the traditional script.

"Mike" then asked Cassidy to meet him with the documents a few days later at 10 A.M. on a residential street just off Route 1, half a mile north of the sprawling Belvoir military complex.

"Don't wear your uniform," the Russian said.

"I have to," Cassidy replied, "I'm working."

Then wear an overcoat, Polikarpov instructed him. Cassidy said he would but pointed out that the coat would be olive drab and would still bear his sergeant's stripes.

Before the scheduled meeting with Polikarpov, Cassidy joined two of his FBI handlers at the chicken restaurant on Route 1. The agents handed him documents that had been cleared to be given to the GRU officer.

At the rendezvous with the Russian, Cassidy produced the material. "I have to have it back," he warned.

"No problem," Polikarpov said, "I'll have it back this afternoon." Around 3 P.M., they met again, and Polikarpov, having had time to photograph the documents, gave them back to the sergeant.

Later, Cassidy met the FBI men again at the restaurant, returned the documents to them, and was debriefed. The same procedure was followed in a subsequent series of meetings. Polikarpov pressed for any and all information Cassidy could get on nuclear power. In each case, Polikarpov took the documents from Cassidy in the morning and, like clockwork, returned them in the afternoon so that Cassidy could supposedly slip them back into the army's files.

No money changed hands at the first rendezvous, but Polikarpov paid Cassidy for the documents he brought to their later meetings. Cassidy turned the money over to the FBI agents.[5]

In March 1960, Polikarpov handed Cassidy off to a second "Mike,"

---

[5] Under government rules, the FBI was allowed to use the Soviet money it received in this manner to pay the actual costs of the double-agent operation. Any amount over that had to be turned over to the Treasury. One of the ironies of the espionage activities of the cold war is that the Russians actually ended up paying part of the cost of their own deception in SHOCKER. The money flowed both ways, of course; during those years, hundreds of thousands of dollars were paid by the CIA and other U.S. intelligence agencies to sources who were actually working for the KGB or the GRU, or equally for both sides.

who took over the meetings. Polikarpov and Cassidy continued to play volleyball at the Y on Thursday evenings. The FBI identified WALL-FLOWER's new control as Gennady Dimitrievich Fursa, another GRU officer, who was listed simply as an "attaché" in the political section of the Soviet embassy. But Fursa missed two meetings, and the FBI had Cassidy express his concern to Polikarpov at one of their volleyball games.

Although Cassidy continued to pass documents to the Russians under the FBI's guidance, he was distracted in 1960 by personal problems. "My marriage was souring," he said. One of his army buddies, also a noncommissioned officer, was put on orders for Korea. "It gave me an idea: Why not me, too? This may be the way to save the marriage. My marriage vow was very important to me. I felt I had to try to make it work. Maybe if we were separated for a while things might be different. Maybe a year away from home might patch things up."

WALLFLOWER's plan to leave the United States for an overseas post dismayed the FBI, but the bureau had little choice but to go along with Cassidy's wishes. The human factor was central to the success of any espionage operation; it could not be ignored. Cassidy clearly wanted to get away from Washington for a time. The army and FBI approved his transfer to Korea.

Before he left in September 1960, the Russians gave him recontact instructions for his return. That was welcome news to the FBI, since it meant the operation might not be over after all.

"I was told to take a red crayon and crush it on the sidewalk in front of a photography store in Washington," Cassidy recalled. "And the next day I was to walk with a pipe in my mouth and a book in my hand on a residential street in Maryland, and someone would come up to me with a code phrase. The contact would ask, was a certain movie house nearby? Cassidy was to give a prearranged reply.

WALLFLOWER memorized his instructions. He would see, when he came back from Korea, whether his wife, or the Russians, were waiting for him.

WALLFLOWER

When Joe Cassidy began his dealings with the Russians in the late summer of 1959, it was still the era of tailfins and jukeboxes, the last decade of a Main Street and Norman Rockwell America. Microchips, MTV, and the Internet were light-years away.

It was the height of the cold war. A little more than a decade earlier, on March 5, 1946, Winston Churchill had delivered his famous speech at Westminster College in Fulton, Missouri. "From Stettin in the Baltic to Trieste in the Adriatic, an iron curtain has descended across the continent," he warned. "Behind that line lie all the capitals of the ancient states of Central and Eastern Europe."

At home, the 1950s had seen the rise and fall of Senator Joseph R. McCarthy of Wisconsin. Although he ultimately self-destructed, the legacy of suspicion he sowed by exploiting a supposed communist menace at home influenced domestic politics and American foreign policy for decades. Dwight Eisenhower was in the White House. Schoolchildren hid under desks during air-raid drills as protection against a feared nuclear Armageddon. More than 100,000 citizens built fallout shelters and stocked them with water, canned food, and flashlights.

Abroad, the CIA overthrew the governments of Iran and Guatemala and attempted unsuccessfully to unseat President Sukarno in Indonesia. The Soviets, meanwhile, crushed the revolt in Hungary, maintaining their grip on Eastern Europe.

It was a time of spies, of secret battles fought in the shadows, and not only in distant places such as Vienna and Berlin. The American public read about a series of sensational Soviet espionage cases in the United States itself, including the arrest, conviction, and execution of the "atom spies," Julius and Ethel Rosenberg.

In this cold war environment, the FBI under J. Edgar Hoover was not content merely to detect and catch Soviet spies; when possible, it tried to run agents against them. Thus, in 1958, the FBI and the army began planning what eventually became known as Operation SHOCKER.[1]

In those years, the FBI had a classified program known as DESECO, for Develop Selected Contacts. The purpose was to develop sources who could provide information about the targets of the KGB, the GRU, and other East-bloc intelligence services.

According to Charles Bevels, an FBI agent who ran SHOCKER for several years, the case originated under the DESECO program. "The FBI interest," Bevels said, "was to identify the contacts made by the Soviets. If we could turn the contacts around to work for us, that was to our ad-

---

[1] The code name changed over the years, partly for reasons of security but also to distinguish various phases of the case. The operation's first code name was CHOWLINE. Later, both the FBI and the army used the code name ZYRKSEEZ (the phonetic spelling of Xerxes, the Persian king who ruled in the fifth century B.C.). By 1971, the code name SHOCKER had been adopted by the Joint Chiefs of Staff, and the same year the FBI chose the code name PALMETTO for the University of Minnesota professor in what became the final stage of the long-running affair. Also in 1971, the FBI coined the code word IXORA for a startling offshoot of the case. To avoid unnecessary confusion, the operation is generally referred to here as SHOCKER, the name used at the highest level of the Pentagon, although it was not a cryptonym used by the FBI.

vantage. But, in addition, under the program certain people were selected to be put into contact with the Russians."

Because the double agent passes genuine classified information, even though the documents have been cleared for that purpose, his handlers want some benefit in return. One reason for transmitting real secrets, of course, is to convince the opposition that the agent is trustworthy. In turn, that opens up the possibility of a grand deception, of eventually slipping in bogus documents, false information designed to mislead and confuse an adversary government.

Inside American intelligence agencies, operations of this kind are known variously as deception, double-agent, or counterespionage operations.[2] In the 1990s, the FBI's National Security Division, in its internal documents, more often used the term "perception management" to describe these operations. But this latest term of art boils down to the same thing as its predecessors—tricking an adversary into believing false information by persuading it that a source is selling America's secrets.

The central purpose of Operation SHOCKER was to build up to a major deception of the Soviet Union. In addition, SHOCKER had several other objectives: to learn the identities of the GRU's officers in the United States; to discover how it recruited Americans as agents, and how it ran them; and, by the questions the Russians asked of the source, to learn what gaps existed in the Soviets' knowledge of the American military.

The FBI also hoped that the operation might flush out Soviet "illegals"—spies operating without benefit of diplomatic cover. Intelligence officers working out of the Soviet embassy in Washington, the Soviet mission to the United Nations in New York, or UN headquarters, could be watched and their contacts sometimes identified. Illegals, by contrast, are normally almost impossible to detect, since they can be anywhere and blend in with the general population. But an illegal put in contact with WALLFLOWER might be spotted and identified.

From the FBI's perspective, there was one other fringe benefit to the

---

[2] There are some nuances and differences among the various terms. Not every double-agent operation, for example, involves transmitting false information to an adversary service.

operation. The GRU agents occupied with running an agent under FBI control had less time to spot and recruit real spies.

According to Phillip A. Parker, a former senior FBI counterintelligence official who played a key role in Operation SHOCKER, another advantage the bureau gained from a counterespionage operation, even if the Russians eventually caught on, was that "dangles . . . make them suspicious of the real guys—the real walk-ins."

Every double-agent operation, however, carries within it a risk. For the most part, real secrets are given away to the opposition, information that could prove harmful to the United States. Ideally, a delicate balance is maintained between the risks and the benefits.

In Operation SHOCKER, the FBI was responsible for all operational aspects. Together with the army, the FBI screened and selected a military man to be dangled to the Russians. The bureau ran the agent. The army provided the agent as well as the "feed"—the classified materials to be released. Within the Pentagon, an elaborate system of secret panels reviewed the feed. Ultimately, the Joint Chiefs of Staff approved the documents given to the Russians. The entire procedure was supersensitive and highly secret.

After months of planning, and a good deal of pulling and hauling between the bureau and army intelligence, the FBI was ready to move. Early in 1959, Joe Cassidy was told by his commanding officer at Belvoir to report to a meeting at the post library.

"When I got up there, there were twenty-five to thirty other top-grade sergeants, and I thought, What's going on here? Somebody said, 'I think it's a security problem.' We were called in one by one. There were two civilians there.

"They asked me how long I'd been in the army, what my name was, where I worked. Just general things like that." Cassidy was puzzled by the odd interview.

"About two days later, I was told to report to the intelligence office. The same two civilians were there." As Cassidy later found out, the two men across the table were Donald A. Gruentzel and John Buckley, both special agents of the FBI. Gruentzel, the lead agent, was a stocky, sandy-haired Midwesterner known around the bureau as "Gruntz" or "Madman," the latter sobriquet a tribute to his aggressive driving style.

Gruentzel has been credited by his counterintelligence colleagues with creating Operation SHOCKER and recruiting Joe Cassidy as its star actor. Gruentzel was not a man who talked much about himself, but he was respected as a very tough agent. He earned a law degree at Creighton University, in Omaha, and had joined the bureau in 1951. His father had worked in a restaurant, and Gruentzel loved to cook. "Nothing fancy," said one FBI man, "Gruntz was a meat-and-potatoes man. He could cook dinner for two dozen people or fifty people."

Like Charlie Bevels, Gruentzel and Buckley worked out of the FBI's Washington field office on the S-3 squad, the counterintelligence unit that monitored the GRU.[3]

Cassidy was puzzled at first by their questions. "They started asking had I ever played volleyball." The FBI, as it turned out, had come to the right man. "In my early days as a first sergeant at Fort Lee, Virginia," Cassidy recalled, "my Company E would play A Company in volleyball. We played for a case of Coke for every three games won. A Company ended up owing us some fifteen hundred cases of Coke."

The FBI men asked Cassidy if he would mind playing volleyball at 6 P.M. every Thursday at the Y in Washington. "I said, No, I wouldn't mind. At that time they revealed who they were. It was clear I was being dangled. I knew I was bait, but I didn't know for what purpose or what country was the target. I was excited about it.

"They told me I was to linger after playing and see what happened. They said, 'You might be approached by someone with a foreign accent.' I asked, What am I supposed to do then? Just go along with it, they said. And go in uniform. They gave me the code name WALLFLOWER."

In this almost casual way, Joe Cassidy, with no previous training in intelligence or espionage, was launched on a career as a spy. He had no way to know that it was to become his life's work.

---

[3] S-2 was in charge of counterintelligence against the KGB in Washington. S-1, known informally as "Deep Snow," handled Soviet cases of especial sensitivity. All three squads were supervised by Ludwig W. R. Oberndorf, "Obie" to all in the bureau.

ORANGE PEELS FOR BREAKFAST

Joe Cassidy's earliest memories are of the orphanage to which he was sent at age three, an institution with the grim, Dickensian name of the Home for the Friendless.

He was born on June 25, 1920, in Erie, Pennsylvania, the third of five children. His father was a foreman at the electric company. "My mother died from TB when I was about three years old," Cassidy recounted. "My youngest sister, Maxine, died, I'm told, shortly after birth. I do not remember my mother or my young sister. I faintly recall being at the grave site at the burial of my mother, and someone gave each of us a ring."

His father, suddenly a widower and unable to care for the children, placed Cassidy and an older brother and sister in the Home for the Friendless. Cassidy's younger sister, Shirley, was taken in by a childless couple.

Cassidy and his siblings hated the orphanage. "My breakfast every morning all those years consisted of a bowl of milk with pieces of bread broken into it." It wasn't enough for a growing boy. He supplemented his diet by scavenging for scraps, even garbage. "I can remember finding discarded orange peels which I washed off and ate. I was hungry much of the time."

Two stern overseers, Miss Moon and Miss Richardson, ran the orphanage. "We were given chores to do, and one of mine was to make beds. I would leave breakfast early, and on the way to the dorm I'd pass a cabinet where food was kept. The keys were almost always left in the lock. I would sneak in there and find something to eat." Cassidy was so little at the time that he had to stand on a stool to reach the forbidden food.

"One morning, I took a banana. I had eaten about half of it when Miss Moon entered the dorm. I shoved the banana under the mattress. She came over to me and sat down, and the half-eaten banana squished through the peel and then through the metal springs and plopped on the floor. Miss Moon heard the banana fall and really gave me hell. And from then on, the keys were never left in the lock."

The Home for the Friendless was a frugal place, and its officialdom had calculated that the orphans' shoes would wear out more slowly if they were worn only in winter. "During the summers, we were made to go barefoot, which I hated. I was always stubbing my big toe. To this day I don't like to go barefoot except in the shower or to bed."

About the only happy moments for Cassidy were on Sundays, when his father visited. His father brought a bag of candy, but he was required to hand it over to Miss Moon or Miss Richardson, who divided it up among the children. Cassidy and his brother and sister complained to their father that they had little enough to eat, as it was. But there was no place to hide from the formidable Miss Moon, since anyone coming to see the orphans was restricted to a community visiting area. "My Dad's solution was to bring the Sunday funnies, and with me on his lap and my brother and sister beside me, he would open the paper in front of him and read us the funnies while we hid behind the paper and ate the candy."

After five years in the orphanage, Cassidy and his siblings got a reprieve. His brother, Robert, was about to become a teenager, which meant he was too old for the Home for the Friendless. "My Dad persuaded his mother, who lived in Lock Haven, Pennsylvania, to come to Erie and provide a home for us."

To Cassidy, by now age eight, his grandmother was like an angel of deliverance. No more sodden bread for breakfast, no more orange peels. "There was plenty of love and togetherness. We all finally got to know each other. In the orphanage, my sister lived with the girls, my brother was with the older boys, separated from me. We would see each other from time to time, but it wasn't family." At long last, in his grandmother's house, Cassidy could enjoy a normal childhood.

For a boy who had literally been starved for years, the corner grocery store was nirvana. "We found out that the grocery store carried a running tab for families in the neighborhood. My Dad paid the bill every two weeks on payday. Well, I thought this was great—on the way to school in the morning I would stop in and get a dozen chocolate cookies. Next time, it was two bananas, or an orange and two apples." The boy, still psychologically conditioned by his years in the orphanage, worried that someone might examine the grocery bill and confront him. But his father never said a word.

As a teenager growing up during the Depression years, Cassidy got into the usual boyhood mischief, none of it serious. When he was fourteen, his father remarried, and his grandmother moved to her own apartment. A year later, while in the ninth grade, Cassidy asked his father if he could quit school. "He finally agreed if I had a job." Cassidy found one at four dollars a week, working for the Mehler Beverage Company up to sixty-five hours a week as a helper on a soft-drink truck.

Cassidy's hometown, although the third-largest city in Pennsylvania, had none of the historic importance and social distinction of Philadelphia and none of the wealth and power of Pittsburgh. Situated on Lake Erie, in the far northwest corner of the state, Erie was geographically cut off from the rest of Pennsylvania. It was an industrial town with harsh, frigid winters that brought huge snowdrifts and that seemed to last half the year.

But if life in Erie was lackluster, and the hours on the job long, anything was an improvement over the orphanage. And Cassidy soon found work much flashier than hauling root beer. His best friend, Ray Dailey, knew Jack Parris, who owned a local nightclub. Although Prohibition had been repealed two years earlier, admittance to the Parris Social and Athletic Club was speakeasy style. "To enter you rang a bell at the top of the stairs, and an eight-inch slot would open, and a buzzer was pressed to let you in.

"They had slot machines, and pool tables in the rear, up over the Richmond Brothers clothier on State Street, and we went there often to shoot pool. Then we got to watching the floor show on Saturday nights. Soon it evolved to helping out at the bar when they were very busy. Washing glasses, et cetera. One night I was asked by a patron to fix a couple of Tom Collinses, and before long I was a regular bartender.

"Jack was quite an entrepreneur. He was raised in a poor Italian family and soon not only owned the club but a model and hobby supply store, which I ran for a while, and a neon-sign company. We became good friends, and a lot of times he would give me his Packard to drive some of the showgirls home."

For a sixteen year old, tooling down State Street with showgirls in a fancy car was a definite step up from hauling soft drinks. But Cassidy did not entirely neglect the spiritual. "Although my family was Presbyterian, and we went to Presbyterian Sunday school, all my friends were Catholic. On Saturday night, we'd tend bar, work all night, and then go to mass. We ran two floor shows, the last one at two A.M. We'd close at five-thirty, wash glasses, and straighten up the place. We would leave the bar at five forty-five, run over to the cathedral a few blocks away for six o'clock mass, and then back to Clark's restaurant for breakfast on Jack's tab. I've gone to Catholic church ever since."

By now, Cassidy had a steady girl, Ray Dailey's sister, Pat. "We always bought the five-cent new song list each week, and we listened to the Lucky Strike Hit Parade together on the radio.

"These were Depression days. Wages were low, but we could buy ground beef four pounds for a quarter. My grandmother helped me buy a car for thirty-five dollars. Gas was seven or eight cents a gallon, and they cleaned your windshield and checked your oil and tires."

When Cassidy was eighteen, he found work at Erie Forge and Steel Company as a laborer, laying railroad ties. It was tough work, but soon the war in Europe brought better jobs at higher wages. Cassidy was offered a job as third helper on the open-hearth furnace. Wearing dark glasses and long-sleeved wool shirts to protect themselves from the intense heat, the helpers shoveled sand into the furnace, to repair holes caused by the extremely high temperatures.

"There were about five guys in a circle, taking turns," Cassidy recalled. When the furnace's hydraulic doors opened, a machine called a charger fed scrap metal into the flames. "What comes out is molten steel."

After a few months, Cassidy was promoted to second helper. He still had to shovel sand into the furnace, but now he also got to tap it out. "When it's time to tap it out, you open up the back of the furnace. You poke an air hose into the back of the furnace until the molten metal starts to pour. The crane operator takes the ladle and pours it into an ingot, about fifteen feet by six feet."

It was hard work, but by now Cassidy was a rugged, handsome young adult. After Pearl Harbor, the steel plant was working overtime, and Cassidy's friends were going off to war. Because his job was considered essential to the war effort, there was little chance he would be drafted. But Cassidy chafed to join up.

"By late 1942, most of my buddies were in the service, and one of my best friends had already been killed. I told the personnel office I'd like not to be exempt from military service at my next call-up. They honored my request, and I was drafted in February 1943." Private Cassidy reported to Fort Lee, in Petersburg, Virginia, for basic training, and then was selected to attend school to become a drill instructor.

He rose rapidly through the ranks, and after a year he was promoted to first sergeant, skipping several grades. Cassidy also got engaged to Pat Dailey, but he did not often go home to Erie to see her, because of the expense and lack of leave time.

Hilda Marie Prince, a young woman from Petersburg who worked in the PX, noticed the good-looking sergeant. When Cassidy's grandmother died in the late summer of 1943, Prince heard about it and urged Cassidy to stop by before he left on emergency leave for the funeral.

He did. "She had a bag of food for me to take on the trip." Cassidy was touched by the gesture. When he returned, they dated and were married after the war. "Eleven months later, we had a daughter, Shelby Jean." But Cassidy's marriage to Hilda went rapidly downhill. "As I look back now, I do believe she saw me as a ticket out of the burg—Petersburg, that is—because the marriage was a bust right from the start."

In 1947, Cassidy was transferred to the First Cavalry Division in Japan and detailed to the 302d Reconnaissance Company. His wife and daughter remained in the states. After a year, he was shipped back to Fort Lee, where he remained until 1952, when he was assigned to the Far East Command. The Korean War was under way, and Cassidy, again without his wife, was sent to Japan, expecting he would end up in Korea. Instead, he was detached from his unit and assigned to Kokura, Japan, as an administrator in the office that identified the remains of GIs killed in action and shipped them home for burial. It was a grim but fortunate assignment for Cassidy; almost everyone in his old outfit was killed in the war.

A year later, the army allowed dependents to join their spouses in Japan. Hilda and Shelby Jean arrived in Kokura. Hilda was finally out of Petersburg, but she was unhappy in Japan. She wanted to return home but took a job in the PX and stayed on until Cassidy's tour ended in 1955. They returned to the states and bought a home in the Strawberry Hill section of Alexandria, Virginia. That December, a son, Barry J., was born into their cheerless marriage.

Cassidy was assigned to a clerical job in the adjutant general's office at nearby Fort Belvoir. It was dreary work, and when Cassidy heard of an opening at the base's nuclear field office, he applied and was accepted. The office supervised a school for nuclear power plant operators, as well as the Belvoir power plant itself.

In April 1959, Cassidy earned a high-school general-equivalency degree, twenty-four years after he had dropped out of the ninth grade. Four months later, he was called in for the interview that was to change his life forever.

Joe Cassidy, nightclub bartender, steelworker, and career army man, unexpectedly metamorphosed into WALLFLOWER, a neophyte spy and counterespionage agent for the FBI, working against the highly trained, professional officers of the Glavnoye Razvedyvatelnoye Upravlenie. On the face of it, the match seemed unequal.

Could an amateur such as Cassidy really be expected to fool the Russians? If the Soviets ever discovered the truth, they might retaliate against him. He was playing a potentially dangerous game; if he lost, he realized, he might just end up dead.

CHAPTER

5

RECONTACT

When Cassidy left for Korea in September 1960, he told the second "Mike" that he expected to return in December 1961. But he did not make it back until February 1962.

The FBI, anxious to keep Cassidy in play against the Soviets, wanted him near Washington. The arrangements were made quietly. Much later, Cassidy was told that his records had been flagged; he was not to be given new assignments by the army in the usual manner. Cassidy received orders to report from Korea to the Maryland Air National Guard office at Edgewood Arsenal, on the Chesapeake Bay, fourteen miles east of Baltimore.

Cassidy landed in San Francisco and took a bus across the country. He had hoped the time away might improve relations with his wife. It did not. "When I got back to Alexandria, I called my wife, and she picked me up. At the house, I said, 'I've been assigned to Edgewood.' 'Well,' she said, 'you're going to be assigned there by yourself. I'm not going with you.' So I slept on the couch that night."

Angered and disappointed but not entirely surprised by the final breakup of his family, Cassidy reported to Edgewood. After he found a furnished apartment, he drove to Newport News, Virginia, to get his teenage daughter, who was living with an uncle. His son, now six, stayed with his mother.

As soon as Cassidy and his daughter were settled in at Edgewood, he got in touch with the FBI. His bureau handlers fretted that the army's delay in returning him to the states might have spooked the Russians. Although it was two months later than planned, the FBI decided to have Cassidy follow his instructions for recontacting the GRU. There was little else the bureau could do.

Cassidy drove from Edgewood and crushed the crayon in front of the photography store in downtown Washington. The next day, as instructed, with pipe in mouth and book in hand, he strolled along a residential street in Maryland. But no Soviet spy appeared to inquire about the nearest movie theater.

For several months, until May or June, Cassidy dutifully crushed crayons in front of the photo store on the designated days and walked the specified street with pipe and book.

Nothing happened.

"The bureau tried different ways to recontact the Soviets," Cassidy said. "They put up an index card at the Y saying, 'Lost watch,' and it gave my name and phone number at Edgewood. There was no response."

Finally, in August 1963, the FBI tried a risky and unorthodox ploy. "Don Gruentzel came up with the idea. I met him in Washington one day. He wrote a note that said, 'I'm back from Korea' and gave the telephone number of my office at Edgewood. It said, 'I'm the person you were involved with at Belvoir.' We got in his car and drove to Sixteenth Street, across from the Russian embassy. There were some kids, maybe ten or twelve years old, playing on the street. He called one over and gave him the note and told him to deliver it to the embassy and give it to who-ever came to the door. Don gave him fifty cents. I said, 'Maybe you should have given him the fifty cents when he came back.'

"From where we were parked, we were in a position to see what hap-pened. We watched the kid deliver the note. The person who opened the door didn't look around. He took the note and went inside."

Not many days afterward, Cassidy was in his office in Edgewood when he received a phone call. "It was a foreigner, speaking very slow in a low voice. . . . He said he was glad I had returned from Korea, and he arranged a time and place for a meet, near Greenbelt, Maryland." WALL-FLOWER was back in business.

The meeting took place on September 19. This time, neither Polikar-pov nor Fursa appeared. A third Russian, Boris G. Kolodjazhnyi, showed up. He was listed as first secretary of the Soviet embassy, but to Cassidy, predictably, he introduced himself as Mike.

Cassidy's assignment to the National Guard was of little interest to Kolodjazhnyi. But the GRU officer was well aware of the main activity at Edgewood, the army's chemical-warfare center.

There, in the laboratories at Edgewood, army scientists operating under the tightest secrecy experimented with and developed the nerve gases that were the most lethal agents in the nation's controversial arse-nal of chemical weapons.

The Russians now believed they were close to achieving one of their prime objectives: penetrating a major U.S. defense activity. From their perspective, Cassidy's new assignment proved that even a noncommis-sioned officer was worth recruiting, because he might, in time, have ac-cess to information of enormous value. The GRU man pressed Cassidy. "He knew what was at Edgewood. He wanted to know about the chemi-cal center. I told him I didn't know anything."

The bureau set out to remedy the problem. It began orchestrating Cassidy's transfer to the nerve-gas laboratory, a process that took several months.

In October, Cassidy met again with the GRU. This time, yet another officer showed up. His name was Mikhail I. Danilin, and he was to become Cassidy's principal Russian handler. The fourth Mike served as Cassidy's Soviet control for eight years, longer than any of the others. On the State Department diplomatic list, he appeared as an attaché in the cultural section and later as an embassy third secretary. As was the case with his predecessors, he was an officer of the GRU.[1]

At six foot one, Danilin was a big man, as tall as Cassidy. He was soft-spoken, quiet, handsome, and dark haired. He, too, pressed Cassidy for everything he could learn about nerve gas. They met again three times in the spring of 1964.

As Cassidy recalled it, the strings for his move to the nerve-gas laboratory were pulled by Special Agent James F. "Jimmy" Morrissey, who later succeeded Don Gruentzel as his case agent. A short, clever Boston Irishman, Morrissey was a leprechaun with a law degree, a fanatic Red Sox fan, and a man of great charm, with a natural talent for counterintelligence.

"Morrissey brought a guy from army personnel to talk to me," Cassidy said. Soon after, Cassidy was recommended for promotion, and on June 10 he moved into a slot in the Weapons Development and Engineering Laboratories (WDEL) at Edgewood, known as "Weedle." The companion lab at Edgewood, the Defense Development and Engineering Laboratories (DDEL), was called "Deedle."

In October, Danilin met again with Cassidy. The GRU officer was, of course, delighted to hear that Cassidy had been transferred to the weapons lab. Cassidy was where the Russians wanted him. Danilin asked where Cassidy worked in the lab and what documents he saw. He bombarded Cassidy with all sorts of questions about nerve gas. "He was interested in formulas and method of delivery," Cassidy said. Danilin also inquired about incapacitants developed at Edgewood—such as BZ, which can cause disorientation and temporary paralysis—and riot-

---

[1] Of all of Cassidy's Russian case officers, Danilin was the only one actually entitled to call himself "Mike," since his first name, Mikhail, is the Russian equivalent of Michael.

control agents such as CS. His main interest, however, as might be expected, was in nerve gas.

Cassidy was not a scientist—he had never even gone to college—but one of his jobs at the weapons laboratory was to file the documents produced by the chemists and engineers.

The Strangelovian world in which Cassidy now found himself was one that operated in deepest secrecy, with almost no public knowledge of its existence. Nerve gases are among the more horrible weapons ever developed, no less deadly than nuclear bombs and biological agents such as anthrax, Ebola virus, or the bubonic plague. A tiny drop of nerve gas, inhaled or in contact with the skin, can kill almost instantly.

Closely related to common insecticides, nerve gases were unknown until the approach of World War II. Appropriately, they were first developed by the Nazis. In 1936, Dr. Gerhard Schrader, a chemist with I. G. Farbenindustrie in Germany, had discovered the first nerve gas by accident while researching compounds to kill insects. He synthesized an organophosphorous ester known as tabun, or GA.

Soon, Schrader and Nazi scientists were developing far more powerful nerve gases: sarin, also known as GB, which Schrader discovered in 1938, and soman, known as GD. The Nazis built a nerve-gas production plant in Breslau, disguising its output under the code name Trilon, a popular soap. At the end of the war, the Soviets captured German stocks of nerve gas, dismantled the plant in Breslau, and transported it back to the Soviet Union. U.S. Army intelligence found Dr. Schrader, however, and obtained the nerve-gas formulas from him. As a result, American scientists, too, were able to replicate tabun, sarin, and soman. In the 1950s, British and American scientists developed another powerful nerve gas, VX.

By the 1960s, both the United States and the Soviet Union had extensive chemical- and biological-warfare (CBW) programs, which were important targets for intelligence operations. Edgewood was a prime objective for the Soviets, as were Fort Detrick, Maryland, the government's center for germ-warfare research, and Dugway Proving Grounds, a huge restricted area sixty miles southwest of Salt Lake City that tested both chemical and biological weapons.[2]

Sarin, soman, and VX remain the world's three principal nerve gases today. All three work by inhibiting the action of cholinesterase, a key enzyme that controls the body's nervous system, including breathing, brain function, and muscle movement.

Cholinesterase neutralizes the buildup of acetylcholine, a nerve-impulse transmitter, in the body. Acetylcholine must be present for an impulse, or message, to jump from one nerve ending to the next. This is how humans are able to think, breathe, and move.

But when nerve gas inhibits the production of cholinesterase, nothing neutralizes the acetylcholine, and the nervous system in effect runs on fast-forward, spinning wildly out of control. As one government official put it, "All three nerve gases work by making people forget to breathe." The respiratory muscles convulse, and death follows, generally from asphyxiation.[3]

The term *nerve gas* is a misnomer, since the chemicals are actually liquids delivered in a fine mist by an aerosol spray. Sarin has perhaps become the best known nerve gas, in part because it was used by the Aum Shinrikyo cult in a terrorist attack in the Tokyo subways during the morning rush hour on March 20, 1995, killing twelve persons and injuring five thousand. (Two months later, the cult leader, Shoko Asahara,

---

[2] Something went terribly wrong at Dugway during a nerve-gas test on March 14, 1968. Some 6,400 sheep were killed in two Utah valleys, apparently by a cloud of VX. Although the army has never officially taken responsibility for the sheep kill, it has skirted close to an admission. A month after the sheep died, the army said evidence "points to the Army's involvement." In January 1998, Colonel John Como, Dugway's commander, said that a test of "a lethal chemical agent at Dugway . . . may have contributed to the deaths of the sheep." Despite the army's half denials, the government compensated the ranchers for their lost animals.

[3] Atropine, a derivative of the deadly belladonna plant, is a principal antidote to nerve gas. Belladonna, which means "beautiful lady" in Italian, is a highly poisonous plant of the nightshade family with purple or red flowers. Another antidote is 2-PAM, pralidoxime chloride, one of a class of chemicals known as oximes that restore the normal action of cholinesterase. 2-PAM, however, is ineffective against soman (GD) after two minutes. Both atropine and 2-PAM, along with an injector, are contained in the MARK-I kits provided to U.S. troops.

was captured and charged in the attack along with forty of his followers.)

All nerve gases are organophosphorous compounds. Although they are lethal, they have different properties and varying degrees of effectiveness. Some, for example, require smaller doses than others to kill people. Some nerve gases penetrate clothing better than others. Scientists also speak of "persistent" or "nonpersistent" agents. That is, some more-volatile gases, such as sarin, evaporate quickly and are considered nonpersistent. Others, such as VX, evaporate much more slowly and can remain in an area, still deadly, for a week or two.

Sarin (GB) is a colorless, odorless liquid. A 1996 Material Safety Data Sheet issued by the army's Chemical and Biological Defense Command at Edgewood states that "effective dosages for vapor are for exposure durations of 2–10 minutes."[4] Soman (GD) is described as a "colorless liquid with a fruity odor. With impurities, amber or dark brown with oil of camphor odor." Like sarin, it can kill in two to ten minutes. VX is odorless, but, unlike sarin and soman, it is viscous, with the consistency of motor oil. It can be colorless or slightly yellowish. One drop on the skin kills. The army's safety-data sheet warns: "Death usually occurs within 15 minutes after absorption of a fatal dosage."[5]

Bernard Zeffert, a former chemist at Edgewood, perfected VX for the army. "We got VX from the Brits who created it," he said. "When people in the process lab were gearing up for production of VX, they got poor re-

---

[4] The army's chilling official description of sarin goes on to warn:

> Symptoms of overexposure may occur within minutes or hours, depending upon dose. They include: miosis (constriction of pupils) and visual effects, headaches and pressure sensation, runny nose and nasal congestion, salivation, tightness in the chest, nausea, vomiting, giddiness, anxiety, difficulty in thinking and sleeping, nightmares, muscle twitches, tremors, weakness, abdominal cramps, diarrhea, involuntary urination and defecation. With severe exposure symptoms progress to convulsions and respiratory failure.

[5] Scientists express the degree of deadliness of a nerve gas with the term *LD* (for lethal dose) *50*, meaning the amount that will kill 50 percent of those exposed to it. The smaller the amount needed to reach LD50, the stronger the agent. For VX absorbed through the skin, the LD50 is ten milligrams for a 154-pound man. For skin exposure to soman, the LD50 is 350 milligrams.

sults." Zeffert and Jefferson C. Davis, Jr., tackled the problem. "We conducted an experiment and published a paper, in-house only, on the bond energies of phosphorus and sulphur."

As a result of their work, Zeffert and Davis received the patent, along with the army, for a link in the process of making a precursor of VX. Davis, who had a master's degree in chemistry when he entered the army in 1954, was sent to Edgewood. In his early twenties, he suddenly found himself making nerve gas. "Among the GIs there was a sort of black humor about it," Davis recalled. "We'll do what the army wants for two years."

The scientists on the permanent staff of Edgewood Arsenal had a pleasant life. Their laboratories were located on a scenic, wooded peninsula that stretches into the northern end of the Chesapeake Bay, south of Havre de Grace. They lived in nearby towns like Bel Air, comfortable suburbs of Baltimore. They married, raised children, and went to work in their labs, making some of the deadliest concoctions known to humankind. Few would admit to any qualms about their work. Like some nuclear scientists, many found justification in the fact that the Soviet Union also had chemical and biological weapons. Soviet scientists thought much the same way.

"By and large, it was a 'we better keep up' kind of mentality," recalled Davis, later the chairman of the chemistry department at the University of South Florida. "We had a sense of duty at the time." But Davis said his own views changed. "The more you learn, the more you wonder about the saneness of it all. I think later a lot of people were not happy that that sort of stuff should be developed or used. I feel we should destroy the reserves of nerve gas and never use it." But the disenchantment Davis felt later was not typical. Many of the scientists at Edgewood argued that using nerve gas was actually a more humane and sure way to kill enemy soldiers than leaving them bleeding to death on a battlefield.

When the Edgewood scientists retired, many continued to live around Bel Air as they slipped into their seventies and eighties. They remained a close-knit group.

Benjamin L. Harris had been technical director of the army's chemical labs for eleven years when he left Edgewood in 1981. The retired nerve-gas scientists, he said, formed a club called the GOBs, for Good Old Boys. In the early 1990s "the Good Old Boys still met in Edgewood every Friday at Vitali's restaurant, in a motel at the junction of Route 24 and I-95." By 1997, their ranks had dwindled to four. "Now they meet at Denny's, across the road."

Not all the ex-scientists at Edgewood joined the GOBs. Saul Hormats was definitely not a member of the club. White-haired and bespectacled, in his mid-eighties when interviewed for this book, Hormats was a maverick who had broken with his fellow scientists and publicly opposed the development and use of nerve gas. Born in Troy, New York, he grew up in Baltimore, earned a chemical-engineering degree at Johns Hopkins University in 1931, and three years later started at Edgewood. He worked there for thirty-seven years, serving as deputy director and then director of development, before he retired in 1972. Not one given to false modesty, he described himself as "the godfather of chemical warfare in the United States."

Hormats explained how Edgewood was organized into a research group, which worked on the nerve gases, and a development section, which designed a production facility. "Production plants were scattered around the country, one at Pine Bluffs, Arkansas, for example.

"We ran toxicity tests on animals—mostly mice and dogs. It was done by our medical division. We had to make damn sure the stuff was stable, effective, not flammable, et cetera. It was then put into a one-fifty-five-millimeter shell, and sometimes an eight-inch shell, or a four-point-two mortar shell. All with GB."[6]

Just to the north of Edgewood Arsenal is the army's Aberdeen Proving Ground, a weapons-test area. "Aberdeen would take a shell and fire it to see the trajectory, strictly for munitions testing. Target effects were all done at Dugway," said Hormats.

---

[6] In addition, the army in the mid-1960s had a wide variety of weapons capable of delivering both GB and VX, including 105 mm howitzers, 105 mm rocket launchers, and Honest John and Sergeant missiles. The air force had thousand-pound bombs containing 198 gallons of GB.

At Edgewood, the scientists concentrated primarily on sarin (GB). But they progressed to more compounds designated with letters of the alphabet, beyond GA (tabun) and GB. They skipped over GC, for fear that it might be confused with phosgene (CG), an older poison gas used widely in World War I.[7]

The Edgewood chemists also experimented with soman (GD), and conducted research on a nerve gas designated only as GE, an ethyl version of sarin. They experimented as well with cyclo sarin (GF), a colorless, odorless nerve gas that is apparently as lethal as its cousins. According to Jeff Smart, Edgewood's official historian, "We only standardized GB. We decided to declare it the main agent and produce it on a large scale." Although no one at Edgewood would confirm it, there is some evidence that the scientists also may have conducted research into GH, a nerve gas that combines an organophosphorous compound with isopentyl alcohol.[8]

The chemists at Edgewood were not content with this research. They strove at great length and at considerable expense to develop an even more powerful nerve gas. In the end, however, the technical problems they encountered were insurmountable. But this failure was to become the core of Operation SHOCKER.

From the questions the GRU asked Cassidy, it was clear the Soviets were anxious to know which nerve gases were being produced and put into weapons. Had the United States decided to choose one of the three gases, or was it developing more than one?

The GRU was also eager to discover whether the United States was developing a binary system to deliver nerve gases. In a binary system, the

---

[7] Phosgene chokes its victims and can cause death by asphyxiation. It was also rumored among the scientists at Edgewood that GC was a code sometimes used in military medical records for gonorrhea.

[8] Iraqi scientists working for Saddam Hussein reportedly developed a nerve gas that is an analogue of GH, using isobutyl alcohol.

chemicals that combine to form nerve gas are kept separate—in two compartments in an artillery shell, for example—and mix only on approach to a target. A binary system is a much safer way to store the gas and reduces the danger to pilots and troops who must handle it. Moscow also wanted to know if the scientists at Edgewood might be working on newer and even deadlier forms of nerve gas. At a meeting in May 1965, Danilin asked Cassidy to find out the formula for the version of VX produced in the Edgewood lab. He gave Cassidy a hollow battery as a concealment device, as well as a specially treated sheet of carbon paper for secret writing. The carbon would enable Cassidy to send a message to the Russians on what appeared to be a blank piece of paper.

As it turned out, in asking Cassidy for information about binary weapons, the GRU was inquiring into matters at the cutting edge of American nerve-gas technology. According to William C. Dee, a veteran official at Edgewood, Ben Witten, chief of organic research at the facility, came up with the concept of a binary system in 1957. In a test chamber at Edgewood, and in field tests of VX at Dugway, it worked.[9]

Saul Hormats, however, stopped the development of binary weapons in the 1960s. "It was put on ice by me for two reasons," he said. "So that other countries wouldn't get it. I didn't want third-world nations making them in a barn in the boondocks. And second, it had no military value whatsoever. With the straight GB you had more agent in the shell; it is more efficient than the binary. The binary shell is a base ejection shell, which means the nerve gas shoots out the back of the shell and goes up in the air. With unitary munition it bursts right on the target. It is a different kind of shell, and it works better."

The United States did not begin production of binary artillery shells until 1985, almost two decades later. By the late 1980s, 155 mm binary

---

[9] The precise way that binary nerve-gas weapons work is classified, but scientists familiar with them said that as the shell is fired, the contents push back in what is called a setback. The setback ruptures the disk that keeps the two chemicals apart. The rotation of the shell in the air mixes the two components. By the time the shell nears the target, the chemicals have mixed and produced nerve gas.

shells containing sarin were being produced, Dee said, each containing 6.5 pounds of the gas.

"I was furious when Reagan revived binary weapons," said Hormats. But by that time, of course, he had retired and left Edgewood.

In March 1966, Danilin gave Cassidy a rollover camera, a spy gadget developed by the Soviets to copy documents that was a kind of predecessor of today's handheld scanners. "The camera was about the size of a pack of cigarettes," Cassidy recalled, "but not as thick." Cassidy simply rolled the camera over the document, and it automatically took a picture. He could capture an entire page in three passes of the camera. Cassidy did not have to extract the film. "I would give the whole camera to the Soviets and exchange it for a new one." Over time, the GRU gave Cassidy three rollover cameras.

FBI technicians examined these cameras, and one detail bothered Charlie Bevels. "They all had high serial numbers," he recalled. "I wondered: Who else has these things?"

An indication of the GRU's trust in Cassidy was the fact that Danilin did not interrogate him on where or when he was able to use the rollover camera without being seen. At one point, Danilin did suggest that Cassidy take the material into the men's room to copy it. That was not an option, Cassidy explained; there were no doors on the stalls at Edgewood. "I could have taken the documents to my car," he said. "But they didn't ask, and I didn't explain."

The documents that Cassidy photographed and passed to Danilin were selected by army intelligence and approved at the highest echelon of the Pentagon, the Joint Chiefs of Staff.

One of those who ended up clearing the "feed," as counterintelligence agents call such material, was Tom O'Laughlin, a former FBI agent who by 1962 had moved over to the Pentagon, as the direct result of a diktat by FBI director J. Edgar Hoover. According to Bevels, O'Laughlin ran afoul of Hoover's edict that FBI agents had to meet strict weight standards. "Hoover had a physical and found that his weight was higher than the Metropolitan Life standard," Bevels said. "He went on a diet and felt so good he decided everyone would have to do it. . . . [Tom] had a lot of trouble making weight."

The problem with the feed, of course, was the need to balance Cassidy's credibility with the requirements of secrecy. These contradictory demands could never be completely reconciled. As in every such operation, some secrets had to be given away in order to protect the double agent. Officials in Washington were thus passing secret information to the Soviets, the disclosure of which by anyone else could have resulted in a long prison term for violation of the federal espionage laws.

The difficult balancing act often led to tensions between the FBI and the Joint Chiefs. The bureau wanted to keep the Russians convinced by passing significant documents, but the Pentagon was reluctant to part with its classified secrets.

Bevels recalled the conflict. "It was hard to get the military to give us stuff. Sometimes we wanted to put classification stamps on documents that weren't classified, and we had trouble getting clearances from the military even to do that."

The meetings with Danilin almost always took place in the parking lot of a bowling alley in Springfield, Virginia, a Washington suburb. There, Cassidy passed the documents that he had photographed.

"We would meet at nine P.M., always on a Saturday night. I suppose this is when America is out partying and has its guard down."

Danilin, overjoyed to have a mole inside Edgewood, urged Cassidy to obtain everything he could on the nerve-gas program. He emphasized he wanted as much as possible about the chemical formulas and the makeup of the binary system. "He would say, 'Find me anything you can on binary.' He wanted information on all the nerve gases. He asked about VX. He asked about sarin. He asked about GD—'Get everything you can about it.' "

After two years, and with the Russians well hooked and pushing for every scrap Cassidy could provide, the counterintelligence agents in the FBI decided the moment they were waiting for had arrived. Danilin and the GRU trusted Cassidy.

It was time for the deception.

CHAPTER

6

THE DECEPTION

Joe Cassidy was a plainspoken man, not by nature guileful. But the FBI agents who originally recruited him had unexpected good fortune; the modest master sergeant possessed the one quality that would carry him through. Joe Cassidy was a natural actor.

And that quality was precisely what the FBI was counting on as the bureau and intelligence officials in the Defense Department began planning the deception late in 1965.

In intelligence operations, deception material is also known as disinformation. Ironically, the very word *disinformation*, although adopted by

U.S. counterintelligence, appears to have originated with the Russian word *dezinformatsiya.*[1]

In 1959, the KGB created a disinformation department known as Department D, part of the First Chief Directorate (FCD), headed by General Ivan I. Agayants. Its duties included fabricating documents and planting false intelligence to confuse and mislead foreign governments.

In the Pentagon, an elaborate machinery existed to create and approve disinformation. False information was controlled by a whole series of secret boards under J-3, the operations umbrella of the Joint Chiefs. The FBI's requests for deception material dealing with nerve gas were referred to one arm of J-3, the United States Evaluation Board (USEB), a little-known interagency intelligence committee. Its members were the heads of the intelligence organizations of the military services, along with representatives from the FBI and the CIA.

The USEB was the first panel to rule on any deception operation that involved the military. After the USEB, the proposal moved over to another unit under J-3, the Special Assistant for Clandestine and Special Activity (SACSA). After SACSA approved the plan, since SHOCKER was an army project, it was sent to the army's deputy chief of staff for operations (DCSOPS, pronounced "dess-ops"). Finally, after DCSOPS signed off on the proposal, it moved to the army's Office of the Chief of Research and Development (OCRD), which prepared the feed for the FBI.[2]

---

[1] The FBI's official intelligence glossary defines disinformation as "carefully contrived misinformation prepared by an intelligence service for the purpose of misleading, deluding, disrupting, or undermining confidence in individuals, organizations, or governments." Leo D. Carl, *The International Dictionary of Intelligence* (McLean, Va.: International Defense Consultant Services, 1990), p. 110.

[2] The Department of Defense has declined to make any comment about Operation SHOCKER. For four years, the United States Army Intelligence and Security Command (INSCOM), in Fort Meade, Maryland, insisted in response to several Freedom of Information Act requests by the author that it had "no record" of Operation SHOCKER under that or any of the several other code names used for the operation over more than two decades. As far as the army was concerned, it never existed. At the author's behest, Kenneth H. Bacon, Assistant Secretary of Defense for Public Affairs, asked the secretary of

At FBI headquarters, the deception operation was supervised by Eugene C. Peterson, a veteran counterintelligence agent in the Soviet section. A big, burly, professional counterspy, Peterson had the face of a boxer—a broad pug nose with a horizontal scar between intent blue eyes, a face with a lot of miles on it. In the course of his twenty-eight-year career with the FBI, he worked on most of the major Soviet cases of the cold war.

Despite his tough-looking exterior, Peterson was an affable, pleasant man from Aberdeen, South Dakota, where his father drove a laundry truck and his mother worked as the firm's bookkeeper. Peterson enlisted in the army air corps out of high school, then graduated from Northern State Teachers College in Aberdeen in 1951 and joined the FBI. He began his counterintelligence career in Puerto Rico in 1960. Four years later, Peterson was transferred to headquarters to work against Soviet spies. He rose to chief of the Soviet section in 1976.

Although an elaborate structure of Pentagon boards and committees had approved SHOCKER, the actual control of the operation rested in the hands of a small number of people—Peterson at FBI headquarters, successive case agents at the Washington field office, and across the Potomac in the Pentagon, Taro Yoshihashi, the army's top counterespionage expert. A quiet, self-effacing man who worked deep in the intelligence bureaucracy, Yoshihashi was a double-agent specialist and thus the FBI's point of contact inside the Defense Department.

Born in Hollywood, California, to a Japanese-American family, Yoshihashi earned a degree in psychology from the University of California at Los Angeles and joined the army in 1942, not long before the rest of his family was evacuated to a relocation camp in Cody, Wyoming. Assigned to General Douglas MacArthur's headquarters in Brisbane, Australia,

---

the army, Togo D. West, Jr., whether any information about the operation could be released. West ordered a review. On May 27, 1997, Bacon responded to the author, saying that the files had indeed been located but remained classified and would not be released. When subsequently pressed, Bacon said, "There is a security issue here." He declined to elaborate.

Yoshihashi maintained files on all Japanese Army units with the help of MAGIC, the decrypted messages obtained after the United States broke the Japanese code.

After the war, the army sent him to investigate the biological-warfare experiments conducted by the Japanese against civilians in Manchuria. He was assigned to the Pentagon in 1968. As a double-agent specialist, Yoshihashi was also the army's representative on the staff of USEB.

As in the case of many obscure government panels, USEB's staff really ran it. "In the five years I was there," Yoshihashi recalled, "the principals at USEB only met once, in January of 1972. The meeting was in the basement of the Pentagon in one of the J-3 offices." James J. Angleton, the CIA's controversial chief of counterintelligence, showed up for the rare meeting. Angleton, who trusted no one, had nearly destroyed the CIA trying to unearth moles who he was convinced were burrowing away inside the agency.

At the meeting, he was true to form. "Angleton was the agency representative. At one point he said, 'I have a lot of interesting information I could give you, but I'm not sure about your security here.' I thought, what a lot of b.s."

Although the CIA, through its membership on USEB, was aware of the nerve-gas deception, it exercised no operational control. In the jargon of the intelligence world, Cassidy was the FBI's "asset," not the CIA's, nor the army's.

"The army's role was merely providing support," Yoshihashi noted. "It was a bureau operation. I would get requests from Gene Peterson.

"The bureau would bring in documents from Edgewood and say can we release these? Gene or the bureau's liaison agent would bring the documents over to the Pentagon. Then I would go to DCSOPS for approval. In some cases, I would make a recommendation that material should not be released. Most of the documents that we approved, except for the deception, were true information."

Yoshihashi and Peterson, while responsible along with a few other officials for managing the operation, did not deal directly with Cassidy.

That was the job of the case agents in the field. And during the deception phase of SHOCKER, that meant Jimmy Morrissey.

In the fall of 1964, a major shift of positions had occurred in the FBI's Washington field office. Ludwig Oberndorf, the counterintelligence chief, was assigned to headquarters. Special Agent William J. Lander took over S-3, the GRU squad. At the same time, Donald Gruentzel, who had been Cassidy's case agent, was promoted to supervisor of S-2, the KGB squad. It thus fell to Jimmy Morrissey to run Cassidy during the most sensitive phase of the operation.

In its final form, the plan was, in a sense, a triple deception. "There were G-series gases up to letter H," Yoshihashi said. "The deception was to say we now have GJ. It was fictitious." Secondly, the claim of a new and powerful GJ nerve gas might lead Moscow to conclude, by implication, that the Edgewood scientists had also created a nerve gas labeled GI. The third aspect of the deception was that the bogus documents to be passed to Moscow by Cassidy were also to reveal that GJ existed in binary form.

The decision to tell the Soviet Union about a breakthrough nerve gas designated GJ had a grain of truth embedded within it, since the Edgewood scientists had in fact tried to do so and failed. The effort had taken place, but the results disclosed to the GRU were false.

Most former officials privy to the deception declined to discuss it. One ex-FBI agent familiar with Operation SHOCKER, however, agreed to talk about the deception, the most sensitive phase of the long-running case, on the condition that he not be named. "We had spent a lot of money, and we thought, hell, make them do it. It was hoped the operation would lead the Soviets in turn to spend time and resources on trying to develop the same weapons system, in binary form. It was a 'we tried and couldn't so let's make them spend money on it' attitude."

The FBI's files confirm this purpose. In December 1965, FBI headquarters informed the Washington field office that the deception operation had been authorized based on material developed by the army. The deception would involve a lethal chemical agent, many times more effective than any then available. For "technical" reasons, it was said, the United States had decided not to deploy this weapon but would pass the information to the Soviet Union in a controlled manner. The objective was to cause the Soviets to conduct extensive research and to commit money, personnel, training, and material to replicate or defend against a chemical agent that the United States had not actually produced and therefore had no intention of using.

Another former FBI official, who also insisted on anonymity, was willing, cautiously, to describe the nerve gas that the Soviets were led to believe had been developed. "It was very unstable and could not be stored, so it could not be put in a weapon. It would not maintain its toxicity. *And there was no antidote for it.* So the idea was, we give it to the Soviets, they make it, and then discover it's unstable and no antidote exists, so it can't be used. Because how would they protect their own troops?"

Now the double-agent operation had escalated into a risky, high-stakes gamble. For at its core, the deception over nerve gas was designed to mislead Moscow into believing that the United States was ahead in the chemical-warfare arms race.

Any deception operation carries with it a risk. The documents passed by Cassidy to Mikhail Danilin contained enough true information mixed in with the false to get the Russians to believe all of it. The risk was that Soviet scientists might find the true information valuable and use it to make breakthroughs that had eluded America's scientists.

The Joint Chiefs, the army, and the FBI agents who actually ran the operation knew and weighed the danger. But they also knew that the Soviets were already engaged in full-scale research and production of nerve gases. The competition between the two countries to develop newer and more lethal nerve gases was already a reality. Because of that, the officials in Washington reasoned, it was worth the risk to try to lead the Soviets down an expensive false trail.

Another ex-FBI official said the scientists had reassured the bureau that the formula could safely be passed. "We were assured it wouldn't work," he said. "So it sounds great and looks great, but it will break down at the end. It was made in the lab but never put into production." Had the bureau considered the risks? "Yes," he replied, "they did, but since they were assured it wouldn't work, they felt it would be OK."

One of those who worried about where the operation might lead was Henry Anthony Strecker, who served in a senior post in army intelligence at the time.[3]

The whole business made Harry Strecker nervous. "I remember sitting in on a bureau briefing with Gene Peterson where they talked about an operation out of Edgewood," he said. "We called it *spiel* material, which means 'play' material. I remember a nerve gas we didn't make. Someone at the briefing expressed concern that if we drove the Soviets to looking into a bogus formula, is there a legitimate concern we might drive them to a breakthrough we don't want them to have?"

---

[3] Strecker was assigned from 1965 to 1968 to the army's Office of the Assistant Chief of Staff for Intelligence (OACSI, but often called just ACSI and referred to in-house as "oh-ax-see" or "ax-see"). His successor was Taro Yoshihashi.

CHAPTER

7

WASHINGTON GAME

Early in 1966, Cassidy began passing the false information about nerve gas to Mikhail Danilin. From the Soviet embassy in Washington, the disturbing intelligence about GJ, the powerful new chemical weapon developed by the United States, was relayed to Moscow.

The deception phase of Operation SHOCKER continued for three and a half years, until July 1969. Throughout this period, the GRU pressed for more information about the new nerve gas, and Cassidy obliged with more documents—some real, some fake.

Cassidy's importance to the Russians had suddenly increased spectacularly. New, more secure arrangements were needed to pass the vital film coming out of Edgewood and to transmit instructions to the sergeant. In March 1966, Danilin unveiled to Cassidy two kinds of spy paraphernalia that were to be used for communication between them.

First, he introduced Cassidy to microdots—tiny, circular specks of film on which vast amounts of data could be reduced to a size no bigger than a printed period. He was to receive future instructions on microdots, Danilin explained. To enable Cassidy to enlarge the microdots to make them legible, Danilin gave him a portable microdot reader.

At the same meeting, Danilin gave Cassidy a short course on how to make an artificial, hollow rock. From that time on, Danilin said, the GRU's microdots and the rollover cameras from Cassidy were to be exchanged inside fake rocks. The rocks, he explained, needed to be so realistic-looking that they could safely be left in a park, in the woods, or even on a street.

"He told me how to take the rollover camera and wrap it in wax paper, then tinfoil over that, and then cover it with plaster of paris. Plaster of paris is a gray powder. You add water and mix it in a bucket, and it has the consistency of dough or Spackle. You mold it around the tinfoil and let it harden. It made a coating about a quarter of an inch thick. It would dry in an hour. Sometimes I'd rub sand or dirt in it. The rocks were light gray, or darker." Cassidy quickly became expert at fashioning the phony rocks. To any casual observer, they were indistinguishable from real ones.

Now the meetings and exchanges of material between Danilin and Cassidy began to follow a set procedure, a sort of espionage ballet. The choreography seldom varied.

"First I would go to a drop site and leave my rock, with the rollover camera inside. The drop sites were listed in the instructions. A lot of them were near Burke, Virginia," a Washington suburb. Cassidy then drove to a designated point in nearby Springfield. While he was en route, a Soviet retrieved Cassidy's rock. In Springfield, " 'Mike' would be waiting on the street. Or I would park and walk a block to where he was waiting. Then he would get in my car and we'd drive to the parking lot of the bowling alley. Always at nine P.M. At the personal meetings, nothing would pass. We'd part around eleven."

This way, the Russians reasoned, if something went wrong and the FBI swooped down on the parking lot, neither man had any documents.

They were just two people chatting by a bowling alley. At the meetings, Danilin discussed the previous batch of material Cassidy had provided and what he might be looking for next. "When we left the bowling alley we'd drive in my car to wherever he said, and I would drop him off. It was always different from where I picked him up but always in Springfield."

Cassidy then drove to a prearranged spot to pick up a fake rock that Danilin had left for him before their personal meeting. Inside were instructions in secret writing, a microdot, and cash. The instructions listed more drop and pickup sites and the dates of future meetings.

"The next day I would give the rock to the FBI." Although Cassidy had the portable microdot reader, it was much easier for the FBI to blow up the microdot in its laboratory and relay Moscow's instructions to Cassidy. Neither Cassidy nor the FBI would easily have found a microdot inside a rock, but Cassidy was always told where to look. Those instructions came on what appeared to be a blank sheet of paper with secret writing, or SW as it is known in the espionage trade. Cassidy then steamed the sheet of paper and the message became visible.

Usually, the microdot was tucked away in a slit in a matchbook cover that was placed inside the rock. One matchbook had a picture of a Mississippi River paddle steamer; the SW instructions told Cassidy to look under a particular section of the paddle wheel.

In addition to enlarging the microdots to full-page size, the FBI photographed the entire contents of every rock retrieved by Cassidy, including the cash. These were all recorded on eight-by-ten color prints.

The bureau watched most of Cassidy's meetings with Danilin, and it kept the Russian's apartment under surveillance. The FBI also tried to follow and photograph Danilin when he cleared drop sites, but that was extremely difficult in the remote, wooded areas of northern Virginia favored by the Soviets. The Russians chose such isolated areas because it was fairly easy to spot anyone who might be following them. Normally, a Soviet agent also had a partner watching his back.

"Physical surveillance of Soviets at a drop was almost impossible," Charlie Bevels said. "They were aware of it, and they ran countersurveillance. Once Danilin was scheduled to clear a drop in a very dark, rural area. The lab wanted to use infrared film to get a picture of him clearing the drop. I said no. Because when you use an infrared flashbulb, if you are looking straight at it, you can see it go off. I didn't want to take the chance."

On another occasion, the bureau was frustrated in its surveillance efforts by the unexpected. "I remember one personal meeting they had at the Rose Hill shopping center in northern Virginia, off Franconia Road," Bevels said. "We had cameras, and we were in a house that the owners left at our request. We assured them that the house will not be disturbed, there would be no shooting. We had given them twenty-five dollars; go out to dinner, we'll be here a couple of hours. But at Rose Hill some guy in a huge tractor trailer, Interstate Movers was their name, parked it right in our way. We couldn't see anything."

The GRU understood that Cassidy was not passing secret documents for ideological reasons. As far as the Soviets knew, he was betraying his country for dollars. Since Cassidy never split open the rocks before handing them over to the FBI, he never knew exactly how much money they held. But according to Charlie Bevels, "the rocks often contained ten thousand dollars at a time, usually in a little Baggie, rolled up inside the rocks. Sometimes there was more than that."

But at the meetings with Danilin, Cassidy, playing his role, continually pressed for more money. If the Soviets tended to think of Americans as greedy and materialistic, then he would meet their expectations. "I was always crying for money. I have a teenage daughter, child-support payments for my wife, I have to buy food, clothes, insurance. The piddling amounts you're giving me aren't worth the chance I'm taking."

Despite Cassidy's complaints to the Soviets that he was being underpaid, the money was rolling in, albeit into the FBI's coffers to finance the operation. With the GRU paying Cassidy tens of thousands of dollars, the Russians worried that he might display his new wealth conspicuously. His Soviet handlers warned him to spend money carefully and to avoid buying anything that would attract attention.

Intelligence work is highly compartmentalized. Although Taro

Yoshihashi monitored the operation from the Pentagon and was deeply involved in the feed, he never met Joe Cassidy, though he admired him from afar.

"I felt Cassidy was one of the most competent double agents we ever had," Yoshihashi said. "For example, when he bought a freezer, he said to the Soviets, 'I have enough cash now to buy this, but I did a down payment just like everybody else.'"

When Cassidy needed to write to the GRU, he was instructed to use the special carbon paper he had been given earlier. He recalled how it worked: "The carbon was reddish but dark, it looked normal except for the red color. I would take a sheet of ordinary paper and make a pencil mark to show the writing will be on that side. I would put the special carbon on top of the paper, another paper on top of the carbon, and clip the three together. Then I would take a pencil and write the message. It left no visible marks on the bottom sheet. I'd give the top sheet to my FBI handler and save the carbon paper to use again. I was left with a blank sheet of paper with the invisible writing. I would put that sheet with the secret writing in the rock."

Cassidy used this method to confirm a meeting date or a drop site or to answer requests from Danilin. "Sometimes he would ask whether I could get him something, and I would respond in a letter that I could or could not, or I was still looking for it. Sometimes I wrote to say a drop site they proposed was no good, it was in an area where there were too many people around."

Cassidy got on well with Jimmy Morrissey. As it happened, he had a lot in common with his new case agent. Both were born into working-class Irish American families, and they hit it off from the start.

Morrissey was a quintessential Boston Irishman, with a soft New England brogue. Born in Charlestown, the blue-collar neighborhood of triple-decker houses that sent John F. Kennedy and Thomas P. "Tip" O'Neill to Congress, the FBI man was one of five children of immigrants who came over from County Waterford around the turn of the century; his father was a freight handler at a cold storage warehouse.

In the "wilderness of mirrors," as counterintelligence has been called, seemingly unrelated spy cases often interlock, their threads becoming entangled with one another. So it was with one GRU case that had an impact on Morrissey and, at least indirectly, on Cassidy. In New York in January 1962, FBI agent John Mabey made one of the most important recruitments of the cold war. He persuaded Colonel Dimitri Fedorovich Polyakov of the GRU to pass secrets to the FBI. Mabey gave him the code name TOPHAT. Polyakov, who rose to the rank of general, provided information of enormous value during eighteen years as a spy for the United States.[1]

TOPHAT told John Mabey that he had trained a GRU agent whom the FBI had persuaded to cooperate, and who provided leads that enabled the bureau to arrest a GRU team of illegals, Robert K. Baltch and his wife, Joy Ann. The couple had taken the identities of a Roman Catholic priest from Amsterdam, New York, and a housewife in Norwalk, Connecticut, neither of whom were aware that their identities had been stolen by Russian spies. Jimmy Morrissey handled the Baltch case. It was only after completing the assignment that Morrissey was able to take over as case agent for Joe Cassidy.

Polyakov had also provided leads that led the FBI to investigate Herbert W. Boeckenhaupt, a young air force sergeant who repaired code machines for the Strategic Air Command. Boeckenhaupt was meeting secretly with a GRU officer in Washington.

The FBI's counterintelligence agents customarily worked several cases at a time. The Boeckenhaupt case was also assigned to Morrissey, who by then was simultaneously juggling the Cassidy operation. On Halloween of 1966, the FBI arrested Boeckenhaupt in California. He was charged with betraying the Strategic Air Command's codes to the Soviets, convicted in May 1967, and sentenced to thirty years.

During the summer of 1966, the GRU informed Cassidy that they would communicate with him from then on in encoded SW, as well as in plain text on microdots. A six-digit numerical code, he was told, was to

---

[1] In 1985, Polyakov was betrayed to the KGB by the CIA's Aldrich H. Ames, and three years later he was executed.

be keyed to a dictionary and concealed on pages of SW. The coded messages would back up the microdots.[2]

In August, Cassidy picked up a hollow rock containing a rollover camera, a microdot, and a three-by-four-inch miniature dictionary. Entitled *The Universal Webster*, it was part of a series called Langenscheidt's Universal Dictionaries, published by Barnes and Noble.

Cassidy explained how the code worked. "Each six-digit group led to a word. Suppose I got a message with the number 243124. I would go to page 243, then to the first column because of the 1, then to the twenty-fourth word on the page. The word might be *meet*, the first word in a message that said, 'Meet me at Springfield bowling alley nine o'clock Saturday ten October.' "[3]

In March 1967, Cassidy recovered another rock containing an addition to the code, a numerical key designed to make the code a bit more difficult to crack. "To each group I would add 062520, my birthday. The sum would then work with the dictionary the same way."[4]

Although the deception phase of Operation SHOCKER was designed primarily to persuade Moscow that American scientists had developed the

[2] Although Danilin did not explain why the microdots were in plain text and the SW encoded, the logic was not hard to follow. If one of the hollow rocks left for Cassidy was somehow found—by a child playing, for example—the finder would not see the microdot, and the piece of paper would appear blank. Encoding the text of the SW provided another layer of security.

[3] The dictionary had 413 pages set in two columns of type. The Soviets instructed Cassidy that the first three digits indicated the page number, always between 100 and 413, the fourth digit indicated the column, and the last two digits indicated the placement of the word.

[4] Now, however, the code became a little more complicated. Because the fourth digit of his birth date was number 5, the number given to Cassidy always had a 5, 6, or 7 as the fourth digit, so that the sum when added to 5 would indicate column one or two. For example, one actual message Cassidy received contained the number 135685, which, added to his birth date, produced 198205, which meant the word "last." The next number was 249692, which, added to his birth date, resulted in 312212, which led to the word "Saturday." The message also included 152685, which, when added to his birth date, produced 215205, indicating the word "March." Thus the numbers were part of a message scheduling a meeting in New York City for the last Saturday in March, 1975. The code was laborious to translate, but it worked.

nerve gas GJ in binary form, there is evidence that documents dealing with deadly biological weapons were passed to the Soviets as well.

Charles Bevels, who succeeded Morrissey as WALLFLOWER's case agent, said an army scientist at Fort Detrick had worked on a biological agent called Strain X that became part of the deception operation. "Joe passed the biological information. His job at Edgewood was administrative, he had no technical knowledge. His story [to the Russians] was that he came across this report at Edgewood."

Although Bevels could not recall the nature of the disease or toxin labeled Strain X, another former FBI man, John J. O'Flaherty, who later followed Bevels as Cassidy's case agent, said that among the materials passed to the GRU by WALLFLOWER were documents dealing with "botulinum toxin type E." In all likelihood, this was Strain X.

Toxins are poisons produced by some microorganisms and plants; snake venom is also considered a toxin. The CIA used shellfish toxin for the tiny poison darts developed by its technical experts to kill human targets, although CIA director William E. Colby testified to the Senate intelligence committee in 1975 that "I do not know of any actual use."[5]

Because toxins are so lethal, they are attractive to biological-warfare scientists around the globe. Botulinum toxin, produced by *Clostridium botulinum* bacteria, is among the world's deadliest poisons. It can result in paralysis and death.

Stephen Prior, president and CEO of DynPort, a company in Reston, Virginia, that produces all the vaccines for the Defense Department to counter a potential germ-warfare attack, explained that botulinum bacteria "can elicit seven different toxins, A through G. The strains of *Clostridium botulinum* were isolated by various scientists. Each strain produces one or more toxins."

---

[5] Select Committee to Study Governmental Operations with Respect to Intelligence Activities, United States Senate, 94th Congress, vol. 1, "Unauthorized Storage of Toxic Agents," p. 19. The dart, which the CIA preferred to call "a nondiscernible micro-bioinoculator," was fired by a noiseless dart gun, accurate up to 250 feet. The victim would feel nothing when struck, and no trace of the microscopic dart would be found through any later medical examination of the dead person. The agency also stockpiled cobra venom.

Scientists at Fort Detrick concentrated on the Hall strain of botulinum (named after the scientist who first isolated it), since it produces large amounts of Type A toxin, which is one of the most lethal forms of botulinum. "In animal studies," Prior said, "type E is one of the more potent toxins but less potent than type A."

Type E was discovered as the cause of two serious outbreaks of botulism in 1934, one in New York State that was traced to canned herring from Germany, and the other in Dnepropetrovsk, Ukraine, also due to fish.[6] Type E is most often found lurking in the soils of Alaska, northern Europe, and Japan.

According to Benjamin Harris, Edgewood's former technical director, the formula for yet another deadly toxin may also have been passed to the Russians. Asked whether he was aware of any deception operations during his years at Edgewood, Harris replied, "I know they were engaged in that as a matter of course. I was aware of one incident where we were asked by the intelligence people to supply information on a toxin that was not a good candidate for use as a weapon.

"It was ricin. It was considered a toxin because it was produced by a living organism, the castor-bean plant. We did not consider it a good candidate because it was difficult to come by in large quantities and had not been synthesized at that time." Harris was never told in so many words to what use the information was put, but he said his impression was that it was passed to the Soviets.

The Edgewood scientists did not consider ricin a good weapon, but the KGB did. During the evening rush hour on September 7, 1978, Georgi I. Markov, a Bulgarian émigré, writer, and opponent of the Soviet-backed regime in Sofia, was walking in London when a man jabbed him in the back of his right thigh with the sharp tip of an umbrella. Mumbling an apology, the man disappeared into the crowds. Four days later, Markov was dead, the victim of a tiny metal pellet containing ricin toxin.

---

[6] Charles L. Hatheway, "Toxigenic *Clostridia*," *Clinical Microbiology Reviews* 3 (January 1990): 71.

After the collapse of communism, the new government of Bulgaria admitted that its spy agency had been responsible for the famed "poison umbrella" murder of Markov. More details were provided by General Oleg Kalugin, the former chief of counterintelligence for the KGB, who said that General Sergei Mikhailovich Golubev, of the KGB's Directorate K, was dispatched to Sofia, along with a second officer, to advise the Durzhavna Sigurnost (DS), the Bulgarian secret service, on the hit. In Sofia, the ricin was tried on a horse, which died, and a prisoner, who did not, because the pellet failed to release the toxin. The KGB also provided the umbrella and the poison pellet that were used to kill Markov. It is at least possible, therefore, that the umbrella attack employed the formula that Benjamin Harris believed had been passed to the Soviets.[7]

Early in 1967, as Cassidy recalls it, two unusual events occurred on one night when he met with Danilin at the bowling-alley parking lot. When Cassidy picked up Danilin, a second man was with him. "This was the only time there were two men, and there was no explanation of why a second person." In the parking lot, "Mike asked, 'What did you put in the rock?'" Cassidy briefed the GRU man on the latest batch of documents he had copied with his rollover camera.

"And then he briefed me on what they wanted me to look for. And the three of us got in my car, a blue Oldsmobile, and drove off to a residential area nearby. Mike motioned me to stop and to get out of the car, which was unusual, because normally only he got out of the car. The normal thing was, after a meeting, I would drop him off and I would stay in the car. So all three of us got out, near a streetlight.

"Joe," Danilin said, "this is my friend Mike, he's a real good guy, and he'll take good care of you."

---

[7] Whether the information about ricin was passed to the Soviets, either in the deception phase of SHOCKER or in a separate, parallel counterintelligence operation, is not clear. In 1985, Vitaly S. Yurchenko, a senior KGB official, told the CIA about Special Lab 100, a laboratory in Moscow where KGB scientists developed and tested poisons for operational use. The Russians may have thus extracted ricin on their own.

Cassidy was startled by what happened next. "[Danilin] gave me a bear hug and released me and held my head in both hands and kissed me on the cheek.

"And he said, 'I'll never see you again.' It was dark, but from the streetlight I could see tears welling up in his eyes and slowly making their way down his cheek. It was a very emotional scene, and I was truly taken aback by it."

To the FBI, Danilin's tears were further evidence that the GRU man completely trusted WALLFLOWER. Danilin was parting sorrowfully from a revered and valuable agent. And if the Soviets believed in Cassidy, they might also believe in the bogus nerve-gas formula he had given them.

CHAPTER

8

AND THE VOLGA TURNED WHITE

The Soviet nerve-gas program—the equivalent of Edgewood Arsenal, Dugway, and the other facilities in the United States—was run in secret laboratories in Moscow and in equally guarded test sites and production plants located along a five-hundred-mile stretch of the Volga River.

In Moscow, research and development was conducted at the State Scientific Research Institute of Organic Chemistry and Technology, at 23 Shosse Entuziastov, four and a half miles due east of the Kremlin, not far from Izmailovo Park, the site of the capital's popular flea market. There, scientists experimented with sarin, soman, and VX and sought to create newer and deadlier forms of nerve gas as well. Some 350 miles to the east, the test sites and plants stretched almost in a straight line from north to south along the Volga River basin. In the north, in the Chuvash republic, some of the formulas created in the labs in Moscow were produced in a plant in Novocheboksarsk, a suburb of Cheboksary, the capital of the region.

About 250 miles to the south, near the city of Volsk in the Saratov region, were two Shikhany military sites where Soviet nerve gases were developed and tested. Finally, another 250 miles south in Volgograd was the Kirov Chemical Works, known as Khimprom, a major production site. Part of the facility was the Nazi nerve-gas plant captured by the Soviet army after World War II and brought back to Russia. The Moscow research institute also had a branch in Volgograd.[1]

In 1949, Boris Libman, a twenty-seven-year-old Latvian-born physical chemist and chemical engineer, began work at the pilot plant in Volgograd, in the section where nerve gases were produced and tested in small amounts.[2] At the Volgograd plant, Libman's work soon caught the attention of his superiors and by 1958—the year that Operation SHOCKER was created—he was named chief engineer. In 1960, he received the Lenin Prize for his work on both sarin and soman. The prize came with ten thousand rubles, a significant sum at the time.

Volgograd began producing sarin (GB) in the pilot plant in 1949 and went into large-scale production in 1959. It also began turning out small amounts of soman (GD) in the late fifties.

As the Soviet scientists attempted to divine what the United States was doing in its nerve-gas research and production, some of the information filtering to Libman and the officials at Volgograd had been gleaned by the espionage operations of the GRU. The intelligence data flowed to Volgograd from the Moscow research institute, which in turn received it from an arm of Soviet intelligence with the cover name of the Institute of Medical Statistics.

---

[1] Formerly Stalingrad, the river port city was devastated in World War II, but the surrender of Hitler's forces there in 1943 was the turning point for the Soviet army, which then went on the offensive along the eastern front.

[2] In both the United States and Russia, the chemists in the pilot plants typically worked with small quantities and attempted to devise the processes that would take place in a full-scale plant. In a full-scale production plant, chemical engineers turned out nerve gas by the hundreds of pounds or tons. At Edgewood, nerve gases were tested initially in a process laboratory, even before the work moved to a pilot plant.

Additional intelligence information was provided to Volgograd directly by the chemical-intelligence unit of the GRU. The unit passed along data about U.S. research on binary nerve-gas weapons and about BZ, the incapacitant developed at Edgewood.

More important, in 1972 Soviet intelligence learned the actual formula for VX, which had been invented in Britain and shared only with the scientists at Edgewood. Full-scale Soviet production of VX started in 1972 at Novocheboksarsk.

A dozen years earlier, Soviet scientists had read in the openly available literature that the United States was gearing up to produce soman. But the information was incorrect, although production had been under consideration.

At Edgewood in the late 1950s Benjamin Harris had in fact urged his bosses to commit to large-scale production of soman. Harris, a chemical engineer, had served in the Army Chemical Corps during World War II. He had been an assistant professor at Johns Hopkins University when he began consulting at Edgewood on how to handle the sarin that had been captured from the Nazis. "I went around to storage sites and advised people on handling the GB. How to open containers safely." In 1949, Harris left academe for full-time work at Edgewood.

At that time, the scientists at Edgewood and army officials were still debating which of the major nerve gases to choose for large-scale production. Harris did a study of soman (GD): "I came to the conclusion that [its] increased toxicity and other properties made it a more efficient chemical agent."

There was, however, a problem. Unlike sarin, which is produced with ordinary alcohol, soman relies on pinacolyl alcohol, a much more exotic substance.[3] "It was a lot more expensive to manufacture, because it is a much more complicated alcohol, for which a plant would have to be built. There was no large-scale plant available in the U.S. at that time."

But in Harris's view, the cost of producing the pinacolyl alcohol was

[3] Pinacolyl alcohol combined with methyl phosphonofluoridate creates soman, or pinacolyl methyl phosphonofluoridate. The second chemical component of soman is identical to that used in sarin; only the alcohol is different.

outweighed by the advantages. "If one makes a cost-benefits analysis of the cost of delivery of a weapon to the target, the cost of the fill is an insignificant portion of the total. The cost of delivery is much higher.

"Everybody knew soman was more toxic, and it is also more persistent, because the heavier alcohol makes the gas more persistent. Among the gases, GD, soman, is in the middle; it lasts longer than GB, but it's not as persistent as VX. You can make it more persistent by putting in a thickener. I urged them to make GD," Harris said. "I made that recommendation to Sy Silver," Edgewood's technical director at the time.

"We didn't do it. They decided to make GB. It was decided at a high level."

Saul Hormats recalled the decision. "Soman was not used," he said, "because I decided GB was better, more volatile, you get a fast cloud with it. You would have to make a new alcohol for soman, and GB used normal alcohol, already available. You can't buy a big tank-car load of pinacolyl alcohol, but you can buy one of rubbing alcohol."

But none of this was known at the Kirov Chemical Works in Volgograd.

Large-scale production of sarin (GB) had begun at Volgograd in 1959 but the Russian scientists considered soman the best nerve gas they had at the time. They had first learned of it when the Soviet army captured the Spandau lab, west of Berlin, at the end of the war.

"At first, the Russian military establishment was against GD," said a former Soviet scientist who preferred not to be identified. "They were interested in VX. Then they changed their minds. If America had large-scale GD, we must have it."

And so, by 1960, the Russians had committed to large-scale production of soman, in the mistaken belief that the United States was following the same course. But they faced the identical problem of how to extract pinacolyl alcohol. Although relatively simple to produce today—it is used in the manufacture of a number of herbicides and fungicides—at the time, pinacolyl alcohol required five stages of electrolysis to produce. Work began on construction of a separate unit of the vast Volgograd complex to perform the electrolysis and begin full-scale production of soman.

With the Lenin Prize and increasing responsibility for the Soviet nerve-gas program, Boris Libman's star was on the rise. Then, early in February 1965, a frightening event took place that was, for Libman, a harbinger of personal disaster. A levee on the Volga was destroyed by melting snow. At the plant, there was near panic because Libman and the other scientists feared that they might have contaminated a tidal pool behind the levee. If so, there was a real danger that tens of thousands of people in the lower regions of the Volga might be poisoned.

Hurriedly, the scientists began testing the river as far as twelve miles downstream. To their immense relief, they found no traces of nerve gas. After a day and a half, the levee was repaired, and the danger passed.

For Libman, however, the reprieve was short-lived. Four months later, on June 15, he looked out at the river and was horrified at what he saw. The Volga had turned white.

That, as closer inspection revealed, was the visual effect of thousands of fish that had died and turned belly-up. The immense fish kill extended for fifty miles along the river. The nerve-gas plant was immediately suspected as the logical cause.

Libman, however, soon discovered what he believed to be the real source of the ecological disaster: The huge Volgograd hydroelectric power station had closed its gates, and the river was twelve feet lower than normal. As a result, the heat of the sun had made the water warmer. All the dead fish were sturgeon, which are more sensitive to high temperature than other fish.

Libman's protests were to no avail. As the chief engineer at the plant, a nonethnic Russian, and a Jew, he was an obvious target. Nor was it easy for Libman to prove that pollution from the nerve-gas plant had not somehow contributed to the fish kill. Libman might also have been blamed because Moscow had begun a large-scale program of hydropower construction up and down the Volga; to admit that the power station had caused the fish kill might have brought that project to a halt.

On March 9, 1966, Boris Libman was convicted of negligence and sentenced to two years in a prison labor camp in nearby Volsky. At the time, he was forty-three years old. He was stripped of his military medals and fined ten thousand new rubles, which was ten times the value of his Lenin Prize and the equivalent of two years' salary. Six other officials of the chemical plant were convicted and fined but not sent to prison.

In an interview with the author in Moscow in 1993, Vil Mirzayanov, a scientist who worked for years in the Soviet nerve-gas program, blamed the fish kill on the chemical plant. "Boris Libman was chief engineer of the Volgograd plant in charge of soman production. Some of the soman toxins polluted the Volga, and the fish went belly-up. [Aleksei] Kosygin, then the prime minister, ordered someone be made an example, and Libman became the scapegoat."[4]

In the prison camp, Libman worked first as a foreman of a construction crew, building houses. After some months, he was allowed to work in a chemical plant during the day, developing phospho-organic stabilizers for rubber. To do so, he left the prison during the day but had to be back inside by 10 P.M. Any later than that would be considered an escape, and five more years would be added to his sentence.

Although sentenced to two years, Libman was let out after one year because nobody else could start up production of soman at the Volgograd works. The soman production plant opened, with Libman back on the job, in 1968.

In 1972, Libman was transferred to Novocheboksarsk to oversee the full-scale production of VX. The Soviets, however, were not content with mass production of soman, sarin, and VX. Two scientists, Pyotr Petrovich Kirpichev and Vladimir Uglev, were working at Shikhany 1 on a new nerve gas, the like of which the world had never seen before.

Whether the formula for GJ that was passed to Moscow in Operation

---

[4] Mirzayanov's theory about why the fish died might be correct, but full-scale production of soman had not yet begun in 1965, the year the fish kill occurred. The electrolysis plant that was needed to produce the necessary pinacolyl alcohol was still under construction at the time, and major production of soman at Volgograd did not begin until 1968.

SHOCKER inspired this Soviet effort may never be known without access to the closed archives of the GRU. But in 1973, Kirpichev and Uglev perfected the new substance, said to be eight to ten times more powerful than any nerve gas then in existence.

Its name, which means "newcomer" in Russian, was Novichok.

CHAPTER

9

THE NUN

In 1968, Joe Cassidy was living in an apartment building on Moravia Road in Baltimore and commuting to his job at Edgewood Arsenal. He noticed the attractive high-school teacher who lived in an apartment one floor above him, but they had only a nodding acquaintance.

Marie Krstyen in turn was aware of the tall, good-looking sergeant. Occasionally, she glanced out the window and watched him play catch with his son, Barry, who lived with his mother in Alexandria but visited on weekends.

Early in March of that year, the wife of another tenant in the building left in a huff, after stripping the apartment clean. The distraught husband was wandering the hall. Marie Krstyen and Cassidy took pity on the fellow and tried to calm him down. The wandering wife returned in a few days, and Marie and Cassidy started dating. She was forty and had never married; Cassidy was forty-seven.

"On the first date, he took me to the Playboy Club," she recalled. Krstyen was not sure that his choice was such a great idea, but Cassidy, a member, was fond of the prix fixe menu; drinks were only $1.50, as was dinner. On his sergeant's salary, he considered the place a bargain. As the waitresses in their brief, cottontail outfits ministered to the couple, Cassidy began probing to find out more about his new friend's background. For Krstyen, it was a turnoff.

"He kept asking a lot of personal questions," she said. "I didn't like that at all."

Marie Krstyen, of course, had no way of knowing why her date was asking so many questions. In part, Cassidy grilled her out of normal curiosity. However, while he did not need the FBI's permission to see a woman, he was aware that the bureau would want to know as much as possible about anyone he was dating. If it turned serious, he knew, they would have to do a background check.

Despite getting off on the wrong foot that first evening, Cassidy soon recovered and made a decided impression on his schoolmarm neighbor. "He swept me off my feet," she said. "There was something about him that got me. He seemed a very loyal and truthful guy. He seemed genuine." Since Cassidy was living a double life and pretending to the Russians that he was a money-grubbing traitor, he was anything but genuine. But Marie Krstyen had fallen in love.

"He had good manners, he always greeted people, he was a perfect gentleman. Everybody called him the Sarge, and everybody loved him. I was teaching at night, and Joe always checked to make sure I got home.

"I usually went to his place for dinner, because he did the cooking. In the latter part of April, at dinner at his apartment, he presented me with an engagement ring. He just floored me. But I did accept it, and I'd had nothing to drink."

Cassidy remembers the scene about the same way, with one nuance. Marie, he said, had hesitated. "She sat there looking at the ring. But finally, she said, 'Yes.' I put it on her finger. The next day her students whispered, 'Miss Krstyen's engaged.' It went around like wildfire.

"Within a few days I told the bureau I was going to get married. I had already told them I was dating her. So in March the bureau had started checking her out."

What happened next alarmed the FBI and dismayed Cassidy as well. "Marie had mentioned she came up from Atlanta. And I knew she was a teacher, but anything else I didn't know. So I told the bureau she was from Atlanta, and they couldn't find any trace of her.

"So I queried her some more, what did you do in Atlanta? And finally she said she came from Montgomery, from Alabama." Still, the FBI could not find any trace of Krstyen. And why had she changed her story? She seemed to have materialized in Baltimore out of thin air without any past history. Yet that was impossible. Could Krstyen be a Soviet swallow? That was the term that Russian intelligence used for a female agent dispatched to seduce a male target. Perhaps the innocent-looking schoolteacher was actually a Russian working for the GRU, sent to check up on Cassidy's bona fides.

Finally, the FBI solved the mystery. For twenty years, Marie Elizabeth Krstyen had been Sister Miriam Joseph of the Vincentian Sisters of Charity. For part of the time, she had lived behind the walls of a convent. Small wonder that the FBI had trouble with its background check.

Cassidy was relieved at the news, although slightly embarrassed that he had taken an ex-nun to the Playboy Club. But he wondered why Krstyen had not revealed her previous life.

"I never told him I had been a nun," she said, "because I wanted him to be himself. I didn't want him to act different."

But Cassidy had not revealed his secret either. "I never told her about my other life," he said.

In a sort of gift-of-the-magi, O. Henry twist, Marie Krstyen née Sister Miriam Joseph, and Joe Cassidy, aka WALLFLOWER, had concealed their secrets from each other. Even as their wedding date approached, Cassidy was still not authorized by the FBI to tell her the truth. She did not yet know the extent to which her own life was to change when she married a spy.

But why had Krstyen told Cassidy she had come up from Atlanta? "I did say Atlanta," she recalled, "but all I meant was I changed planes in

Atlanta. I had come from Montgomery. I did spend about a week in Atlanta with friends."

Marie's father, John Krstyen, was born in Czechoslovakia and came to America as a child of ten. Her grandfather was Hungarian; later, she wondered if her Eastern European family background had added to the FBI's concern when the bureau finally figured out who she was.

Marie Krstyen was born on March 20, 1927, in Johnstown, Pennsylvania, where her father worked for Bethlehem Steel, fixing machinery. Her mother, Mary Kondash, was the daughter of a local businessman. "Our family was Catholic, my mother converted when we were small. I went to a parochial school, and I wanted to be a teacher, so the nuns said, 'Join the convent.' It was a way of getting a college education."

She had entered the convent, which was in Pittsburgh, at age eighteen. Even early on, there were harbingers of her eventual decision to return to the secular life. Sister Miriam alone would not bow her head during prayer before mealtime and was admonished by the nuns. She was told she was too proud, and was not showing the proper degree of humility. "But I felt humility is truth. And if my feelings were the truth, then why should I bow my head? I consider religion very personal, between you and your God."

For any infractions of the rules, the nuns were forced to kneel at the crucifix in front of some three hundred other nuns in the cafeteria and eat their meals on their knees. Independent-minded, and a touch rebellious, Sister Miriam questioned the practice. She was required to eat several meals on her knees, however, for minor transgressions.

But her goal of a college education was met. "The Vincentian Sisters sent me to Duquesne University, which is also in Pittsburgh, in 1947." The sisters ran schools and hospitals. Sister Miriam taught school and later transferred to hospital work. She was sent by the order to a rural area of southwest Missouri, where she worked in the local hospital and attended Saint Louis University in the summers, earning a master's degree in hospital administration.

In 1958, she was transferred to Saint Jude's Hospital in Montgomery, where she found herself in the midst of the turmoil over civil rights. "All the black patients were sent to Saint Jude's," she said. "Because of that, there were phone threats to blow up the hospital. Martin Luther King came to the hospital several times and visited patients who had been beaten during civil-rights demonstrations, and some white demonstrators. I would meet him at the door."[1]

In the spring of 1965, Sister Miriam Joseph turned thirty-eight. "I wanted to get back into teaching. I asked to change from hospital work and was turned down; they said they would have to train someone else. So in January I left the order." After her brief stopover in Atlanta, she arrived in Baltimore, where her sister Helen lived, and found work as a teacher.

In the spring of 1968, Cassidy's divorce became final. Krstyen and Cassidy set their wedding date for the third week in June, but an obstacle arose. "I was marrying a divorced man and had problems with the church," Krstyen recalled. "I went to different priests. It would have been over a thousand dollars to get an annulment. I'd never been married, and I said to the first priest, he [Cassidy] has nothing to do with this. But I was told, 'You can't receive the sacraments.' "

To be told she could not receive communion and the other rites of the Roman Catholic church was not acceptable to the former Sister Miriam Joseph. Joe and Marie were married in June as scheduled, but it was three years before the issue of the sacraments was resolved. "I finally found a priest who said, 'You go right ahead.' To me, religion is more than some rules a priest makes up. To me, religion is my relationship with God. I go with a peaceful heart and mind to the sacraments."

The wedding took place in the chapel at Edgewood Arsenal. The

---

[1] In May 1961, John M. Doar, an official of the Justice Department's civil rights division, was on the scene in Montgomery when the Freedom Riders were beaten with baseball bats and lead pipes at the Greyhound bus station. Doar also went to St. Jude's to investigate the threats against the hospital. Sister Miriam greatly admired Doar "because he protected St. Jude's. John spent part of one night by the switchboard with me listening to the threats. He had a set of earphones and could listen to the calls coming in." In 1974, Doar was counsel to the House Judiciary Committee that voted to impeach President Richard Nixon.

chaplain who officiated was a Protestant, but he performed a Catholic service. Jimmy Morrissey and his wife attended the wedding, Marie recalled, "but I didn't know who they were."

The bride was in for a shock. "One day shortly after the marriage," she said, "Morrissey shows up at the apartment and flashes his badge. He said, 'Your husband is involved in secret work for the United States, working with the FBI and the military.' He didn't give any details. He said, 'There are times when he will have to go out for the whole evening or overnight.' "

When Morrissey had left, Marie turned to her husband.

"You never told me you were involved in anything like this," she said. "Now I understand why you were asking all those questions about me." Cassidy, her "truthful guy," could only smile and shrug.

After the initial astonishment had worn off, Marie began to worry. "I did not resent the fact that it had been kept secret. I knew there was a reason it had been kept secret. But I had some questions. Was it dangerous? The question was running through my own mind, but I did not press Joe about it. I figured it would become clear in time."

Jimmy Morrissey became a familiar figure in their marriage. Cassidy shielded his wife from much of his activities, but the nature of his mission gradually became clear to her. "I realized it was spy work," she said. "I figured it out. I knew about double agents. I read about them in a spy novel or saw a movie. I figured he was a 'good' spy. But Morrissey never mentioned the country. I didn't know the country was Russia until Joe told me that the FBI had worried I was a plant."

One way or another Marie was drawn into her husband's intelligence work. "Once in the early 1970s," Cassidy said, "we were leaving Petersburg, Virginia, and I had to go somewhere, to a picnic grove, so I could get a shortwave transmission from Moscow. She walked Beau, our silver poodle, and kept watch while I got the transmission."

Cassidy could hardly have concealed his secret life from Marie. Although for the most part he used the rollover cameras to photograph the documents he passed to the Russians, on instructions from the Soviets he also bought a camera and a tripod to copy material. At times, Marie saw Cassidy taking pictures of documents or steaming letters on the stove to develop secret writing.

Marie made sure that the spy paraphernalia was kept out of view. "We kept the equipment in the guest room," she said. "I always made sure the tripod and camera and radio were hidden when we had guests."

Marie Cassidy did not have to wait very long to learn whether her husband's espionage work might be dangerous. In October 1968, only four months into their marriage, Cassidy received a microdot instructing him to travel abroad—something that had never happened before. He was to go to Mexico City for a meeting. The instructions gave the date and the time of night that he was to be on a certain street. He was not asked to bring any documents.

It was an alarming turn of events, for both Cassidy and the FBI. It was not clear why the Soviets wanted to meet Cassidy outside the United States. For the first time, WALLFLOWER might be in real danger.

CHAPTER

10

"THEY MIGHT SHOOT ME"

The KGB was responsible for counterintelligence within the Soviet military, including the GRU. So it was not unreasonable to believe that if Moscow had somehow discovered that Cassidy was an American spy, he could be targeted.

As the poison-umbrella attack on Georgi Markov demonstrated, the KGB had the capability to assassinate its enemies or to provide its allies with the means to do so. In the 1950s and 1960s, the KGB carried out a number of hits, some successful.[1]

In 1954, for example, Nikolai Y. Khokhlov was dispatched to Frankfurt to assassinate the leader of an anti-Soviet exile group. He was

---

[1] In *From Russia with Love*, Ian Fleming, the creator of James Bond, popularized SMERSH as "the official murder organization of the Soviet government." In fact, during World War II, the Soviet army did have special units called SMERSH to spy on the armed forces, liquidate disloyal elements, and track down Nazi agents.

armed with a noiseless gun disguised as a cigarette pack that fired bullets laced with potassium cyanide. Instead of carrying out the hit, Khokhlov defected. But in 1957, Moscow sent Bogdan Stashynsky, who later described himself as a professional killer for the KGB, to liquidate Lev Rebet, a Ukrainian exile leader in Munich. He murdered Rebet with a special gun that fired a spray of prussic acid, the liquid form of cyanide. Two years later, with an improved model of the vapor gun, he assassinated Stefan Bandera, another Ukrainian exile leader in Munich. Stashynsky later fled to West Germany and was convicted of the murders and sentenced to eight years in prison.

In 1964, the KGB attacked Horst Schwirkmann, a wiretap expert for West German intelligence who had been sent to Moscow to debug Bonn's embassy there. After completing his assignment, Schwirkmann visited the famous Zagorsk Monastery, an hour northeast of Moscow. He stopped to admire a painting of the Resurrection. A middle-aged man who had been kneeling and praying by it arose and stood politely behind Schwirkmann, who suddenly felt what seemed like ice water on his left buttock. Within seconds, the West German technician was in agonizing pain, and his skin had blistered. Hospitalized and given intensive medical treatment, he almost lost his left leg but survived. U.S. physicians determined he had been sprayed with deadly nitrogen mustard gas.

Within the KGB's First Chief Directorate, its foreign-intelligence arm, the assassination unit was first the ninth, then the thirteenth department. In 1965, Peter Deriabin, a KGB defector, testified to a Senate committee, "The thirteenth department is responsible for assassination and terror. This department is called the department of wet affairs, or in Russian *Mokrie Dela. . . . Mokrie* means 'wet,' and in this case *mokrie* means 'blood wet.' "

During the time that Cassidy was working as a double against the Russians, then, the KGB was capable of assassinating its enemies, although it may have later abandoned the practice. In 1989, Victor Gundarev, a KGB colonel who had defected in Greece three years earlier, told the author, "Yes, they had *Mokrie Dela.* I don't know a single case in the last fifteen years or more. But there is risk." Because of the perceived risk, however remote today, most Soviet and Russian defectors in the United States, including Victor Gundarev, live under assumed names in the CIA's equivalent of the Justice Department's witness-protection program.[2]

The risk was much greater, of course, during the height of the cold war, when Cassidy was instructed to go to Mexico. At the time, the summer Olympic games were under way in Mexico City, and there were no flights or hotel rooms available; the city was completely booked.

Cassidy kissed his bride good-bye but said very little about why he was leaving the country. "Just that it was involved in that work," Marie remembered.

From Baltimore, Cassidy flew to Dallas, rented a car, and drove to Brownsville, on the Mexican border, hoping to catch a flight from there. He went to a travel agency. "There were no flights to Mexico City, but I was told to keep checking," Cassidy recalled. "I kept checking for several days and finally decided I would have to drive."

Having heard stories of *bandidos* waylaying travelers, Cassidy was not thrilled about the prospect of driving. "The next day the travel agency called and said they had a flight from Matamoros, Mexico, just over the border from Brownsville." Cassidy turned in the rental car, hailed a cab, took it over the bridge to the dusty, decrepit airport in Matamoros, and caught his flight.

On the plane, Cassidy's fears crowded in. The FBI's agents usually watched when he met his Soviet handlers in northern Virginia. Their

---

[2] The KGB went out of existence after the collapse of the Soviet Union in December 1991. In Russia, the spy organization split into two principal parts: The Russian foreign intelligence service, the old First Chief Directorate, became the Sluzhba Vneshnei Razvedki (SVR), which carries out espionage abroad. The Federal Security Service (FSK, later the FSB) became the successor to the KGB's internal-security and counterintelligence departments.

presence offered a measure of reassurance and protection. But counter-intelligence in Mexico might not be possible; the bureau would be operating outside its turf.[3]

Yet if Cassidy did not keep the appointment in Mexico City, the Russians might conclude that he was a double agent. Operation SHOCKER could collapse. Cassidy decided he had to go.

Since the hotels in Mexico City were full, the travel agency had made arrangements for Cassidy to stay with a Mexican family. He had several days to kill while waiting for the appointed night. "I spent a week in Mexico posing as an Olympic tourist. I got tickets to boxing, track and field, and swimming."

Cassidy had arrived early in Mexico City for two reasons. First, he wanted to be sure he got there in plenty of time. "The other reason was a cover story: I went to Mexico to go to the Olympics. That was what I told my family and friends. After all, I had just got married, so why was I flying off to Mexico? I told everybody I already had these arrangements."

Cassidy was no James Bond, sipping magnums of Dom Pérignon and dining at expensive restaurants with gorgeous women. Having been warned about the water and food, he subsisted on beer, which he did not much like, and peanuts at a downtown bar. Cassidy, who grew up on his grandmother's mashed potatoes and gravy in Erie, was partial to simple fare; he shunned the tacos and tortillas. His menu expanded a bit when he discovered that the top-floor restaurant of the Hilton hotel had cornflakes. "I was afraid of the milk," he recalled, "but hell, I was hungry."

Finally, the night of the meet arrived. Cassidy hailed a cab and took it to what turned out to be a desolate, remote barrio on the outskirts of the city. "The meeting was set for nine P.M. I got there [at] eight-thirty or

---

[3] Although the FBI sometimes conducts surveillances abroad in espionage cases, if it informs the local intelligence service, the risk of a leak increases. If it does not do so, and the foreign government discovers it, there may be unpleasant diplomatic repercussions. Moreover, the CIA is unhappy when the FBI operates in foreign countries, since foreign-intelligence operations are primarily its responsibility.

eight-forty-five. I left the cab and walked to the designated spot in the middle of the block.

"There was nothing there, just several houses built out of wooden boxes. The whole area was a slum. There were shacks across the street and a couple smoking, playing some sort of a game, bent over a board. I could see them by the streetlight." Looking around, Cassidy realized he was the only American anywhere in the area. "I felt pretty conspicuous, over six feet, with white, close-cropped hair. I don't know if there was any bureau countersurveillance or whether the CIA was notified. I was hoping the bureau had me under surveillance."

As he stood there in the dark, Cassidy wondered why Mexico and why he was told not to bring any documents. Did the GRU suspect him? Was he about to be kidnapped?

For the first time since it had all begun almost a decade earlier with volleyball and oyster dinners along the riverfront in Washington, he was frankly scared. "I thought they might put me on a plane to Moscow, give me the truth serum, and shoot me."

No one stepped out of the shadows at 9 P.M. Cassidy waited for an hour beyond the appointed time, then walked to the corner and waited another half an hour before a taxi came along. The taxi did not stop, but about ten minutes later it cruised by again, and this time it picked him up.

Disappointed but also relieved, Cassidy flew back to Baltimore and reported to the FBI that the Soviets had failed to make contact. At home with Marie, Cassidy made light of his trip at first. He told his wife he had seen some boxing matches and track-and-field events. He joked about his trouble finding something to eat. It was only some time after his return that he revealed to Marie his fears about the trip.

In December, at his next scheduled meeting with his GRU handler, Cassidy complained bitterly. The new "Mike," to whom Danilin had handed him off, had been identified by the FBI as Oleg Ivanovich Likhachev, a GRU officer listed as a third secretary of the Soviet embassy.

Likhachev was not his real name, however. The GRU man was using his wife's maiden name in his career as a spy, probably to avoid any potential embarrassment to the memory of his father, a decorated Soviet general during World War II. Likhachev's father, General Ivan Chernyakhovsky, was killed in action in February 1945.[4] Had Likhachev been caught in a spy scandal and expelled from the United States or another country, there would be nothing to connect him with his famous father.

"I was steaming," Cassidy recalled. "I said, 'Jeez, Mike, I just got married and you send me off to a foreign country and nobody shows.' He said, 'You were supposed to have been told the meeting was canceled.' That's all he said."

Jack O'Flaherty, soon to become Cassidy's new FBI case agent, had his own theory about the hat dance the GRU put Cassidy through in Mexico. "It could have been a test to see if he would leave the country," Flaherty said. "If he resisted, they might conclude he was under control."

---

[4] In recognition of his service, the Soviet government awarded a lifetime pension to his widow and money to his children, Oleg, the future spy, and his sister, Neonila, until they completed their educations. Likhachev's father-in-law, Ivan A. Likhachev, was a major player in the industrial development of the Soviet Union and ran the Stalin automobile factory for years. He was familiar with American automobile production and design, having toured all the major auto plants in the United States during the early 1930s. He had even worked at Ford plants in the United States for two years.

SUNDANCE

By the spring of 1969, Cassidy had been stationed at Edgewood for seven years, and the FBI began to fret that the Russians might regard it as a suspiciously long time for him to remain in the same job. Moreover, the nerve-gas deception was winding down after three and a half years.

It had been difficult enough to keep Cassidy in the Edgewood lab as it was. Shortly after his marriage, Cassidy was informed by the army that he was being sent to Karlsruhe, Germany. There was some suspicion within the FBI that the army wanted to transfer Cassidy there so it could take over the case. (Because the FBI operates primarily within the United States, if the case moved abroad the army would have jurisdiction.) Morrissey managed to outflank the army and squelch the transfer. According to Charlie Bevels, the FBI had to maneuver around the army bureaucracy more than once.

"Cassidy's name kept showing up on a list for Vietnam," Bevels recalled, "and every six months or so Jimmy Morrissey had to go to the Pentagon and get his name off the list. Joe was uneasy because he couldn't explain it to anybody. He didn't want any special privilege."

The army inadvertently solved the bureau's problem that spring by promoting Cassidy, a master sergeant, to an E-9, the rating for sergeant major. "Since there was no E-9 slot at Edgewood, I had to find a slot," Cassidy said. "I checked and found one open at the United States Strike Command [STRICOM], in Tampa, Florida. I put in a request for transfer."

Unknown to Cassidy, the FBI was orchestrating his move to Tampa. The bureau, Phil Parker recalled, saw a major benefit that might flow from the transfer. "The GRU's officers in the embassy could not meet him in Florida, because of travel restrictions on Soviet diplomats, who were normally confined to a twenty-five-mile radius of Washington." As a result, he said, the FBI hoped that the move would force Moscow to surface a new contact, perhaps an illegal, who might lead the FBI to other unknown Soviet agents.

Nothing is easy in the bureaucracy. If the FBI was going to run an espionage operation out of STRICOM, the military had to be told. Tom O'Laughlin, the ex-FBI man then working for the Joint Chiefs, was designated to bell the cat. He traveled to Tampa and briefed the base commander, a four-star general. O'Laughlin was successful in his delicate mission. The general agreed to accept Cassidy.

Operation SHOCKER was now set to move to Tampa. STRICOM, located at MacDill Air Force Base, was the Pentagon's unified command for a large group of army, air force, navy, and Marine Corps units around the country. The command was created in 1962 by President John F. Kennedy. As its name implies, its purpose was to allow the military to respond quickly to a flare-up anywhere in the world.

In July, as Cassidy prepared to move to Florida, he received instructions from Oleg Likhachev to return on the day after Christmas to Washington, where he would meet "an old friend."[1] While Cassidy would

---

[1] Cassidy had thirty days' leave every year and could get away almost any time, but the Soviets may have reasoned that it would look normal for him to travel around holidays.

have no difficulty getting leave to make the trip north, for the moment these instructions frustrated the FBI's plan to force the Soviets to reveal a new contact.

The following month, Cassidy said good-bye to Jimmy Morrissey and Charlie Bevels, and he and Marie left for Tampa. He contacted the Tampa FBI office and met with Dennis R. Dickson, who served briefly as his case agent. In the files of the Tampa office, WALLFLOWER was given a code number, TP510.[2] He and Marie bought a house on the water in St. Petersburg.

At FBI headquarters, Gene Peterson chose a new code name, ZYRK-SEEZ, for the case that the FBI had up to then designated as CHOWLINE and the Joint Chiefs called SHOCKER. Peterson chose the loopy spelling of Xerxes for a crafty practical reason: He knew he would be able to use it right away, without the usual bureaucratic delay for approval. The panjandrums in charge of such matters could see at a glance that ZYRKSEEZ was unique; it would not have to be laboriously checked against previous bureau code names because there was no way in the world it would duplicate a cryptonym already in the files.[3]

Even so, Peterson was given a hard time over the code name. A few days later, someone from the records branch called him, complaining vociferously about the unusual spelling.

"What's with this ZYRKSEEZ?" the file keeper asked. "We can't pronounce it."

"You don't have to pronounce it," Peterson shot back. "All you need to know is where to file the damn card."

In December, as instructed, Cassidy returned to Washington. On the

[2] TP stood for "Tampa." He was also given another coded designation, TP510-OA. The last two letters stood for "operational asset."

[3] Xerxes, the Persian king, was only indirectly the source of the code name. Peterson rode into headquarters every day with an FBI agent whose initials were F.X. and whose nickname was Xerxes. The name popped into Peterson's head as he was casting about for a new cryptonym. Although Peterson had his own reasons for the phonetic variation, the FBI sometimes deliberately skews code words to give them added security. A mole inside the FBI who overheard the code name ZYRKSEEZ for example, would very likely look in files under the letter X and not find it.

day after Christmas, he waited on a street in Prince Georges County, Maryland, at the designated time. As promised, an "old friend" appeared.

Mikhail Danilin, by now a second secretary of the Soviet embassy, was back from Moscow. He smiled broadly at the sight of the agent he had lamented he might never see again.

After the two men had greeted each other, Danilin instructed Cassidy to pick out several drop sites in the St. Petersburg area. That would be good news to the FBI; the bureau's plan appeared to be working.

Danilin told Cassidy to bring the description of the locations to their next meeting. Once the drops were agreed upon, Danilin said, Cassidy was to buy a camera, photograph military documents from MacDill, and place the film in hollow rocks at the drop sites at designated times and dates. The agent who cleared a drop would leave a paper bag as a signal that the film had been picked up. Cassidy was to return to the drop site each time and verify that the paper bag was there.

Then Danilin explained that "another USSR agent" might clear the drops in Florida. Cassidy agreed to his instructions but grumbled to Danilin about having to come north at Christmas, leaving his wife by herself.

To the FBI, Danilin's passing mention of "another USSR agent" was important additional evidence that the bureau's plan was on target: Given the restrictions on travel by Soviet diplomats, the agent almost had to be an illegal.

In the world of espionage, illegals are a prime catch. Because illegals do not operate under diplomatic cover, they can be anywhere—the woman who works in the hair salon down the street, the friendly clerk in the hardware store, or even the neighbor next door. Unless illegals are identified by a defector, they are virtually impossible to find. Their spying usually goes undetected.

Back in Florida, with the help of the FBI, WALLFLOWER drove around St. Petersburg picking out likely drop sites for the GRU. Most were in residential areas or near stores or office buildings, which would make surveillance that much easier for the bureau. In a park or wooded area, it would be difficult for the FBI to get close enough. Cassidy was to explain to the Soviets that the Tampa Bay area was less rural than northern Virginia, compelling him to select sites in more populous places. As instructed, he also bought a 35 mm camera.

Then, in May 1970, he met his new FBI case agent, a tall Irishman from Brooklyn who still retained a trace of his New York accent along with a lot of street smarts. At age thirty-five, John J. O'Flaherty was already a bureau veteran. The two men took to each other immediately, the start of a lifelong friendship.

At six foot two, Jack O'Flaherty was a handsome, impressive-looking man with an athlete's build. The son of a mounted policeman in New York, he was born in Brooklyn but grew up in the Rockaways in Queens. He went to St. John's University and joined the police force in 1957, working the four-to-midnight shift and attending law school at St. John's by day. "A family friend, Mike O'Brien, encouraged me to apply to the FBI and gave me an application," O'Flaherty said. "From time to time, he needled me, what happened to that application I gave you? So, finally I applied."

He joined the FBI in March 1961 at age twenty-six, worked as an agent in North Carolina, and was assigned to the Cuban squad in New York, his first taste of foreign counterintelligence work. He married and, after a tour in the San Juan office, arrived in Tampa in August 1968.

On July Fourth weekend 1970, Cassidy drove north to Washington for another meeting with Danilin at their old haunt, the parking lot of the bowling alley in Springfield. The Soviets approved most of the drop sites he had selected, and Danilin accepted Cassidy's explanation about why the drops were to be in more built-up areas.

Cassidy received a packet of what looked like ordinary lead of the type that is loaded into a mechanical pencil. He was instructed to crush the lead, dissolve it in water, and use the solution to raise the secret writing he would receive from the Soviets. This replaced the earlier method of steaming.

Almost six months later, Cassidy went to Washington again. On the day after Christmas, he picked up three hollow rocks containing two new rollover cameras to use in addition to his 35 mm camera. There were also instructions from Danilin for the first drop in Florida. The message said: "6 Mar. 9:00. Base of bush by large palm tree at Rafael Blvd. and Snell Island Blvd. (south of stop sign)."

After collecting the rocks, Cassidy met with Danilin, and then drove back to Florida, where he turned the rocks over to O'Flaherty. In Tampa, arrangements had to be made to select the classified documents that Cassidy would photograph for the GRU. An ad hoc committee of representatives of the armed services was created at STRICOM to screen the feed before the Joint Chiefs in Washington gave final approval.

Snell Isle, misnamed because it is really a peninsula along Tampa Bay, is a quiet, mostly residential section a mile and a half long and less than a mile wide. Almost half the area is taken up by a private golf course.

With the first pickup by the Russians scheduled for the night of March 6, 1971, O'Flaherty swung into action. He tried to leave nothing to chance in preparing for the moment of contact. There was a two-story condominium directly across the street from the drop site on Snell Isle. O'Flaherty approached Jerry Koontz, a seventy-four-year-old widower who lived on the second floor, overlooking the palm tree. Koontz was a retired sales manager for Sinclair Oil. "He allowed us to use his apartment."

Also in the line of vision of the drop site, catercorner and a block away, was a building that housed the Tampa Bay Engineering Company. O'Flaherty approached William O'Neill, the firm's president, and asked if the FBI could take over the building on the night of March 6. O'Flaherty never explained the reason, but he assured the executive, "There won't be any shooting." O'Neill agreed.

On the evening of March 6, the stakeout was ready. O'Flaherty waited in the dark in the condo across from the palm tree with his FBI team and a bug-eyed Jerry Koontz, for whom retirement had never been this exciting. "In the front room were two photographers, Fred Webb, who was in charge of the FBI photo lab, and George Austin, and two agents, Joe Hall from the Washington field office, and Larry Doyle from New York. Five of us in the dark, watching."

The two visiting FBI men were counterintelligence agents, experts at spotting Soviets, in case Danilin or anyone else from Washington dared to risk violating the twenty-five-mile rule. The photographers were looking through a night-vision scope.

Promptly at 9 P.M., Joe Cassidy placed three hollow rocks at the base of the palm tree. Inside were rollover cameras with photos of eleven documents, one stamped TOP SECRET, nine marked SECRET, and one CONFIDENTIAL. The document marked TOP SECRET was entitled "CINPAC Keystone Robin (Charlie) Movement Planning Conference (U) MSG DTG 110338Z DEC 70."

If all went according to plan, a Russian spy would appear within half an hour. Would he arrive by car? On foot? O'Flaherty had attempted to cover all the bases. "We had an agent with a tie-clasp camera riding the bus line in case the illegal arrived by bus." Other agents were in the engineering offices as backup, watching from a distance.

Time ticked by as O'Flaherty and the four other FBI men in the condo strained to see any activity around the palm tree, which was nestled against a thick hedge. George Austin was peering through the night scope.

"All of a sudden George says, 'I see a hand,' " O'Flaherty recalled. "We couldn't see anything. But through the night scope he could. The individual had come from the opposite side, from behind the palm tree, and reached through the bushes. His fingers were inches from the rock, groping for it, and then he gave up. He comes out from behind the bushes. My first thought is, Is this a professional spy? He has white slacks on. The last thing he should be wearing." Through the night scope, the photographer could see the man was young, tall, and slender, with dark hair and glasses.

"He comes out front, and the cameras are going. He picks up the rocks and puts them in a bag. And then he walks away, south on Rafael.

Now we've got a person, and he's moving in a direction where we did not have anybody." It was 9:23 P.M.

O'Flaherty silently cursed. The skinny Soviet spy in white slacks was eluding their grasp, and there was nothing they could do about it. Who was he? Had agents been stationed on Rafael Boulevard, they might have been able to get a closer look or a better picture, but it might not be possible to identify the man from the photographs, since he was almost certainly an illegal, an unknown face.

The FBI had decided in advance not to try to follow whoever appeared at the drop. SHOCKER had been running for twelve years, and O'Flaherty was not about to blow the operation by putting men on the street; if the spy became aware that he was being tailed, the game would be over. "We wanted fixed surveillance for security reasons, no cars," he said.

Luck was on the bureau's side. The unknown spy had forgotten to leave a paper bag by the palm tree to signal that the drop had been cleared. He realized his mistake and came back. Seven minutes later, at 9:30 P.M., a light blue Volkswagen suddenly appeared. The man jumped out, with the car's motor running, and left a Publix supermarket bag at the base of the tree. Then he got back in his car and zoomed away.

Through their night-vision scope, the photographers could make out the license plate: 1E-17128. From the condo, O'Flaherty called Joseph F. Santoiana, Jr., the FBI's special agent in charge (SAC) in Tampa, at his home. The SAC called in the license number and asked Tampa to run the plate. By the time O'Flaherty and his team reached the office, they had their answer. The Volkswagen belonged to a rental agency in Miami. Around midnight, teletypes were sent out to Miami and to FBI headquarters in Washington reporting all that had happened.

SHOCKER had surfaced an unknown spy and created a new case. The FBI gave it a separate code name: PALMETTO.

Now the FBI's task was to identify the man. Before dawn, a teletype arrived from headquarters instructing Tampa and Miami to follow up but emphasizing that the surveillance be discreet.

The FBI was moving with an excess of caution. "Sure, we could have staked out the rental agency," O'Flaherty said, "but they [headquarters] were very concerned about blowing the case."

At 7 A.M., Special Agent Sam Jones, of the FBI's Miami office, checked with the rental agency in Miami, an establishment known as Lester-U-Drive-It. Donald W. MacArthur, the manager, identified the man who had rented the car and returned it an hour earlier. He was apparently Mexican but had produced a Canadian driver's license. The name on the license was Gilberto Lopez y Rivas.

MacArthur remembered that when Lopez rented the car, he had said that he had arrived in Miami on a Greyhound bus. Jones reasoned that he might have left the same way. The FBI man went to the Greyhound terminal and spoke to the ticket clerk. Jones brought with him the photographs taken through the night scope. But the clerk shook his head; he could not remember selling the man a ticket.

"You know how many people we get going through here?" the clerk asked. He paused, then recalled something. "Wait a second—bad breath! The guy had bad breath! I remember him now." The clerk had given the man directions to San Antonio. He suggested the most direct route, but Lopez bought a ticket on an earlier bus with stops in New Orleans and Houston.

"Now we alerted all the divisions along the way," O'Flaherty said. "FBI agents were watching the Greyhound terminals in all three cities, New Orleans, Houston, and San Antonio.

"Several agents were getting on buses to try to spot him. The Greyhound with Lopez aboard arrived in New Orleans the next day. The FBI saw him on the bus. Agents boarded the bus in New Orleans and watched him leave the bus in Houston. He took a cab to Houston Intercontinental Airport." The agents did not want to get in too close and did not trail the taxi, though they later interviewed the driver. He said his passenger had entered the terminal. Checking further, the FBI established that he had boarded a Braniff flight to Mexico City. Jean Hadid, a Braniff ticket agent at the airport, identified Lopez.

Lopez was gone, at least for the moment, south of the border. The FBI knew nothing about him yet, except his name, if it was his real one. But

O'Flaherty knew one thing, as he looked back on the kaleidoscopic events of the last forty-eight hours: Something unprecedented in the history of espionage had occurred. The man who called himself Gilberto Lopez y Rivas was the first illegal ever surfaced by a double-agent operation of the FBI.

CHAPTER

12

PALMETTO

Having traced the man in the white slacks to Mexico City, the FBI made an astonishing discovery. Gilberto Lopez y Rivas, on an espionage mission to Florida for Soviet intelligence, had rented the Volkswagen in his true name.

The bureau now had enjoyed two lucky breaks. Had Lopez not initially forgotten to leave the Publix bag at the drop site, or had he used false credentials to rent the car in Miami, the FBI might never have identified the skinny young man who picked up WALLFLOWER's three rocks on Snell Isle.

Gradually, the details about Lopez emerged. The son of Gilberto Esparza Lopez, an accountant, and Rosa Morgado Rivas Lopez, he was born in Mexico City on March 6, 1943, which meant that he was celebrating his twenty-eighth birthday on the day that the FBI agents had watched and photographed him from Jerry Koontz's condo.

Lopez attended the Universidad Nacional Autónoma de México, where he earned a master's degree in 1969. For two years, from 1967 to 1969, while a student at the university, he was a research assistant in anthropology for the International Olympic Committee in Mexico City.[1]

In 1968 Lopez had married another anthropology student, Alicia Castellanos. The couple had a boy, Nayar, and later another child, Ali.

Lopez was a leftist and an intellectual, and it was clear that his central concern—and possibly the driving force behind his decision to engage in clandestine work for the GRU—was his outrage over the treatment of Mexicans and Mexican Americans in the United States.

Fury over the plight of Chicanos in America appeared in almost all of his published writings. In 1971, the same year that the FBI identified him, Lopez published *Los Chicanos: Una minoría nacional explotada.*[2] The book's title reflected his view of the United States as a nation of ruthless gringos exploiting poor Mexicans.

Many Mexicans and Americans have sympathized with the problems faced by Mexican Americans, especially migrant workers who often toil in terrible, unsanitary conditions, performing backbreaking labor for low wages. Millions of Americans supported the efforts of Cesar Chavez to organize the grape and lettuce workers in California. Most of those who champion the attempts of Mexican Americans to achieve a better life, however—even those who are harsh critics of American society—do not act on their views by becoming spies against the United States. Lopez did. Somewhere along the line, probably while he was a student at Mexico's national university, Gilberto Lopez was recruited and trained by the GRU.

Five months after he had flown back to Mexico, Lopez reentered the United States at Brownsville in August 1971, with his family. Through

---

[1] It was in October 1968, while Lopez worked for the Olympic Committee, that Cassidy attended the games in Mexico City and waited in vain in the barrio for the Soviet contact who never came.

[2] Mexico: Editorial Nuestro Tiempo, 1971; 3d ed., 1979. The title translates as *The Chicanos: An Exploited National Minority.* Lopez has also been published in English. See *The Chicanos: Life and Struggles of the Mexican Minority in the United States* (New York: Monthly Review Press, 1973).

records of the Immigration and Naturalization Service, the FBI learned his destination: Salt Lake City. Lopez, as it developed, was returning to school. He was working toward his Ph.D. in anthropology at the University of Utah.

He was placed under surveillance in Salt Lake City, and his apartment was wiretapped and bugged. George M. Owen, an FBI wireman, was sent out from headquarters to install the electronic surveillance on the PALMETTOS.[3]

Even though the drops in Florida were now activated, Cassidy traveled to Washington again on July 3, 1971, to get new instructions and meet personally with Mikhail Danilin.

The GRU officer said he had received the documents that Cassidy had left on Snell Isle, which meant, of course, that Lopez had gotten them safely to the Soviets in Mexico City.

Danilin then told Cassidy what kinds of documents he wanted from STRICOM. He instructed Cassidy to look in particular for documents dealing with future U.S. military exercises. They discussed the dates and locations of the next several drops in St. Petersburg.

Inside the hollow rock that Cassidy picked up before the meeting was a package containing ten thousand dollars and new instructions on a microdot concealed inside a postcard. The package also contained a blank sheet of paper with secret writing that duplicated and backed up the instructions on the microdot.

Cassidy was told he would be sent to Mexico again the following July. This time, Danilin provided detailed instructions for the contact. Cassidy was to stay at the San Marcos Hotel. On July 22, before noon, he was to confirm his arrival by placing a red chalk mark on a white fence pole on Calle Río Lerma, near his hotel. Also described were a dead drop where he would leave his film, a meeting site, and various signal sites. Cassidy

---

[3] Although PALMETTO was the FBI code name for the Lopez phase of the operation, the term was used interchangeably to refer to the case, to Lopez himself, or in plural form to Lopez and his wife, Alicia.

was not thrilled at the news; aside from the risk of meeting the Soviets abroad on dark streets, there were the gastronomic dangers lurking in Mexico City.

The next domestic drop was set for the night of September 10, 1971, at the same palm tree on Snell Isle. O'Flaherty again prepared to station agents in Jerry Koontz's condo and in the engineering company. Learning from the previous drop, O'Flaherty arranged this time for a third observation post.

"The third spot was a private school on Snell Isle Boulevard. I approached the dean, Gordon Tucker. He had to check with the board. Charles Randolph Wedding, who later became the mayor of Saint Petersburg, was on the board, and he approved."

Promptly at 9 P.M., Cassidy made the drop at the base of the palm tree, as O'Flaherty and the agents with him watched. This time, Cassidy left films of a document stamped TOP SECRET, another marked SECRET, and a third marked CONFIDENTIAL, as well as other material.

The document marked TOP SECRET was entitled "USSTRICOM . . . Programming Plan 2-71," dated June 22, 1971. It described the establishment of the U.S. Readiness Command under instructions from the Joint Chiefs of Staff.

The document stamped SECRET dealt with the withdrawal of U.S. forces from Vietnam. It was called "Letter of Instruction for the Eighth Incremental Redeployment of U.S. Army Forces from RVN (U) - AGDA-A(M) (6 JULY 71) OPS OD TR July 14, 1971."

As the FBI agents waited, tension built inside the darkened condo. Then, around nine-thirty, the telephone rang, and O'Flaherty grabbed it. "An agent at the school site called me on an open phone line, a land line as we refer to it. 'Jack, looks like we've got him here. Female driving, child in the car, and another unidentified male.' " Gilberto Lopez was back, this time with his wife, Alicia, their young son, and a second man. The FBI cameras were whirring away.

O'Flaherty continued his narrative: "The subject gets out of the car, a gray Renault, license number LP9414, about a block from the drop site, and starts walking east on Snell Isle Boulevard. He cuts into a yard and again comes out from the bushes. This time he comes right around in front of the tree and picks up the rock. He left a paper bag at the tree. It was a Publix bag both times.

"His wife stops right below our LO, the lookout. She pulls up the car past the intersection and waits for him about a block beyond the drop. He crosses the street, walks a block to the car, right under the engineering firm. He gets in, and they drive off the island at the eastern end."

Three months later, on December 20, the espionage ballet was repeated, with the FBI at the same three observation posts. Inside the hollow rock this time were films of three documents stamped SECRET, including another one dealing with troop pullouts from Vietnam, dated September 24, 1971, and entitled "Letter of Instruction for the Ninth Incremental Redeployment of U.S. Army Forces from RVN(U), - AGDA-A(M) (17 SEPT 71) OPS OD TR."

As Cassidy was placing his fake rock, FBI agents saw a white two-door Vega, with Florida plates, 1E-23144, cruising north on nearby North Shore Drive. At 9:29 P.M., Gilberto Lopez appeared again, on foot, but with a bold new approach, O'Flaherty recalled. "Lopez, his wife, and their two-year-old son walk up. They're holding the kid's hand. Lopez, actively assisted by his wife, began searching the area under the bushes, and they clear the drop. They left in the Vega."

The Russians were picking up the pace. Cassidy had now had three drops and a personal meeting in Washington in only nine months.

Four days after Christmas, although it was not the usual form of communication from the Soviets, Cassidy received a one-page letter, dated Christmas Day, in the mail, addressed to him at his home in St. Petersburg. Inside was what looked like a blank piece of paper. To develop it, Cassidy used the special pencil lead he had received from the GRU. But it was not an easy task.

"The lead was difficult to crush," O'Flaherty said. "Joe was using a rolling pin for a while to crush it into powder and then add water. The idea was to dissolve it and use a cotton swab on the blank page, and it would raise the writing. The lab said the writing itself was prepared from barium, strontium, and lead and raised with tetrahydroxyquinone. The lab identified that as the chemical in the special pencil lead."[4]

As Cassidy swabbed cotton over the blank sheet he had received, the words slowly appeared:

"Dear Friend, Thanks for your efforts Top Secret September document was good. For it I'll pay three thousand for whole September package I owe you six thousand. Don't worry about money, I never failed you."

The letter went on to approve the next series of numbered drop sites. "Places 2, 5, 6, 7 aren't good, so correct our schedule as follows: September ten place ten; December twenty place three . . . I need new Secret document . . . now your film are good. My best wishes for New Year."

The letter also informed Cassidy: "Your trip abroad is canceled." For Cassidy, it was a reprieve from another round of beer, peanuts, and corn flakes in Mexico City.

But for the FBI, the cancellation posed a puzzle. The counterintelligence analysts speculated that it was linked to the FBI's recent arrest on espionage charges of Walter Perkins, an air force master sergeant. Perkins had been the highest-ranking noncommissioned intelligence officer in the Air Defense Weapons Center at Tyndall Air Force Base, in the Florida panhandle. He had had complete access to classified information on sophisticated air-to-air missile systems. He had been arrested by the FBI in October at the Panama City airport as he prepared to board a plane for Mexico City with five classified documents in his briefcase. According to the FBI, Perkins was en route to meet his GRU handler.

At Perkins's court-martial, an air force counterintelligence agent in the Office of Special Investigations said the tip about Perkins had come from the police in Tokyo, where the sergeant had been formerly stationed. An informant said that Perkins had been in contact with Edward Khavanov, a Soviet colonel in the Tokyo embassy. OSI then put Perkins

---

[4] Tetrahydroxyquinone is an organic compound used in chemistry as a titration indicator to detect the presence of barium and other substances.

under full-time surveillance, installing six video cameras in his office that recorded him copying information from classified documents onto index cards. Perkins was convicted and sentenced to three years by a military judge.

In Salt Lake City, where he had been sent to bug and wiretap the Lopezes, George Owen was alarmed at what he saw. FBI agents there, more attuned to following around bank-robbery suspects than Russian spies, were too obvious to suit Owen, according to Charlie Bevels. "Owen came back and told headquarters, 'I've watched those guys handling surveillance. Every bureau car has antennas nineteen feet high.'"

Hearing of Owen's dismaying report, Robert J. Schamay, an FBI counterintelligence agent in Washington, urged that something be done, fast. Schamay, six foot four with the frame of a linebacker, volunteered and became the case agent in Salt Lake City.

Wiretapping and bugging the Lopezes had presented problems, Schamay remembered. "They lived in married housing at the university with one child, the little boy. They were in a two-story concrete building, on the top floor. George had put in the technical coverage, but it was hard to do in a concrete building." Owen installed a dual-purpose microphone that tapped the phones and also allowed the FBI to overhear room conversations. The microphone was concealed in a wall telephone; the FBI had managed to gain access to the spies' apartment long enough to switch the wall phone for an identical "hot" unit. The bureau had also installed a remote surveillance camera, trained on the entrance to the building, that transmitted its pictures to a television screen in the FBI's office downtown. Agents conducted physical surveillance of the couple as well.

Since illegals working as Soviet spies are rarely identified, the bureau wanted to learn as much as possible about the Lopezes and their actions. Eugene Peterson, supervising the case from FBI headquarters, decided to insert an undercover agent who would have the difficult and delicate mission of trying to become close to the PALMETTOS.

Peterson reviewed the files of several hundred FBI agents, looking for just the right candidate. Finally, he narrowed the field to fourteen agents with Hispanic backgrounds. From the list, Peterson zeroed in on Aurelio Flores, a twenty-nine-year-old agent in Miami. Not only was Flores of Mexican-American background and bilingual in Spanish and English, he was almost exactly the age of Gilberto Lopez.

Peterson sent the paperwork up to John P. Mohr, the number-three official of the bureau. Mohr noticed that Flores had a toddler.

"What about the child?" he asked. "There might be a security problem."

Peterson was incredulous. "He's only eighteen months old," he protested.

"Yeah," Mohr said, "but my grandson is eighteen months and he says, 'Grandpa G-man.' "

Mohr had a point, although as events were to unfold, it was not the undercover agent's child who talked out of turn. Headquarters approved Peterson's choice, and Flores prepared to move to Salt Lake City with his wife and son.

Peterson arranged a new résumé for Flores. Peterson contacted a former FBI man who was chief of personnel security for a large private corporation in Miami, and the ex-agent agreed to insert a fake employment record for Flores into the company's files.

Aurelio Flores, a compact man with brown hair and hazel eyes, was born in Del Rio, Texas, graduated from Saint Mary's University in San Antonio, and served as a captain with the army airborne special forces for five years before he joined the FBI in 1970.

To go undercover in Salt Lake City, ideally Flores would have used a completely new identity with backstopped documentation. There was a problem, however. Since the plan was for Flores to approach Lopez as a fellow student, Flores applied for admission to the University of Utah as a graduate student in geography. "We would have had to change my college transcripts if I used another name," he said. "I used my own name."

If Flores succeeded in befriending Lopez, it was possible that the Soviets might check on his background. As a precaution, the bureau asked various government agencies and private companies to alert it if anyone made inquiries about Flores. "We checked to make sure no one was checking on me. We had 'stops' at different places [so that] in case they were asking questions, we would know."

Flores was accepted by the university and arrived on campus in January 1972. Lopez, he discovered, was an avid badminton player, and Flores briefly considered approaching him as a fellow enthusiast. He decided there was a better way.

The PALMETTOS had enrolled their two-year-old son, Nayar, at a Montessori school day-care center not far from the university. Flores did the same with his son.

"The first time I went to the day-care center, I parked behind his car and locked him in. So he had to wait until I left to get out."

In the parking lot, Flores apologized in Spanish for blocking Lopez.

"*Dispénsame,*" Flores said, excusing himself. "I'll get out of your way."

"No problem," Lopez replied. He seemed pleased to meet another Spanish-speaking parent.

In the days that followed, as they both visited the day-care center, Flores gradually got to know Lopez. "We had to wait for the children, and I introduced myself."

Soon, they became friends. Flores was patient. Lopez liked to talk politics, and Flores made a point of being a good listener. "I listened to his ideas on Marxism and Stalin. He was an admirer of Stalin.

"One day [the PALMETTOS] were going to a function at the anthropology department. There were poetry readings for visiting scholars, that sort of thing. They asked me to baby-sit."

Headquarters could scarcely have expected Flores to get any closer to the target. It might have been unprecedented in the annals of espionage: A Russian spy had unknowingly asked an FBI agent to baby-sit for him.

Whenever Lopez planned to travel to Mexico, or to Florida to service one of Cassidy's drops, he told Flores that he was getting ready to take a trip. Of course, from the wiretaps on his apartment, the FBI usually knew that.

Although Flores had not worked undercover before, he proved to be ingenious and creative. One night, Flores and his wife invited Gilberto and Alicia to their home. "I had him over to dinner and saved all the glasses so we had a full set of prints from him and from her. We loaded the plates into the dishwasher, but they didn't notice we didn't put the glasses in. We got very good prints."

Lopez and his wife had very different personalities, Flores recalled. "She was a good swimmer; he was afraid of the water. So sometimes I could get her at the deep end of the pool and talk to her alone. He would stay in the shallow end. She spoke French, some German. She had traveled through France and had lived with a family in France. She was quite a linguist.

"He was more gregarious, talkative, would have made a hell of a salesman. Go right up to you at a party and start talking. She was more the quiet, intellectual one." But Alicia made one basic conviction clear, Flores said. "She hated Americans."

Similarly, Lopez trusted Flores only because of his Mexican background. "Once Gilberto told the two kids, mine and his, that they must always be friends and not fight. He said to them, 'You must get a pencil and stick it into the blue eyes of the gringos.' "

Lopez was paid well for his espionage work. "The Soviets were paying him in cash every time he made a pickup. We had access to his bank accounts. After each visit to a drop site in Florida he would make a deposit in his bank account. They would pay him between eight thousand and twelve thousand dollars per drop." Out of the total, however, Lopez had to pay his tuition and travel expenses.

From the wiretaps, the FBI learned that Lopez was planning to move with his family to Austin in 1972. The Mexican had received a Ford Foundation grant to study anthropology at the University of Texas.

Lopez broke the news to Flores, though he did not realize, of course, that his good friend already knew it.

"I said, 'Great, good luck.' Then I said, 'I'm not that happy here myself.' " Flores had previously mentioned to Lopez that he had grown up in Texas. "He said, 'Maybe you need a change. Maybe you should transfer, too. I'll call you when I get over there.' So when he called, I said, 'I've been thinking about it, and I've decided to go over there, too.' "

Flores applied on his own to the University of Texas and again was accepted as a graduate student in geography. He moved to Austin in 1972.

The FBI had no difficulty gaining access to the duplex the PALMETTOS rented in Austin. "While I was still in Salt Lake," Flores said, "Gilberto sent me a key to his place in Austin."

For the drop on the night of Saturday, April 1, 1972, Cassidy had selected and Danilin had agreed to a site in central St. Petersburg, a popular trysting place bordered by Straub Park and the North Yacht Basin. The FBI took up positions nearby, ready to photograph whoever appeared. At 9 P.M., Cassidy placed his rock at the base of a metal pole of a street sign at the intersection of Bay Shore Drive Northeast and Fifth Avenue Northeast.

Inside were films of seven documents stamped SECRET, and others marked with the lower classifications of CONFIDENTIAL and FOR OFFICIAL USE ONLY. One of the documents labeled SECRET, dated December 23, 1971, again related to the pullout of American forces from Vietnam and was entitled "Letter of Instruction for the Tenth Incremental Redeployment of U.S. Army Forces from RVN."

The pickup proved to be another family affair. At 9:20 P.M., FBI agents spotted Gilberto Lopez and his wife walking near the drop site. Lopez was carrying his son in a backpack. They stopped at the street sign, and Alicia Lopez put down a black-and-white-striped plastic shopping bag.

Looking like an ordinary couple fussing with their baby carrier, Alicia helped take the backpack from Gilberto. He then kneeled as though adjusting the backpack, and as he did so he reached down, picked up the hollow rock, and slipped it into the shopping bag. Then he helped arrange the carrier on Alicia's back. They walked off, Gilberto smiling and carrying the plastic bag. To any passersby, the episode would have looked innocuous. The FBI captured the whole scene on film.

Mission accomplished, the Lopezes returned to their downtown hotel, the Sorrento, for the night. But Lopez, despite the smooth performance, had a touch of television's Maxwell Smart in his spying activities. Once again, he forgot to leave the troublesome paper bag. At 9:52 P.M., he returned to the drop site and remedied his error.

The next day dawned warm, and O'Flaherty spent most of his Easter Sunday morning in a stiflingly hot panel truck, watching the hotel. The Lopezes left, and O'Flaherty followed them to the train station.

"They got on a train to Washington. I gave the ticket agent a hundred dollars in exchange for the bills they gave the ticket taker, as evidence, in case we could trace the serial numbers. We assumed he was on his way to make his drop to Danilin."

When Lopez returned to Salt Lake City, the FBI learned he was planning to take a brief trip to Mexico. "There was some indication he might clear a drop on the way," Schamay said. "In May, we mounted a massive surveillance which started in Salt Lake. We used planes, campers, motorcycles. He drove into Arizona and then through New Mexico. We used a lot of people. We had people at all the exits from the city. First to pick him up leaving was the motorcycle, a special agent dressed like a typical biker. We had other FBI men dressed like cowboys."

To avoid detection, the bureau switched vehicles and people. "The motorcycle went into a pickup truck, then, when daylight came, we used the airplane." The surveillance ended at El Paso, as Lopez crossed the border into Mexico. But the results of the enormous surveillance were disappointing to the FBI. "We never saw him do anything," Schamay said.

In July, Cassidy traveled to Washington once more to meet with Danilin in Springfield. In the hollow rock at the pickup site, Cassidy received twelve thousand dollars and new rollover cameras, photographic equipment, and film. Concealed in the rock as well were capsules containing the same organic chemical compound that was in the special pencil lead that Cassidy had struggled to crush. The capsules, the Soviets hoped, would prove easier to dissolve in water.

At their meeting, Danilin pressed Cassidy to provide more TOP SECRET documents, especially "like you gave last September." But, all in all, from the Soviet point of view, matters were progressing smoothly; there had now been four successful drops in Florida, the secret documents were flowing, and, through Cassidy, Moscow had achieved another intelligence coup. It had penetrated a vital American military center, the United States Strike Command.

When the PALMETTOS went to Austin, the FBI moved its entire surveillance operation. Even before the Lopezes arrived in Austin, the FBI had cased the house they had rented. The couple was moving into one half of a duplex. The bureau discovered that there was a crawl space over both sides of the duplex. Carroll T. Allen, an FBI technical expert at headquarters, was dispatched from Washington to install video cameras in the crawl space and prepare the house electronically before the PALMETTOS moved in. The rooms were bugged, the telephones tapped.

Allen worked in the hot, cramped crawl space of the duplex to install the miniature concealed cameras, which were so small that they operated through two tiny pinholes drilled into the ceiling. "They put in two video cameras," Charlie Bevels said, "one over the top of his [Lopez's] desk, and one from the side."

The sophisticated cameras worked, allowing the FBI to watch the Lopezes inside their home. "Lopez had a secret cache where he kept his espionage paraphernalia, microdot reader, and other material," Bevels said. "So we could see him on video taking out his materials."

The video camera sent back live pictures to a duplex the FBI had rented about five hundred yards away, where the bureau's technicians had all of their equipment. Through the video, the FBI watched Lopez put on a headset and listen to radio signals. The National Security Agency (NSA), the nation's global electronic-eavesdropping arm, had been picking up the encoded signals for a long time but had not known to whom they were being sent.

Then Lopez made a grievous operational error. A former senior FBI official familiar with the case explained what happened. "He took off a headset to say something to his wife, and we heard five-digit coded broadcasts from Moscow or Havana coming through the headset. And we were able to match them with the shortwave broadcasts we had suspected were directed to him. If he had never taken the headset off, we never could have confirmed it."

The headset figured in another incident that took place when Flores was baby-sitting for Lopez's son, Nayar. What happened proved that even the most careful spy cannot protect himself against the unexpected. "One time I had the TV on at my apartment," Flores recounted, "watching a war movie, just Nayar, my son, and myself, in the middle of the afternoon. Gilberto's little boy didn't talk much. In the movie, a ship was sinking, a torpedo hit it or something, and a radioman puts on a headset and starts sending an SOS. The little boy jumps up, runs to the TV, points at it, and says, 'Papa, Papa!' "

When the Lopezes left Austin for two weeks on a trip, the FBI entered the duplex and removed his shortwave radio, which was of East German make. The radio was sent to headquarters, taken apart, and analyzed. "We got back in before he returned and it would be missed," Flores recalled. "So we knew what frequencies he would receive. Later, the Soviets modified the radio and made it digital. We could not hear the signals, but we were getting them from NSA. Our equipment read it as good as his did."

Although the FBI could watch Lopez receiving radio signals, they could not read the content of the encoded messages. Determined to decode the encrypted signals, the FBI again waited until the Lopezes were away on a trip. Using the door key that Lopez had sent to Flores, FBI agents entered the apartment and copied the "one-time pads" containing the random numbers that Lopez used to decode his radio signals.[5] Now the FBI was able to decipher and read all of PALMETTO's messages.

---

[5] One-time pads, usually no bigger than a postage stamp, are printed on nitrated cellulose, which burns instantly. A spy receiving a message in encoded five-digit groups first subtracts the random numbers on the one-time pad and then converts the resulting total into words from a matrix containing the letters of the alphabet. Each page is used only once and burned. Since only two copies of the pad exist, one in Moscow and one in the possession of the spy, the codes are virtually unbreakable.

"He would burn the pages of the one-time pads after using them," Flores said. But destroying the pages no longer made any difference; the FBI had them.

Lopez received a wide variety of encoded messages from the Russians. Flores recalled, "Some Soviet agents were being thrown out of England, and he would get a message, 'Don't worry, you're in no danger.' Some were, 'Cancel plan A, we are doing plan B.' He would be told to go to Mexico or Florida. And some were personal messages, 'Congratulations on your son's birthday,' or your birthday. Or, 'We are very happy with what you're doing. You're doing a marvelous job for us.' The messages were brief."

The video camera enabled the FBI to read some of the messages at the very moment that Lopez decoded them. "When he wrote something on his notepad, we could see it," Flores said. The camera also revealed the tensions in the Lopez household. All was not harmonious on the domestic front, according to Charlie Bevels. "At one point she [Mrs. Lopez] had a gun and pointed it at him and told him to quit bugging her. She was going to blow his head off."

After some months, Lopez and his family moved out of the duplex and into a single-family house in another section of Austin. The couple also acquired a large, unfriendly dog, Flores recalled. "They bought this big black female dog, a German shepherd, named Brea, which means black tar in Spanish. A big vicious dog, barked a lot. I became friends with the dog. I made sure I played with the dog and fed the dog, so if they [FBI technicians] needed to go in, I could go in. But when the PALMETTOs went on a trip, they took the dog with them, so that problem did not come up."

Lopez continued to service the drops in Florida. On the night of September 10, 1972, Joe Cassidy left a rock at a new drop site at Anvil Street and Twenty-sixth Avenue North, in St. Petersburg. The film contained one document stamped SECRET and several marked with lower classifications. The document stamped SECRET must have pleased Danilin because it was the first to deal with nuclear weapons. Dated February 1, 1972, it was entitled "Operational Feasibility in Mating Nuclear Bombs to Aircraft." A March 1971 document marked CONFIDENTIAL was headed "General Flag Officer Staffing in OJCS and JCS Activities."

The factory of the Morgan Yacht Company overlooked the drop site, and O'Flaherty and his agents, having obtained permission from the owner, were waiting on scaffolds along the windows inside. "Lopez arrives at 9:27 P.M. in a white Pontiac with black hardtop, with his wife and son," O'Flaherty said. The car parked at the corner. Lopez got out, knelt at the stop sign, and picked up the hollow rock. He returned to the car, and they drove off.

Nearly two months later, on November 2, Cassidy received a letter from Danilin. The paper inside appeared blank, as usual. When he developed the secret writing and showed it to the FBI, the message was unnerving. Danilin asked *by name* for specific U.S. military documents that he wanted. How could the GRU have obtained such a shopping list of secret documents? The implication was both obvious and scary: Moscow had a genuine mole buried somewhere in the American military, perhaps one who had access to an index or list of classified material but not to the actual documents.

One document Danilin requested was entitled "Vol. II - Joint Strategic Objectives Plan for Fiscal Year 1975–1982 (USOPFY 75–82)." Danilin also asked Cassidy for data on the yield and number of warheads of Minuteman III and Poseidon missiles.

Then in December, five days before Christmas, Cassidy put down another rock at the street sign by the marina along Bay Shore Drive. Inside was film of four documents marked SECRET and of others with lower classification stamps. The document marked SECRET, although not the one Danilin had requested, was dated September 19, 1972, and was called "Nuclear Capabilities Reporting, JCS message No. 5252."

At 9:22 P.M., a yellow compact with Florida plates cruised by the drop site. Four minutes later, Lopez was seen alone nearby, walking south on Bay Shore Drive. At the street sign, he picked up the rock, put it in a camera case, and strolled away. Lopez had checked into the St. Petersburg

Hilton the day before at dawn. He checked out the next day and took a Greyhound bus to Washington, D.C.

The next drop in St. Petersburg took place on April 1, 1973. The Russians had approved a new drop site in a quiet residential area at Eighty-ninth Avenue North and Fifth Street North. Casing the area, O'Flaherty saw that it was next to a construction site. The builder, Aaron Applefield, allowed the FBI to use the model home on the site as a lookout post. Fred and Pearl Redfield, an elderly couple whose home overlooked the drop site, also allowed the FBI to use their house. An agent loitered on the street in a phone booth.

Cassidy put down his hollow rock at 9 P.M. It contained photographs of three documents stamped SECRET and of several others marked with lower classifications. At 9:33 P.M., the waiting agents spotted Lopez driving alone near the drop site in a yellow late-model Fiat. A moment later, Lopez, with his German shepherd on a leash, approached the corner, doing his best to look like a neighborhood resident out walking his dog. He picked up the rock, got back in the Fiat, and took off.

Lopez then drove to Washington. Again not wanting to alarm the spy, the FBI did not tail the car but instead set up a "picket surveillance," with agents stationed along his likely route.

This was the last drop and pickup in Florida. One month earlier, Cassidy, at age fifty-two, with thirty years in the service, had retired from the army. That did not discourage the Soviets, who were making plans to use their mole in a new capacity. WALLFLOWER had left the military but not his life as a spy.

In Austin, the PALMETTO case took a bizarre and astonishing twist. Flores had done his job so well that Lopez tried to recruit him.

"He came by one night and pitched me in my living room in Texas. He wanted to recruit me. He said, 'I have friends in Mexico that work for another government. I told them about you, and they are very interested.' He asked to take a photograph of me 'to show to my friends.' I said sure, so he took a photograph of me.

"He said, 'They won't come here, you have to go to Mexico.' "

Headquarters debated the risks of letting Flores travel to Mexico. "Finally, the bureau said, 'No, don't go. You know too much about the technical side.' The cameras we used in Austin that worked through the pinpricks in the ceiling were the same kind that were used by NASA in the moon landing. We got the cameras from NASA. The bureau didn't want the Soviets to know we had that technology. They were concerned I might be invited to Nicaragua or the Soviet Union and given sodium Pentothal."

There was another reason that the FBI declined to let Flores go to Mexico. "If we operate outside the U.S., we are going to have to let the CIA know about it. The bureau did not want to involve the CIA."

In the summer of 1974, the Lopezes left their books and furniture with Flores and went off to Europe. "They visited the Soviet Union," Flores said. "They told friends they had been all over Europe. It was a cover story. We think he spent the summer in Moscow."

That autumn, Flores prepared to end his undercover role and transfer to the bureau's Los Angeles division. The PALMETTO assignment, and the pretense, had not been easy on his wife. He had already followed Lopez to two cities. "I thought I had done enough. I wanted my son to get into first grade in California and not be uprooted again."

Flores told Lopez he and his family were moving away. "Gilberto was already thinking about leaving Austin. When we were saying good-bye, he said he had applied to the University of Minnesota. He said he might become a professor."

IXORA

When Cassidy, still on active duty, had met with Mikhail Danilin in Washington in July 1971, the microdot inside the hollow rock that he retrieved at his drop site contained an extraordinary set of instructions. Cassidy was ordered, if he detected military preparations for war, to call a telephone number in New York City.

The instructions also provided the "parol," or recognition dialogue, that Cassidy was to speak to the man who answered the telephone. The microdot gave the man's name as Edmund Freundlich, and his address as Apartment 1A, 2770 Kingsbridge Terrace, Bronx, NY, 10463.

The FBI quickly verified that this was in fact the name and address of the man in apartment 1A. Clearly, Edmund Freundlich was a Soviet "sleeper agent," a faceless spy among the millions of people in New York City, whose job was to serve as a sort of one-man early-warning system in the event of a planned nuclear attack on the Soviet Union. A sleeper agent is a long-term spy planted inside an enemy country with orders to engage in a minimal amount of espionage activities, or none at all, so that he can be activated primarily in case of war or an emergency.

While no target was specified, the primary concern of the Russians was obviously to obtain advance news of an attack against the Soviet Union. A warning call that the United States was mobilizing against some other country would certainly have been of interest to the Soviets as well. But whatever other duties may have been assigned to him by Moscow, Edmund Freundlich's most important job was to wait for the phone call that might mark the start of World War III.

If Freundlich ever received a phone call alerting the Soviets to a nuclear attack, the conversation would be cryptic and the meaning indecipherable to anyone who overheard it. On the microdot Cassidy got from Danilin, he was told that if he had to make the call, he was to go to a pay phone, dial the number, and inquire about an order for books.

Cassidy was instructed to say, "Mr. Freundlich? That's [sic] Rex, how about my order for [a number indicating a future date] books?"[1] The number given would signify the number of days until the attack and would depend on the circumstances. In the microdot, Cassidy was given an example of three numbers: 11, 22, and 55. The numbers were to be understood as single digits; thus 11 would mean one day, 22 two days, and so on. For example, if Cassidy called on October 10 and believed an attack was to be launched on October 12, he was to say, "That's Rex, how about my order for twenty-two books?" Freundlich was to respond, "For twenty-two it's okay." After that, Cassidy was instructed by the Soviets to "just hang up the receiver." He was to follow up with a letter, which would appear to be a business letter confirming his book order,

---

[1] Whoever wrote the parol probably did not know English very well and used "That's Rex" instead of "This is Rex. . . ."

but on the back of the letter, using secret writing, he was directed to provide details of the U.S. plan of attack.[2]

There was only one problem with the instructions Cassidy received on the microdot. The phone number he had been given by the Russians was wrong: The last two digits were transposed. Cassidy had been told to call a number ending with 2835. But when the FBI looked up Edmund Freundlich in the Bronx telephone book, it found that his number ended with 2853.

One would suppose that with the warning of a possible nuclear Armageddon depending on Joe Cassidy, the GRU would have made sure that the telephone number he had been given was correct. But the devil is in the details, and things often go wrong in the spy business, as in any other human endeavor. This, however, was a wrong number to end all wrong numbers.

To the bureau, the fact that the GRU had provided the true name and address of its sleeper in New York was seen as further evidence that Moscow completely trusted Joe Cassidy. For the Soviets to share this information with Cassidy was an extraordinary expression of confidence in him.

Operation SHOCKER had now flushed three illegals: Gilberto Lopez y Rivas, his wife, Alicia Lopez, and Edmund Freundlich.

The FBI opened a new case file on Edmund Freundlich. At the bureau's headquarters in Washington, Gene Peterson gave him his own code name: IXORA. Ixora is a tropical plant that Peterson had cultivated in his garden in Tampa, where he worked for the FBI before coming to Washington. "It's also called the iron bush, because the trunk would get a black mold on it," he said. "It has beautiful red flowers. It only blossoms on second-year wood. When you trim it, you

---

[2] The letter would almost certainly arrive after the attack had begun, making it only marginally useful. In a bizarre touch, if the date of the likely attack was more than a week in the future, Cassidy was instructed only to mail a letter to Freundlich rather than use the telephone at all. To the FBI, the Soviet plan did not make a lot of sense. Apparently, the GRU had much more faith in the postal service than do most Americans.

have to know it won't bloom until two years later. It's like forsythia that way."[3]

A reclusive, fifty-two-year-old bachelor, Freundlich seemed an unlikely spy. He appeared to have few friends and to live a drab, colorless existence. But perhaps that is precisely why he was chosen for his role—a gray man who blended almost invisibly into the background.

Edmund Freundlich, according to records of the U.S. Immigration and Naturalization Service, was born in Vienna on April 14, 1919. The family name means "friendly" in German, and is pronounced "Froyndlish."

In March 1938 Hitler's army marched into Austria and the country was annexed as part of the Third Reich. On August 14, five months after the Anschluss, Freundlich, then nineteen, entered Switzerland at Diepoldsau, just across the Rhine from Austria, as a refugee from the Nazis. Freundlich spent the war in refugee camps in Switzerland. According to records of the Swiss police in the canton of Saint Gallen, he spent time in a camp at Schönengrund, near Appenzell, and for four years, from February 1940, he was in a camp at Diepoldsau. The police files show that from November 13, 1944, until April 20, 1945, he was at the immigrant work camp at Zurich-Seebach. He left Switzerland and returned to Austria on August 29, 1945.

But the bare-bones records of the Swiss police do not tell the whole story. Two of Edmund Freundlich's brothers also made their way to Switzerland in 1939 and later to the Dominican Republic. His brother Oswald emigrated to New York in 1951 and went into business chartering cargo ships.

According to Oswald's son, Robert, Edmund's mother, Anna, was a Catholic who converted to Judaism when she married his father, Wilhelm. "Wilhelm was abusive and gambled away his wife's small business. Anna and Wilhelm tried to enter Switzerland at some point but were turned back. I'm not sure if they were stopped at the border or got in and were turned back and went to occupied France. We found their names on the train list, the trains that went to Auschwitz."

---

[3] Ixora, often grown in greenhouses, is named after the Hindu deity Isvara.

Edmund's brother Oswald was also sent to the refugee camp in Switzerland at Schönengrund, where he met his future wife, Gina. A Swiss guard, later honored in Israel for his actions, forged documents and saved Gina and her entire family, as well as other refugees who lacked required papers and would otherwise have been shipped back to Germany and the death camps. "After the war," Robert recalled, "Edmund had a complete breakdown and was institutionalized in Austria, for up to a year. I visited him in 1964. He worked in the Austrian equivalent of our social security. That was the first time I ever met him. It was an overwhelming experience, he looked so much like my dad, it was stunning."

Sponsored by his brother, on April 16, 1968, Edmund Freundlich was admitted to the United States on an immigrant visa, after swearing he would not engage in "espionage . . . or in other activities subversive to the national security." On his visa application, he listed his address as Kirchberggasse 24, Vienna, and his occupation as office worker. His decision to leave Austria for America puzzled Robert's wife, Jill. "For many years he didn't want to come here," she said. "Then, suddenly, he wanted to come." What his family did not know, of course, was that he had been recruited by Soviet intelligence and was to work as a spy in New York.

Jill was fond of Uncle Edmund. "He had almost a childlike quality, he gave very thoughtful, wonderful presents to the children. He was good-looking, tall, he had a poet's face, sandy hair. He was almost six feet tall. He lived in Kingsbridge Terrace, in a very poor neighborhood, mainly Hispanic. He lived in a hovel. His apartment was small and dirty. He kept every piece of paper, newspapers piled floor to ceiling.

"He never married. He never brought a date to family gatherings. He did not seem interested in material things. He was into natural things and holistic medicine. He was a lovely, sweet, genuinely nice person. A good-hearted person. If you didn't get onto politics, anything controversial, he was lovely.

"He had a healthy distrust of the government and was pro-Russia. He hated the way the Americans treated the Indians, pushed them off their land and was still treating them badly. He talked openly about liking the Russians. There would be political debates. Robert would argue with him."

Robert Freundlich confirmed that he got into political arguments with his uncle. "He was not so much pro-Russian as anti-U.S. A highly neurotic man. It was extremely difficult to have rational discussions with him."

A year after Edmund arrived in the United States, he went to work at Pergamon Press, in Elmsford, New York, near Tarrytown, at a salary of $13,000 a year. He commuted by bus each weekday.

This may not have been a random choice of an employer. The man who owned Pergamon Press, Robert Maxwell, born Ian Ludwik Hoch in Czechoslovakia, also fled the Nazis in 1939 and built a publishing empire in Britain and the United States, acquiring the Mirror Group in London, the New York *Daily News,* and the American publishing company Macmillan, in addition to Pergamon. Maxwell was close to the Soviets, and a number of his executives at Pergamon were also from Eastern Europe. Whether Maxwell had any knowledge that he had a Russian spy on his payroll is unknown, but, whether by chance or not, Freundlich obtained work with the one publisher in the United States who maintained friendly relations with the Soviets during the cold war.[4]

Laszlo Straka was president of the publishing house in 1971, when Cassidy was given his microdot instructions. He said Maxwell started the press in the late 1950s as a subsidiary of the British parent company of the same name. Born in Hungary, Straka spent his whole career working for the Maxwell interests.

"We were a scientific-technical publisher, and the American branch

---

[4] Maxwell's financial empire was collapsing at the time of his mysterious death in November 1991. Maxwell, sixty-eight, disappeared during the night from his hundred-foot yacht in the Atlantic, near the Canary Islands. His body was found hours later, floating in the sea. Although Spanish authorities said Maxwell had died of a heart attack, his death was ruled a suicide by Lloyd's of London, which refused to pay his insurance. To support its conclusion, Lloyd's noted that Maxwell had asked his private jet to circle the yacht, the *Lady Ghislaine,* on November 4, the last full day of his life, as though in a final salute.

also published some journals," Straka recalled. "Edmund Freundlich was a low-level employee. He actually worked for a separate company, also headquartered at Pergamon, with the same phone number, called Maxwell Scientific International, which bought and sold back issues of scientific journals. It was run by Dr. Edward Gray, originally Ed Grunberg, a Romanian Jew. It was Dr. Gray, now dead, who hired Edmund Freundlich.

"He worked as a cataloguer of the scientific journals. So he was in the records ends of things. He always carried around his lunch in a little brown bag. I knew he was from Europe. A quiet sort of man, kept to himself."

Straka confirmed that Maxwell had strong links to the Russians. "The English Pergamon did a fair amount of Soviet translations, and Maxwell considered himself a sort of ambassador to the Soviets and visited Russia frequently. We distributed Soviet scientific journals in the U.S."[5]

Robert Miranda, a former vice president of Pergamon, also remembered Freundlich. "He was a sort of a recluse type of a guy, very smart but a loner. He collected all kinds of material, he was a continuous collector of junk. I wondered if it had to do with his years in the camps."

Lori Miranda, Robert Miranda's daughter, worked directly with Freundlich. "I worked for the microfilm department, and Eddie worked with back issues. We all sat in the same room. The thing I remember most about him, he was a pack rat. The microfilm used to come in little square boxes. Every once in a while I gave him the boxes, and he was very excited. Offbeat, but a nice guy.

"One time he drew a picture of a thumb and put it on the wall and wrote, 'Press here.' People would come over and press it. It was a joke. Eddie enjoyed that."

Freundlich was placed under surveillance by the FBI, and his apart-

---

[5] On November 14, 1991, shortly after Maxwell's death, *The Times* of London reported that the British Foreign Office was investigating allegations that the Soviet Communist Party had aided Pergamon Press financially by placing it in the category of "friendly firms" that were given priority in settling Soviet debts.

ment was wiretapped. His own brother had trouble feigning interest in Edmund's life. The FBI listened to Edmund on the telephone, talking on and on to his brother, and Oswald would start to snore.

Donald F. Lord, a former FBI agent and one of many assigned to watch IXORA, said the bureau discreetly moved into Freundlich's apartment house. "We had an apartment in the same building. He was on the ground floor. We were on the third floor. But we could see him from the window when he went out and walked across the courtyard. It was frustrating. He didn't do anything. He would just ride the subway or walk around the Bronx."

Charles T. Weis, who headed the bureau's GRU squad in New York, remembered the lookout post because he had lugged a spare bedroom set from his house and wrestled it into the Bronx apartment with the help of another FBI agent.

"We had spot surveillance on IXORA because he was so predictable," Weis said. "Initially we were on him all the time. It wasn't necessary to maintain continuous surveillance once we established a pattern—what time he went to work and when he came home and what he did on weekends.

"We could see whatever he did, which wasn't very much. He was a real lost soul."

Edgar Dade formed much the same impression of IXORA. "He was a strange bird, pale complexion, frail, you would never think he was a spy. You would never think he was anything."

Dade did remember one incident. Late at night, Freundlich left his apartment and took a trip by subway to Manhattan. "I was on the surveillance," Dade said. "It was difficult because the train was almost empty." Dade watched as Freundlich got off in midtown and went to the main post office, where he mailed a letter. "In Soviet intelligence procedure, that was considered a safer way to mail a letter," Dade said. The probable reason, he explained, is that if a spy is seen dropping a letter in a mailbox, it can be retrieved by a counterintelligence agency more easily than if it is mixed in with thousands of letters at a central post office. "He was definitely doing something," Dade added. "You don't normally

THE SPY

Army sergeant Joseph E. Cassidy and Marie Elizabeth Krstyen on their wedding day in June 1968. He had not revealed to her that he was a spy for his country, playing a dangerous double game against Soviet intelligence.

THE NUN

Marie Krstyen in her previous life as Sister Miriam Joseph of the Vincentian Sisters of Charity. Not wanting to chill their courtship, she did not tell Cassidy she had been a nun for twenty years, spending part of that time in a convent.

David Wise

James F. "Jimmy" Morrissey, the FBI agent who ran Cassidy during the crucial deception phase of Operation SHOCKER, when nerve gas secrets were passed to the Soviets.

Special Agent John J. O'Flaherty orchestrated the operation in Florida that successfully flushed two Soviet "illegals," code-named PALMETTOS.

David Wise

Charles Bevels (*below*), who succeeded Morrissey as case agent, says biological warfare secrets were also passed to Moscow.

Donald A. Gruentzel was credited by his colleagues with creating Operation SHOCKER and recruiting Joe Cassidy.

THE RUSSIANS

Mikhail I. Danilin, Cassidy's principal handler for the GRU, Soviet military intelligence. So convinced was Danilin that Cassidy was stealing nerve gas secrets for the Russians that he wept when they parted.

Oleg I. Likhachev was Cassidy's Soviet control in both Washington and New York. Ten Russian spies were sent to the U.S. in an espionage case that ran for more than two decades.

THE NERVE GAS CENTER

Aerial view of Edgewood Arsenal, east of Baltimore, as it appeared in the late 1960s. In the guarded base, American scientists working in top-secret laboratories developed deadly nerve gases in a race with Soviet scientists. It was here that Joe Cassidy, in an FBI deception operation, passed Pentagon nerve gas secrets to Soviet intelligence. The building circled on the right is the pilot plant that produced the nerve gases developed in the labs.

The Weapons Development and Engineering Laboratories at Edgewood, where Cassidy had access to nerve gas formulas.

As instructed by the Russians, Cassidy, with pipe in mouth and book-sized package in hand, waits for a Soviet contact on a street in Brooklyn.

The tiny dictionary used by Cassidy to decode Morse radio signals from Moscow and instructions in secret writing from his Soviet handlers.

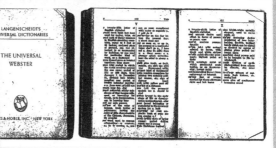

The Zenith Royal 7000 Trans-Oceanic shortwave radio the GRU instructed Cassidy to purchase in 1973.

DAVID WISE

Spies try to keep a low profile and, at all costs, avoid attracting attention. But Cassidy, to his dismay, found himself dragooned into the spotlight with Kathie Lee Gifford in a nightclub at Disney World.

THE PALMETTOS

A Mexican couple working for Soviet intelligence, Gilberto Lopez y Rivas and his wife, Alicia Castellanos Lopez, were under FBI surveillance as they retrieved microfilm documents hidden by Cassidy in hollow fake rocks. In this series of photographs, the Lopezes, code-named the PALMETTOS by the FBI, were captured by a concealed camera.

April 1, 1972, 9 P.M., Cassidy places his hollow rock at the base of a street sign in St. Petersburg, Florida.

At 9:20 P.M., Lopez, carrying his young son, approaches the drop site with his wife, who holds a striped plastic shopping bag.

Lopez, pretending to transfer the baby carrier to his wife, reaches for the rock, visible at base of pole.

Lopez hands the baby carrier to Alicia. The rock is gone, slipped inside the striped bag.

Mission accomplished, the PALMETTOS walk away. Lopez carries the bag with the rock. To a casual observer, they would have seemed a typical young couple out for a walk with their son. The rock held seven microfilmed documents stamped SECRET, including one detailing American troop deployments in Vietnam.

April 1, 1973, Soviet agent Lopez is back in St. Petersburg to clear another dead drop, posing this time as a neighborhood resident out walking his dog.

The Lopezes, again with son, stroll nonchalantly toward another drop site on Snell Isle, St. Petersburg. Lopez appears to be munching an apple.

The family that spies together . . . Their work done, the PALMETTOS stroll away.

JON WISE

THE PURSUERS

"My sole goal was to close this case with an arrest." Veteran counterintelligence agent Phillip A. Parker was determined to capture the PALMETTOS. The Justice Department thwarted his efforts.

Eugene C. Peterson supervised the case at FBI headquarters.

DISASTER IN MINNESOTA

Gilberto Lopez surfaced as a professor at the University of Minnesota in 1976. Operation SHOCKER cost the lives of two FBI agents, Mark A. Kirkland and Trenwith S. Basford, when their Cessna crashed in a rainstorm in the lake country of northern Minnesota as they conducted an aerial surveillance of the PALMETTOS. Only the tail section and pieces of the fuselage are visible as residents in boats attempt rescue operations.

PETER LESCHAK

Two Minneapolis FBI agents killed on duty in airplane crash

By Tom Davies
Staff Writer

"It was cold and very rainy, cloudy and blowing," another FBI agent who had been in the area Thursday said, "like a November rain that you expect to turn into snow at any minute."

FBI agents Trenwith Basford and Mark Kirkland flew into that weather Thursday afternoon in northern Minnesota. Basford, known as a very conservative pilot, apparently tried to bring the plane down on Dewey Lake, about six miles north of Coleraine.

On the third try, the plane's single engine stalled and the Cessna 172

and crashed into the water about 50 feet from shore. Basford, 60, and Kirkland, 39, were killed instantly.

The agents, FBI spokesmen said Friday, were on routine business at the lake, helping Duluth authori-

no indication of foul play, the spokesmen said, just bad weather.

Basford had just celebrated his 35th year with the FBI and face mandatory retirement in December. Kirkland had been an agent for five years and had worked as clerk in the agency for eight years before that.

Basford will be buried in Austin, Minn. Kirkland will be buried in Centerville, Minn. Funerals for both will be in the Minneapolis area on Monday — Basford's at the Cathedral Church of St. Mark, Kirkland's at the Church of Jesus Christ of Latter Day Saints, Douglas Dr. and 29th Av. N.

The front-page story about the plane crash in the *Minneapolis Tribune*, August 27, 1977. The FBI released a cover story saying the two agents were on "routine business" when they were killed. The truth about their mission was never revealed.

Kirkland grew a beard so he could mingle undercover with Lopez's students on campus. He is shown here with his two-year-old son, Kenneth, shortly before the plane crash.

COURTESY OF LETITIA BASFORD

Special Agent Basford, who was piloting the Cessna, loved the outdoor life in Minnesota. Here he runs his boat in the lake country.

Special Agent Mark Kirkland and his fiancée, Julia "Julie" Searle, share a happy moment during their engagement in 1972.

"What happened to the dream?" The cold war cost lives; the plane crash left Julie Kirkland widowed and alone with her two young sons, Kenneth (*left*) and Chris, and their Irish setter, Clancy.

THE SLEEPER

Edmund Freundlich, code name IXORA, was already working for Soviet intelligence in Vienna when this photo was taken in the 1960s.

Immigration form showing Freundlich's admission to the United States on April 16, 1968. A Soviet "sleeper" agent in Manhattan, his mission was to warn Moscow if the U.S. was planning a nuclear attack.

IXORA as he looked in New York City in the 1970s. No one, not even his American relatives, ever suspected he was a spy.

The rock. If IXORA received a call from Cassidy warning that the Pentagon was making preparations for war, he was instructed by Moscow to climb this huge rock in Central Park and transmit a signal by special radio to the Soviet mission to the United Nations a few blocks to the east.

THE WHISTLE-
BLOWER

Soviet nerve gas scientist Vil
Mirzayanov was under KGB
surveillance and facing a
possible long prison sentence
when photographed by the
author in Moscow in 1993.
At great personal risk,
Mirzayanov warned publicly
that the Russians had
developed and concealed
Novichok, a nerve gas said
to be ten times more
powerful than any
possessed by the U.S.

DAVID WISE

AP/WIDE WORLD PHOTOS

Moscow's infamous Lefortovo Prison, where Mirzayanov, fired from his job,
was repeatedly interrogated by the KGB.

DAVID WISE

RECOGNITION AT LAST

February 2, 1974: As Marie Cassidy looks on, Army Chief of Staff General Creighton W. Abrams pins the Distinguished Service Medal on Sergeant Major Joe Cassidy in a secret ceremony at the Pentagon. A few moments later, Cassidy had to give back the medal. The army feared that if seen it might endanger the security of Operation SHOCKER.

The medal

Both Cassidy and his wife received certificates at the Pentagon ceremony.

September 16, 1980: As Operation SHOCKER drew to a close, the FBI honored Cassidy and his wife in another secret ceremony. His case officers gathered to honor them, and both Cassidys received certificates of appreciation for their service. *Left to right*, James Morrissey, Donald Gruentzel, Joe Cassidy, Marie Cassidy, Jack O'Flaherty, and Charles Bevels. Cassidy displays the medal he was finally allowed to keep.

UNITED STATES DEPARTMENT OF JUSTICE
FEDERAL BUREAU OF INVESTIGATION
WASHINGTON, D.C. 20535

September 16, 1980

Sergeant Major Joseph Edward Cassidy, USA (Ret.)
5030 Dover Street, N.E.
St. Petersburg, Florida

Dear Sergeant Cassidy:

It is a pleasure for me to join my associates in thanking you for your accomplishments in the sensitive area of national security. You have over an extended period of time assisted FBI personnel in achieving our goal whenever called upon and your efforts were absolutely vital to our country's defense. I am personally most grateful and I know I speak for my colleagues as well in wishing you the very best in the future.

With warm thanks,

Sincerely yours,

William H. Webster

William H. Webster
Director

FBI director William Webster's letter to Cassidy was carefully couched to reveal nothing about the operation.

"A TYPICAL OLDER COUPLE..."

Joe and Marie Cassidy bought a house and retired to a pleasant, quiet community in the Sun Belt. They told no one of their double life. To their neighbors, they appeared a typical older couple, enjoying their golden years.

go all the way downtown from the Bronx at night by subway to mail a letter." Freundlich often traveled around New York City, mostly by subway, and some of his trips—such as his late-night excursion to the main post office—appeared to be related to an intelligence purpose.

On December 9, 1971, with the bureau listening in on his telephone, Freundlich received a cryptic call late at night. The call might have been a warning of some kind of military action. Freundlich left the building and did not return until after 2 A.M. To the FBI agents who followed him at a discreet distance, Freundlich appeared to be "dry-cleaning" himself in the classic manner of a spy, changing trains and doubling back on his trail, in an effort to lose any possible surveillance. It was an exercise that agents on both sides usually carried out before a meeting. He was not seen meeting with anyone that night, however.

Jill Freundlich recalled one mysterious facet of "Uncle Eddie's" life. "Edmund had one friend in the U.S. whom he referred to as 'Amigo.' He never mentioned his name."

The FBI was anxious to learn more about Freundlich and to determine, if possible, how he would communicate with the Soviets if he ever received a warning call from WALLFLOWER. Although Cassidy's instructions were clearly meant to provide Moscow with advance warning of a U.S. attack on either the Soviet Union or another country, the FBI decided the instructions were general enough that he might be justified in making the call if a conflict anywhere in the world resulted in American forces being put on a high state of alert.

In May 1972 the military forces of India and Pakistan clashed in Kashmir. That could have been a sufficient pretext for the call, but at the time, U.S. forces were still deployed in Vietnam, and on May 8, they mined Haiphong harbor. Because of the possibility that the mining might escalate the conflict, STRICOM and American forces worldwide went to a DEFCON 4 state of alert.[6]

Following instructions from the FBI, Cassidy placed a call to Freund-

---

[6] DEFCON stands for "defense condition." There are five categories of alerts. The lower the number, the greater the level of readiness. For example, DEFCON 5 is the normal

lich at his apartment and gave the parol inquiring about his supposed order for twenty-two books. He followed up with a letter in which, in secret writing, Cassidy advised Freundlich that the U.S. military had gone on a worldwide alert, which was true, with forces in the Pacific at a higher degree of alert.

To what extent the FBI considered the risk that the phone call might trigger a Soviet reaction is uncertain.[7] Since the warning came in the context of an escalation in Vietnam and a possible war on the Indian subcontinent, rather than an attack on the Soviet Union, perhaps they felt the danger was minimal. Yet the phone call warned of possible war; Cassidy stuck to the script and did not say anything specific about Kashmir or Haiphong. The language of the parol gave no clue that the warning related to regional conflicts; only the follow-up letter pointed to Asia. One might conjure up a scenario out of *Dr. Strangelove*, in which the Soviets, panicked and persuaded that the United States was about to initiate a nuclear war, launch a preemptive first strike. As with the deception over nerve gas, risks were taken in the cold war that may have seemed reasonable at the time but in retrospect are chilling.

As soon as Freundlich received Cassidy's warning call, he left his apartment and was gone for several hours. The FBI agents who had him under cautious surveillance believe he put his report in a dead drop near a building on the Grand Concourse, in the Bronx. But they could not be sure of that.

As Robert C. Loughney, one of the FBI agents, put it, "After IXORA got the call, and he reacted, the question was how close to get with our surveillance. If we went forward with a full-court press, he would know we were into his knickers."

In July 1972, two months after his telephone call to Freundlich, Cassidy traveled to Washington to meet with Mikhail Danilin. At the meet-

---

state of alert; DEFCON 2 means war is imminent; and DEFCON 1 means hostilities have begun. On May 8, when U.S. forces went to DEFCON 4, the Pacific Command was already at DEFCON 3 because of the Vietnam War.

[7] If officials at headquarters did weigh the risk, they did not communicate this to the Tampa office, according to Jack O'Flaherty.

ing, Cassidy recounted, "I mentioned I had called the New York contact. And Danilin was surprised. He looked a little bewildered but passed it off right away and didn't question me. It was clear to me he didn't know what I was talking about."

The FBI concluded that no one in the GRU had told Danilin about Cassidy's call. Certainly, Freundlich was under standing orders to report any call from Cassidy and possibly other sentinels. Perhaps there were real Soviet spies in the American military with similar instructions; there was no way to know. The cryptic call IXORA had received six months earlier might have come from a real spy. But either the GRU had cut Danilin out of the loop, for some internal bureaucratic reason, or it had simply neglected to keep him informed.

Danilin may well have let his organization know exactly how he felt about what had happened. On November 2, when Danilin asked Cassidy for specific military documents by name—implying the existence of a genuine mole—he also ordered him to destroy the instructions and parol for the telephone warning.

He was directed to have no further contact with Edmund Freundlich. Uncle Eddie would receive no more calls from Joe Cassidy. But the FBI had plans for IXORA.

CHAPTER

14

THE BIG APPLE

In June 1973, four months after he retired from the army, Cassidy got a letter from his Soviet controllers instructing him to purchase a short-wave radio.

"Buy a new Zenith Royal 7000 radio," the message said. "Do it outside your home city and without registering your name. Pay in cash."

Cassidy acted on his instructions. "I bought the radio for around two hundred and fifty dollars, a Zenith Royal 7000 Trans-Oceanic," he said. "I still have it." The Russians provided him with certain times and frequencies to listen to Radio Moscow on the mornings of the first and third Mondays of each month. The messages were transmitted in Morse code, in a cipher keyed to the same miniature dictionary, *The Universal Webster,* that Cassidy had been given by the Soviets nearly seven years earlier. He used the dictionary to decipher the coded messages.

In early September, Mikhail Danilin left Washington for the last time.

Cassidy was told in the June letter that his next personal meeting, with a new "Mike," was to take place in December in New York City where Russian intelligence officers worked under diplomatic cover at the Soviet mission to the United Nations and in the UN secretariat. "Return in your package both special cameras unless you have a new job with an access to classified documents," the instructions continued. "Your messages to me are okay but in the future try to leave larger margins on both sides on the top and at the bottom of the sheets you are writing on. . . . Do not forget to steam my letter before developing."

Finally, the letter asked Cassidy to brush up on his cryptography. It included sixteen six-digit groups containing a coded test message. "To refresh your skill in reading my coded messages try to work out this one," the letter said.

A few days before Christmas, Cassidy drove north from Florida to keep the rendezvous with the Russians. "I had to drive," he recalled. "If I flew, it would look funny going through security with a hollow rock full of film."[1] The fake rock, it had also occurred to him, might look to security like a good place to hide drugs. Aside from Cassidy's concerns about airport security, he was going to need a car in New York to go to all the drop, signal, and meeting sites specified by the Russians. In the end, however, O'Flaherty decided to transport the rock north.

In New York, Cassidy checked into a motel in Howard Beach, Queens, which, to the vast embarrassment of both Cassidy and the bureau, turned out to be a hot-sheet motel, whose patrons used it for quickie sex. Next day, WALLFLOWER moved to the Hilton near John F. Kennedy International Airport.

Meanwhile, O'Flaherty flew to New York from Tampa, carrying a gym bag with the hollow rock, which contained the two small cameras and films of secret documents that Cassidy had photographed before he retired. O'Flaherty, with his FBI credentials, would have no trouble

---

[1] At the time, Americans were just becoming accustomed to security precautions at domestic airports. Six months earlier, on December 15, 1972, the FAA had imposed the rule that all passengers and carry-on baggage be screened by metal detectors and X-ray machines or searched by hand.

going through security. But no one at the airport bothered to ask why he was traveling with a rock in his carry-on bag. In New York, fortunately, O'Flaherty had not been booked at the seedy motel; he stayed with his mother in Rockaway Point, Queens, in the house where he had grown up.

Cassidy's instructions from the Russians, were, as always, detailed and meticulous. "Come to New York City on December 22, 1973 (Saturday)," he was told. "At 2 P.M. leave your stuff at the following place: From 104th Street in Queens walk west along 165 Avenue to its dead-end. Put your package behind the right side of the concrete wall with railings preventing cars from going further." If for some reason the dead drop was not suitable, he was given a "reserve place" in Brooklyn.

The meeting place with the new "Mike" was to be an antique shop in Brooklyn. "At 4 P.M. come to the entrance to 'Bea's As Is' at 3004 Avenue J. Stay there for 3–5 minutes then walk slowly along right side of Avenue J, turn right to New York Avenue, turn right to Avenue K, towards Nostrand Avenue. Have a book size package in yellow wrapping in your hand and a smoking pipe in your mouth."

The instructions then supplied the seemingly odd parol that was to be used for identification. "If someone approaches you and asks: 'Could you tell me where is the nearest drive-in theatre?' You should answer: 'Beltsville Drive-in is the nearest I know but the best one is Rockville Drive-in Theatre.' "[2]

If no one approached Cassidy, he was told to "repeat the whole thing on the next day."

After the personal meeting with the new "Mike," Cassidy was in-

---

[2] On the face of it, the parol seemed fairly wacky, since both Maryland cities were more than two hundred miles away. Perhaps Danilin, being unfamiliar with the geography of New York, simply stuck to locations he knew. On the other hand, in the unlikely event that the Soviet spy went up to the wrong person—not too many people would be walking around Brooklyn with a pipe and a yellow package—whoever was approached would certainly not recommend a movie theater in Rockville. Conversely, in the one-in-a-million chance that a real stranger came up to Cassidy and asked directions to a drive-in theater, his reply would be so baffling that there certainly would be no danger of Cassidy mistaking the person for his Soviet contact.

structed to go to a dead drop in Brooklyn to pick up his rock: "My package will be between the pole and metal fence going along 36 Street."

The GRU was not making matters easy for Cassidy in the Big Apple. To signal that the pickup had taken place successfully, he was to drive all the way to the Yorkville section of Manhattan and place "a horizontal line with a red marker on the lamp pole located at the south-eastern corner of the intersection of the First Avenue and 90 Street (near Mobil Gas Station) in Manhattan, NYC." But not just anywhere on the pole. "It should be put on the side of the lamp pole facing First Avenue and as high as approximately 3–4 feet from the ground." The Soviets undoubtedly wanted the mark to be facing the street at that height so it could easily be seen from a car driving by.

If Cassidy failed to establish contact with the GRU on either day, he was given several alternate dates to appear at the antique shop. He was directed to "come to New York City on the last Saturday of last month of each quarter (March 30, June 29, September 28, December 28, 1974 . . . etc.) until we meet at 4 P.M. Stay at the entrance to 'Bea's As Is' Shop." But if he received a postcard signed "Mike," he was to appear at the shop at 4 P.M. two weeks after the date on the card.

O'Flaherty met Cassidy in New York and gave him the hollow rock. At 2 P.M. Saturday, Cassidy hid the rock in the dead drop in Queens. Then he drove to a shopping mall in Flatbush to kill time until the meeting. At 4 P.M., he was waiting in front of the antique shop, yellow package in hand and pipe in mouth. FBI agents had the shop and the entire area under surveillance.

Cassidy did not have to start down the complicated route he had been given. A man approached and asked about the nearest drive-in theater. Cassidy gave the required reply. They began walking slowly along the street, talking as they went. The Russian introduced himself, not surprisingly, as "Mike." He proved to be none other than Oleg I. Likhachev, the same officer who had handled Cassidy for a time in Washington four years earlier, before Cassidy had been transferred to MacDill.

Likhachev, now stationed in New York, explained that the rock that Cassidy was to pick up in Brooklyn after their meeting would contain a vial of acetone, which he was to use in the future as the first step in developing secret writing. The Soviets had coated their invisible writing with a new, protective chemical layer that required the use of acetone as a solvent before steaming the pages and crushing the capsules to develop the writing as before.

When Likhachev confessed he had not yet retrieved the rock that Cassidy had left two hours earlier, Cassidy complained and pretended to be highly upset. The previous "Mike," he let Likhachev know, had always cleared the dead drop quickly. Any delay, Cassidy implied, was jeopardizing his security. He did not need to spell out the reason for the GRU man; if someone accidentally happened on the rock, opened it, and turned the film over to the authorities, the documents might be traced back to Cassidy.

Likhachev sought to soothe his agent. "We really like you," he said. "You're number one with us."

Now that Cassidy had returned to civilian life, Likhachev encouraged him to find employment that would continue to give him access to information of interest to the Russians. He suggested a mapmaking agency or a government printing office where regulations or manuals were produced.

As they strolled along the Brooklyn streets, Likhachev worked the conversation around to his main purpose.

"Do you have any trouble getting on military bases?" he asked.

"No," Cassidy replied, "I have a sticker on my car."

"We'd like you to make several trips around the country," Likhachev said. "You'll be traveling around checking bases." He then assigned Cassidy to go to the Dugway Proving Grounds in Utah, the nerve-gas test site, and to several other military bases.

"At Dugway, where you see humps, especially look for humps with pipes on them, let me know. And anything else you can find out about Dugway." The Russian also asked Cassidy to travel to Key West and find out how many submarines were based there. He was instructed as well to visit the Orlando naval-training center and a nuclear-ammunition depot at the air force base in Charleston. Finally, he was told to spy on a 1,700-acre former army base at Slidell, Louisiana, across from New Orleans on the north side of Lake Pontchartrain. The base, once used as an artillery range, had been turned over to the Louisiana National Guard. The Soviets apparently suspected the army was hiding nerve-gas stocks at Slidell because they directed Cassidy to look for twenty mounds with pipes sticking up from them, the same configuration he was told to look for at Dugway. But Likhachev told Cassidy, without explanation, not to travel to the West Coast or New England.

Finally, Likhachev pressed Cassidy to find a replacement for himself, now that he had left the army. "He wanted me to try to develop other sergeants," Cassidy recalled. "Did I know a sergeant who could do the work I was doing? He said, 'There is a weakness in every man. We try to exploit it.' "

Cassidy realized he was in a delicate position; how could he satisfy the Soviets and still get out of the assignment? Cassidy remembered Nicky, a master sergeant at Edgewood Arsenal who had a job similar to his but in the other lab (DDEL). "I went up to Edgewood and took him and his wife to dinner—to renew my friendship, to see if he was still there and had the same job."

With the FBI's approval, Cassidy passed on the sergeant's name to the Soviets. Behind the scenes, the bureau then warned Nicky that he might be contacted by a foreign intelligence service. The sergeant did receive a phone call from a foreigner, but the caller hung up.

Later, the Russians urged Cassidy to set up a meeting between one of the Soviets and the new sergeant. But Cassidy refused, and he hit upon a good excuse. It was too risky for him, he warned the GRU. "I told the Soviets I didn't want to divulge to the sergeant what I was doing."

After the meeting with Likhachev, Cassidy drove first to the dead drop to pick up his rock, then into Manhattan to leave the red mark on the lamp pole in Yorkville. Afterward, he made the long drive back to Queens to meet with O'Flaherty and other FBI agents waiting at the house in Rockaway Point.

O'Flaherty recalled the scene. "We sat at the kitchen table and got a hammer and broke open the rock gently. We counted the money and looked for the microdot and the secret writing."

It was close to midnight when Cassidy drove back to the Hilton. It had been a long day. But now, as a civilian, he had a new assignment; he was to crisscross the country spying on military bases for Moscow.

Cassidy headed home for Florida, but there was a problem. It was the time of the gas shortage, and he was running low. On his way from New York, he drove through Springfield, Virginia, where Charlie Bevels lived, and at 2 A.M. "we gave him twenty-five gallons of gas," Bevels recalled. "I think it was Christmas morning."

For Cassidy, it was another Christmas Day spent on the road, away from Marie. It was getting increasingly hard to explain to the neighbors.

For some time now, the couple next door had been expressing curiosity about why Cassidy traveled so often. "In Saint Petersburg," Marie Cassidy said, "the Mitchells, Bill and Betty Mae, especially Betty Mae, a school administrator, were suspicious. They wondered why Joe would go away for several days at a time. I would say, 'You know the military. Especially Strike Command, they're all over the place.' No one else ever suspected."

A SECRET MEDAL

By 1974, Joe Cassidy had been living his hazardous double life for fifteen years, pretending to the Soviets that he was a traitor to America. Other than his wife, Marie, he could confide in no one. Not even his children or his closest friends had a clue.

Those inside the government who did know the truth decided that, after so many years, Cassidy's extraordinary service to the nation deserved recognition. The problem was that any award or accolade would have to be secret.

Early in 1974, Cassidy was told that he would be given a medal in private by the president of the United States, Richard Nixon.

"The presentation was supposed to be in the White House by the president," Cassidy said. "But because of Watergate, I was told it wouldn't be possible. He was resigning or heading toward resignation." The award ceremony was switched to the Pentagon.

Cassidy, modest to a fault, said, "I didn't care it wasn't the president. I was surprised I was going to get anything." Still, he was impressed by the initial news. "To go to the White House and get a medal? I was surprised."

Accompanied by Marie, Cassidy arrived at the Pentagon for the ceremony. Gathered around Cassidy were the FBI case agents who had watched over him for fifteen years: Jimmy Morrissey, Donald Gruentzel, and Charlie Bevels from the Washington field office, and Jack O'Flaherty and Dennis Dickson from Tampa. On hand as well was Eugene Peterson, the deputy chief of the Soviet section, who had supervised the operation for a decade. Instead of Nixon, General Creighton W. Abrams, the chief of staff of the United States Army, presented the medal to Cassidy on February 2.

Creighton Abrams, the son of a railway mechanic, was only five foot nine, but as compact as one of the tanks that he commanded in World War II, when he led a battalion onto the beaches of Normandy and later punched through the Nazi lines that had encircled the 101st Airborne division at Bastogne.[1]

It was a proud moment for Cassidy. Wearing a seersucker jacket and a summer tie—he had just arrived from Florida—the former sergeant major, a tanned, white-haired, handsome figure, stood erect in the flag-bedecked office as General Abrams pinned the Distinguished Service Medal on him. The award is the fourth-highest U.S. military decoration, and the highest civilian noncombat medal. The accompanying citation read:

> The United States of America
> To all who shall see these presents, greeting:
> This is to certify that the President of the United States of America authorized by act of Congress July 9, 1918 has awarded

---

[1] At the time of the Pentagon ceremony the former U.S. commander in Vietnam was suffering from lung cancer, but it would not be diagnosed for another two months. He underwent surgery in June to remove his left lung but died on September 4, 1974, at age fifty-nine.

the Distinguished Service Medal to Sergeant Major Joseph Edward Cassidy for exceptionally meritorious service in a duty of great responsibility.

Marie Cassidy, too, received recognition from the government for her contribution to Operation SHOCKER. General Abrams presented her with the army's certificate of appreciation and a citation, prepared and dated a month earlier, that read:

> Mrs. Joseph Edward Cassidy
> On the occasion of the retirement of her husband from active duty with the United States Army has earned the Army's grateful appreciation for her own unselfish, faithful and devoted service. Her unfailing support and understanding helped to make possible her husband's lasting contribution to the nation. Given under my hand this 2nd day of January 1974 Creighton W. Abrams (signature), General, United States Army, Chief of Staff.

After Abrams pinned on the medal and congratulated the Cassidys, the five FBI agents lined up behind Cassidy and his wife for an official photograph. Everyone was smiling.

Except for that brief moment when the picture was taken, there was no way that Cassidy could be allowed to wear his decoration; if seen, it might endanger the security of the entire operation. As soon as the secret ceremony was over, General Abrams took the medal back.

Cassidy, accompanied most of the time by Marie, and Beau, their miniature poodle, began spying on military bases around the country for the GRU and writing detailed reports for the Russians on what he found. First, however, he sent the reports to the FBI. "They would screen them and tell me what I could give to the Russians." The bureau provided him with a per diem allowance for his expenses on the road. Although Marie Cassidy did not make the drive to Dugway, she was at her husband's side as he reconnoitered the bases at Key West, Charleston, and Slidell, Louisiana.

As a retired career military man, Cassidy, as he had explained to the Russians, had a sticker on his car that gave him access to any base in the country, whether army, navy, air force, or marine. He, Marie, and the dog could drive right in.

Cassidy used the special carbons that the Russians had supplied to record his observations in secret writing. When done, he steamed the pages to seal in the chemicals, then folded them several times to make them as small as possible in order to fit inside the fake rocks he passed to the Soviets.

Cassidy had already demonstrated that he was a good actor, and his handwritten memos proved him a good reporter as well, with a clear writing style and a trained eye. His report from the air force base at Charleston was a typical example.

The 437th Military Airlift Wing of the Military Airlift Command is stationed here. Inquiries revealed they provide airlift services, combat equipment and troops, to all parts of the world for all of the Dept. of Defense. They employ C-141 Starlifters but I did see a few other types of planes. Takeoffs and landings were numerous throughout the days I was there—so much so I thought there must be a training mission also but could not confirm.

There are about 8000 military and civilian personnel assigned. I roamed the base at will but found no ammo dumps. About 8 miles southeast of this base (see #2 on map), I located a U.S. Navy base. . . . I saw 10–15 large warships, several large landing crafts, at least 3 submarines which I was told were nuclear powered. These ships were anchored on the Cooper River. The roadway on the Cooper River side was fenced the entire length and all entrances to this area manned by guards. . . . A badge was required to gain admittance to any area on this side of the road.

Signs on buildings and fence of this area read "Mine Assembly

Group" "Fleet and Marine Warfare Training Center" "Missile Submarine Training Center" "Submarine Squadron Four" "Nuclear
Material Supply Center" and "Mercury Exclusion Area."

Eight miles north of the base, Cassidy's report continued, he found
an installation with a sign at the entrance that read POLARIS MISSILE FACIL-
ITY ATLANTIC. He added: "I could not gain admission to this place but
could only see large administration building and a few smaller buildings
within. . . . A military shopping area was located for the next ½ mile and
was outside fenced area." Nearby, he reported he saw a sign for the General Dynamics Corporation, "indicating government contractors were
active in the area."

Next, Cassidy came upon a nearby naval weapons facility. "I pro-
ceeded to this facility and [in] about 1/2 mile I came to the guard gate
(see #6 on map). Because of the military sticker on my car I am never
questioned on entering a military base," Cassidy reported. "But at this
one I was stopped and asked the nature of my business."

Now, for the first time on his trip, Cassidy was in a potentially tight
spot. He knew he might have had some difficulty explaining matters.
*Well, you see, I'm a Russian spy, but I'm not really a Russian spy, because I'm
actually working for the FBI, and no, I have no way to prove what I'm saying,
but please, fellows, I'm not making this up, you've got to believe me.* Cassidy
also knew it might be a trifle awkward to explain away the map in the
car on which he had pinpointed the location of every military base for
miles around.

He need not have worried; security was loose as a goose. "I did not
identify myself," he wrote, "but explained I happened to be in the area
and would like to see the base. He waved me through." With a sigh of relief, Cassidy drove through the gate. Inside, "there were several guarded
roads leading to interior of this area. As I left the facility returning to
Route 52 I noticed the whole length of the south side of area along road
was fenced and signs reading 'Gov't Property' (See #7 on map). About
1½ miles there was a gate with guard shacks inside and sign reading 'Mu-

nitions Trucks Entrance.' There was some activity inside and several Navy pickup trucks were observed. . . . On one fence was sign 'Group 8.' "

At Slidell, Cassidy had disappointing news for the Soviets, who had hoped he would find evidence of a clandestine nerve-gas storage area. There were no signs of the kind that warned "No Admittance—Gov't Property," and he added, "The whole area seemed a very unlikely place for 20 semi-underground repositories." At Dugway, Cassidy had reported seeing the mounds with pipes sticking up out of them. There were no mounds at Slidell, nor did the base have roads of the sort that the army might use for transporting a cargo as delicate as nerve gas. "The road to the city airport, dump and golf course is one of the better ones in the area," Cassidy reported, "but it is partially dirt and all chuckholes."

As a consolation prize, Cassidy told the GRU that he found a Slidell Computer Complex that belonged to NASA and was completely fenced and protected by uniformed guards. "About 200 cars in parking lot," Cassidy noted.

On April 20, 1974, Cassidy was back in New York City for the second time. He drove to a drop site and put down a hollow rock containing reports of his trips to military bases in Florida. At 4 P.M., he met Oleg Likhachev in front of a radio repair shop on East 233d Street in the Bronx. As the two walked along the street, Cassidy filled Likhachev in on the results of his reconnaissance. Likhachev asked Cassidy a lot of rapid-fire questions, whether he had obtained civilian employment with a printer, where he was hiding material from his wife, and what bases he would travel to next.

After their meeting, Cassidy went to pick up the rock the Soviets had hidden near the New York Botanical Garden. Cassidy began walking north on Webster Avenue toward the rock, which was secreted in a space between a garage wall and the end of a fence. As he did so, something spies always fear seemed about to happen.

Just as Cassidy approached the drop site, a little girl leaned over and reached for the rock. Dead drops are not foolproof; there is always a chance that someone will pick up one of the hollow rocks and discover its contents. The little girl almost had the rock in her grasp when her mother shooed her away.

Relieved, Cassidy scooped up the rock and hurried off. To signal he had cleared the drop, he then drove into Manhattan to leave a line on the same lamppost he had marked five months before. After that, he again joined O'Flaherty at the house on Rockaway Point.

Breaking open the rock, WALLFLOWER and the FBI agents found an A&P matchbook with the word *Raincheck* on the cover. Under the second *c* was the microdot with new instructions.

On October 19, Cassidy returned to New York for another meeting with the Soviets, and once again the unexpected happened at a drop site. At 2 P.M., Cassidy was supposed to leave his rock at the base of a tree near the end of a footbridge that crossed the Belt Parkway in Brooklyn. As he approached the drop, he saw smoke billowing up. A teenager had flicked a cigarette into a trash heap near the tree. Someone had turned in an alarm, and the New York City fire department was on its way; Cassidy could hear the sirens getting closer. He hesitated, then decided to stick to the plan. He dropped the rock and fled.

Only minutes after Cassidy scrambled out of the way, there were fire trucks and hoses all over the place. In an apartment building overlooking the site, the two FBI agents covering the drop could hardly believe the pandemonium unfolding before their eyes. This was definitely not in the script. Special Agent Jim Lancaster, whose Deep South accent marked him as an alien in Brooklyn, recalled the scene. "There was this fire, and the rock was right by a tree. Me and Ricky Shapiro were looking out the window and we said, 'Oh god, the fire department is going to see this funny rock, and it's going to burn up.' "

To the agents' relief, the rock and its flammable contents survived the blaze intact. Two hours later, Cassidy was walking along Sixty-fourth Avenue in Queens, as he had been instructed to do on the microdot in the matchbook, when Likhachev fell into step beside him. Cassidy told the GRU man that he had looked for a civilian job in Tampa at the United States Readiness Command (REDCOM), as STRICOM was now called, but none was available.

Likhachev asked how the Morse transmissions were going, whether Cassidy was receiving them at the "principal time." Cassidy said he was; he had not had to use the alternate transmission times that the Russians had provided as backup.

At their next meeting in March, Likhachev said, he would explain a new code. Likhachev asked whether Cassidy might be able to obtain topographical maps; after discussing that, they parted. Cassidy drove to Brooklyn to pick up Likhachev's rock, then into Manhattan to mark the same lamp pole, and back to Rockaway Point to meet with the FBI.

Cassidy continued visiting and reporting on military bases around the country, and in March he returned to New York, drove to Brooklyn, and hid a hollow rock on the south side of Holy Cross Cemetery, near Cortelyou Road. Two hours later, he rendezvoused with Likhachev on a park bench in Brooklyn. After their meeting, he drove into Manhattan, and this time he left a piece of yellow tape facing outward on a lamppost at York Avenue and Ninety-first Street. The day ended, as usual, at Rockaway Point.

Six months later, in late September, Cassidy was back in Brooklyn, hiding a rock at another cemetery two hours before he met Likhachev near the Fort Hamilton athletic field. They discussed Cassidy's latest surveys of military bases, and the Morse transmissions. Likhachev said a new person would be his contact at the next meeting in April 1976; Cassidy should be ready to use the parol, since they did not know each other. But the new Mike, Likhachev assured him, would be up to speed on the case.

Cassidy then picked up his rock at a dead drop in Brooklyn, left a signal in Manhattan, and returned to the kitchen table at O'Flaherty's mother's house, where the rock was broken open. For the first time, it contained two microdots, because the message from the Soviets was longer than usual. It directed Cassidy not only to spy on additional military bases but to try to obtain emergency planning documents from city, county, or state offices.

Although there had still been no discussion of the "new code" that Likhachev had mentioned, the secret writing in the rock instructed Cassidy to travel to a location in the Bronx for a meeting on the first Saturday after he received a Morse transmission with twenty groups or to go to a dead drop in the Bronx for a pickup if he received a coded radio message with twenty-four five-digit groups.

In April, Cassidy was back in the New York area, this time to leave a rock at a drop site in suburban Yonkers with more reports on military bases. The FBI had seen Likhachev moving around New York several times with Vladimir Vybornov, who was listed as a "public relations officer" at the Soviet UN mission. His wife, Aleksandra Vybornova, also worked in the public relations office. The bureau predicted that Vybornov would turn out to be the new Mike, and it was right.

On April 10, FBI agents watched Vybornov fill a dead drop near Pinebrook Boulevard in New Rochelle, in Westchester County. He was accompanied by a woman, believed to be Aleksandra. Cassidy cleared the drop, left a piece of yellow tape on a lamp pole at 201st Street in Manhattan, and traveled to Rockaway Point. There was no meeting this time with Vybornov, but instructions on a microdot inside another A&P matchbook told him to prepare for a meeting with the new Mike in October.

Cassidy's report to the FBI of his first meeting with Vybornov, on October 9, 1976, was detailed and meticulous, as usual. At 2 P.M., he left his rock at the base of a street sign at Palmer Avenue in the Bronx. The rock contained a report of his reconnaissance of military bases in Georgia.

He then drove around to kill time before the meeting. "I parked the car just off Gun Hill Road . . . at approximately 1552 hours. I waited in the car until 1557 hours and I then walked to the spot arriving at 1600 hours." Cassidy pretended to be waiting for a bus. "I noticed a person in dark clothes w/umbrella at the corner of NW Fenton and Gun Hill. . . . This person stopped in front of me and as I looked at him he asked me about a drive-in and when I responded he smiled and said 'Hi I'm another Mike.' We shook hands."

As they strolled along the street, the sixth Mike talked about the wet weather and wanted to know where Cassidy had parked; he had not brought his own car, he said, because of the rain. The new Mike not only had a halting command of English, but it was soon apparent he was not cut out for a career in espionage. Vybornov, it became clear, wanted to break all the spy rules because of the inclement weather.

He asked Cassidy to drive back to the drop site at Palmer Avenue, retrieve the rock he had just left there for Vybornov, and bring it directly to the Russian. They would then simply exchange rocks in Cassidy's car. This was an unprecedented request, a total departure from spy etiquette. It flouted the GRU's elaborate procedure for using dead drops to avoid risks. But first, Vybornov had a lot of questions. As they continued walking, he asked if the microdots were legible. Cassidy said they were OK. He then told Cassidy to be sure to keep the secret writing paper wet when he developed it. That puzzled Cassidy, who explained that he dipped the paper in acetone, but after steaming it the sheet dried out rapidly. There was no way to keep it wet. Vybornov did not respond and Cassidy concluded that the Russian was in over his head.

The new Mike then grilled Cassidy closely about his children and household, apparently to reassure Moscow that his family, friends, and neighbors remained unaware of his espionage activities. "He said, 'Do you hear from your son and daughter?' I told him I hadn't heard from my son since he graduated from high school. 'How about your daughter?' " She was busy with a new career in nursing in Alexandria, Cassidy replied. "He asked if I received correspondence from friends and relatives. I said very seldom. He said, 'Do they visit you?' I said we have very few houseguests."

Vybornov persisted, Cassidy's report to the FBI continued. "He said, 'What kind of a house do you have, something like this?' and he pointed to a two- or three-story rowhouse we were just passing. I said no, Mike, and smiled. 'We don't have houses like that in Florida. I live in a house all by itself and on one floor.'

"He said, 'Does your wife know anything about this?' I said, 'No, nothing and I want it kept that way.' He asked if neighbors were friends

of mine. I said a few of them were. He said do they visit? I said I'm not on
a social basis with neighbors. We speak when we see each other during
the day and that's about it.

"He asked how finances were and I told him not so good. He said
there was $4,200 in my package and . . . he hoped this would help." Cas-
sidy, who always complained he needed more money, replied, "But Mike,
I'm missing the big paydays."

He reminded Vybornov that he had provided the name of Nicky, the
sergeant at Edgewood, but had not been paid for that. "I missed the payday on Nicky," Cassidy protested. Vybornov adopted a sheepish expression as though he agreed.

Vybornov, Cassidy reported to the FBI, then pressed for a document
outlining a plan for industrial mobilization in an emergency that Cassidy had said he had access to at a local university. "We are very much
interested in it. We would very much like to have that but not if you have
to expose yourself. Do not take and reproduce if you must give your identity. Do not give name, address, phone number—nothing. It's not worth
it to us, but get it if you can."

As they walked along Eastchester Road toward Gun Hill Road, they
were nearing the drop site. "He said he would walk very slowly up this
road and that I was to get the car, pick up my package, and then pick him
up . . . about five blocks away. . . . I told him I would be back in six or
seven minutes."

Cassidy retrieved his rock, got in his car, cruised along Eastchester,
and spotted Vybornov in the middle of the block. "As I pulled to the curb
he came over and got in. I pulled my rock from my jacket pocket and gave
it to him. . . . He pulled his from his raincoat pocket." There was no need
to put tape on the light pole, Vybornov said, "because I already know
you have [the rock]." It was the only time that Cassidy and a Russian
had simply handed the rocks to each other.

"He had opened the door and was getting out. I noticed he had left his
umbrella in the car in his haste to leave and I hollered and opened the
door and extended it to him. He made several stabs at it before he caught
the handle. . . . To me he lost his composure—seemed he was very anx-

ious for us to separate and me to get the hell out of there." WALLFLOWER gunned his car and took off.

Inside the rock handed to Cassidy was a message in secret writing. It provided his schedule for 1977, called for drops and meetings in April and October, and gave the dates and times of the radio transmissions he was to receive. It asked him to provide the industrial-mobilization plan, and to reconnoiter a nuclear-ammunition depot at the air force base in Charleston.

The message also instructed Cassidy, in case the Soviets should ever lose contact with him, to go to New York City on the last Saturday of January, April, July, and October and wait, pipe in mouth in front of the antiques store in Brooklyn at 4 P.M., holding the usual book-sized package with yellow wrapping. If contact was not reestablished, he was to try again the next day.

In Cassidy's appraisal to the FBI of the meeting, it was plain that he had been underwhelmed by Vybornov. "He seemed to have his game plan and stuck with it. This did not include any comments or discussion from me—just answer the questions. He was far from being polished like, say, Mike #1. He had hard features and could pass for a longshoreman or a lumberjack. He wanted to dominate the meeting—and did—and was very confident, bold, hard as a rock, until he started out of the car when he seemed to lose all his composure in attempting to grab the umbrella."

Cassidy kept his cool at his meetings with the Russians, and he did this time as well, despite Vybornov changing the procedures and peppering him with questions. But he found each encounter with the Soviets nerve-racking. "I was always on pins and needles worrying that I was going to blow it," Cassidy confessed. "I was worried I would contradict myself or make a mistake and blow the thing apart." Cassidy was on edge even though the Russians never indicated the slightest suspicion that he was anything but a genuine mole.

"I felt they trusted me and believed me," he said. "I had a job to do and I wanted to do it."

Marie Cassidy remembered that her husband usually had trouble sleeping before a meet. "He had sleepless nights, plenty of that, and stomach problems. He would eat very little before he'd go." The former nun said she had no appetite on those nights either.

"I was worried about the danger," she said. "I could see how nervous he was before a meeting. There were middle-of-the-night meetings. So I burnt my candle and prayed."

THE PROFESSOR

In 1976, **Gilberto** Lopez y Rivas, busy as he had been with his espionage activities, finally received his Ph.D. from the University of Utah.[1] By then, he was back in Mexico City, where he had been working as a researcher at an anthropological institute. But he did not remain there, as Robert Schamay, who had been the FBI case agent in Salt Lake City, learned in October.

"I was out hunting on a mountain in southern Utah in October of 1976, and a game warden knocked on the trailer. He said I had a phone call. I come off the mountain and find a pay phone in a little dinky town, and it's Gene Peterson. I have to be in Minnesota as soon as possible."

Peterson, by now Soviet section chief at FBI headquarters, was con-

---

[1] The title of his dissertation was "Conquest and Resistance: The Origin of the Chicano National Minority in the Nineteenth Century (A Marxist View)."

tinuing to supervise the spy case. He ordered Schamay to cut short his hunting trip and get moving. "Next morning," Schamay recalled, "I was off the mountain, back home in Salt Lake, packing, and on Monday I'm on a plane to Minneapolis."

Two years before, while still a student in Austin, Lopez had told Aurelio Flores that he might be moving to Minnesota. Headquarters had plucked Schamay off the mountain because the bureau had learned that the PALMETTOS had in fact surfaced there. Gilberto Lopez y Rivas, Soviet spy, was now an assistant professor of Chicano studies at the University of Minnesota. Professor Lopez had the distinction, in all likelihood, of being the first Russian spy ever to become a member of the faculty of that institution. The university, of course, knew nothing of his other, secret life.

Manuel Guerrero had brought Lopez to Minneapolis. Guerrero, then chairman of the university's Department of Chicano Studies, was short one professor for the fall semester. "We advertised in the *Chronicle of Higher Education*," Guerrero said. Lopez had answered the ad and traveled to Minneapolis for a job interview. "I hired him," Guerrero continued. "He was hired on the basis both of his résumé and the interview. Gilberto was a very amicable, social person. He made a lot of friendships."

Lopez, his wife, and their children settled into faculty housing off Fourth Street, on the ground floor of a two-story garden apartment. The FBI wiretapped the place; it did not attempt to install room bugs as it had done in Austin.

Alfredo Gonzales, a colleague in the Chicano studies department, recalled that while Lopez served on the faculty, a Spanish club made a film called *Minnesotanos Mexicanos*. "It was a documentary of Mexican Americans in Minnesota, and he is shown in the film twice. He is tall, very thin, and slender, with dark brown hair, light skin. A European type, not Indian. He had a strong voice, a heavy accent but good English. I knew him socially, but he never once mentioned his political views. He never discussed politics. He had strong views on the historical treatment of Chicanos. He never mentioned the Soviet Union. He loved to talk about opera, and art, and history."

The university offered Chicano studies as a major for undergraduate students. The faculty taught a wide variety of courses dealing with the history and social status of Mexican Americans, bilingual education, and the Spanish language. The university bulletin for the summer of 1977, for example, lists a typical course taught by Professor Lopez. Entitled Chicano History, it offered four degree credits and covered "Mexican American history, including such areas as migration, labor movements, Chicanos in agriculture, the 'pachuco' phenomenon, border conflict, and regional history."[2]

The FBI watched Lopez and listened to his telephone conversations to try to determine whether he was still servicing dead drops for the GRU while exploring Chicano history for his unsuspecting students. The bureau's counterintelligence agents hoped that Lopez would lead them to one or more Soviet spies.

After Robert Schamay flew in from Utah, he remained in Minnesota for three months. His primary task was to brief Mark Kirkland, who had been assigned as the case agent by the Minneapolis office. "Mark had the ticket on it," Schamay said. "He was a nice, hardworking kid from Salt Lake, anxious to do a good job."

Around the same time, Charles W. Elmore, a thirty-one-year-old FBI agent in New York, asked his fellow agent Jim Lancaster about the PAL-METTO case. Elmore was from the West Coast and wanted badly to get back there. Perhaps, he thought, if he volunteered to go out to Minnesota to help on the PALMETTO case, he would be rewarded with his office of preference. A quiet, good-looking man, Elmore was single and had no ties to New York. More important, he was fluent in Spanish. He won a transfer to Minneapolis and went to work translating the wiretaps of the Lopezes' apartment.

Back in Washington, Phil Parker had been transferred to FBI headquarters from the Washington field office early in 1976. He had been head of S-3, the GRU squad in the field office. Now Parker was deter-

---

[2] "*Pachuco* is a term for a cool guy, a Mexican American in the 1940s who wore zoot suits and was considered a hipster," according to Lisa Navarrete, director of public information for the National Council of La Raza.

mined to do something about the PALMETTOS. At headquarters he became the case supervisor and the major player in the events that unfolded.

"It had been my squad's case," he said. "I had participated in surveillance of several of the meetings between WALLFLOWER and the Russians. Both stationary and rolling surveillances"—meaning stakeouts in a building, or cars driving around in the area.

At headquarters, Parker was assigned to the Soviet section of Division 5, the intelligence division.[3] He was forty years old. A tall, handsome Virginian, Parker defied the conventional straight-arrow appearance long adhered to by FBI agents, a code that had been strictly enforced by J. Edgar Hoover and lingered on even after his death. Parker sported a handlebar mustache that made him look like an old-fashioned movie villain or a bartender in a Wild West saloon, for which he took a great deal of good-natured ribbing from his less flamboyant colleagues. When it came to counterintelligence work, however, Parker was all business.

He had not set out in life to become a counterspy. In fact, Parker might never have joined the FBI had the pay been better for high-school teachers. He was born in Chesapeake, Virginia, across the Elizabeth River from Norfolk. His father had been a radio operator on merchant ships, and his mother worked as a printer. Parker attended public schools, went to college for a while, and in 1955 joined the air force, which sent him to Syracuse University to study Russian.

The air force then assigned Parker to England in an intelligence job, where he met his future wife, Jill, an attractive Englishwoman from Bedford. After returning to the states, Parker finished college, and then earned a master's degree in Russian at Indiana University. He also traveled to the Soviet Union, visiting Moscow, Leningrad, and five other cities.

Back home, Parker taught Spanish and Russian at a local high school and coached junior-varsity football. Parker enjoyed teaching but was trying to support his now-growing family on $5,500 a year. In 1965, at age twenty-nine, he applied for a job at the FBI.

[3] In 1993, the intelligence division was renamed the national security division.

The bureau sent him to its training base at Quantico, Virginia, to learn to shoot, then to the Seattle office, and then to language school in Monterey to study Bulgarian. In 1967, he was assigned to the Washington field office, where he acquired the basics of counterintelligence work and followed Bulgarian spies around the capital. Three years later, Parker moved to the GRU squad.

"The GRU was our main target," Parker recalled. "We also handled some Polish and East German cases. We worked out of the Old Post Office building. The squad had great morale. We turned some Soviets. Our job was to identify which ones were intelligence officers." In 1973, Parker was promoted to head of the squad. Three years later, he was transferred to headquarters.

"When I went to headquarters," he said, "my sole goal was to close this case with an arrest."

The FBI had sent Mark Kirkland to the Minneapolis division in June 1973. He was twenty-eight. It was there that he began flying with Tren Basford on aerial surveillances. Kirkland and his wife, Julie, moved into their farmhouse in Minnetonka and started a family. Their first son, Kenneth, was born in 1974, and a second son, Christopher, was born in 1976, the same year that Mark was handed his first big case—the PAL-METTO file.

From an early age, Kirkland's ambition was to be an FBI agent. He was born into a Mormon family on August 8, 1944, and grew up in Centerville, Utah, north of Salt Lake City. "Centerville was a very small town, but he was kind of a rebel," Julie Kirkland said. "He had a motorcycle and bleached his hair white once." He went to high school in nearby Bountiful, and then struck out on his own.

"He was only eighteen or nineteen when he left to be an FBI clerk. His parents were very unhappy that he was leaving town. He couldn't wait to get out of Centerville."

Kirkland moved to Los Angeles, enrolled in California State University, and began working for the FBI in the spring of 1964. He was tall, dark-haired, handsome, and single. Two years later, he married a young woman who also worked as a clerk in the bureau. They had a daughter, Kristin. Kirkland and his best friend at the FBI, Ron Williams, had both joined the army reserve, and they each did a three-year hitch in Germany, where Mark worked in intelligence. Kirkland returned to the states and to the FBI in the summer of 1969. Soon afterward, his youthful marriage ended in divorce.

A year later, Julia Searle, who had grown up in Venice, California, graduated from high school there and landed a clerical job at the FBI in Los Angeles while attending college at night. She was eighteen, with dancing eyes, a pug nose, and long brown hair. Kirkland was eight years her senior. He worked the night shift, on a different floor, but they met, early in 1971, and began dating. Mark and his friends called her Julie.

That same year Kirkland graduated from Cal State, and the following January he and Julie were wed at the Mormon temple in Los Angeles. Three months later, at age twenty-seven, he was appointed a special agent of the FBI.

Julie Kirkland's parents were both teachers. Her father had a doctorate from UCLA and taught theology at Santa Monica City College; her mother gave private lessons in piano and music theory. Like Mark, Julie came from a Mormon background.

Three months after their marriage, the FBI sent Kirkland to Oklahoma City, for what the bureau calls a "first office" assignment. Less than a year later, he was assigned to Minneapolis.

Julie Kirkland soon became aware that her husband was working on a big case, although she did not know its nature, or the code name PAL-METTO. Mark said little about the case. But he grew the scraggly beard and long hair, and Julie realized he was operating undercover. Having worked for the FBI herself, she was able to put some of the pieces together. "I knew the name Lopez, I knew they were at the university, and Mark had installed the equipment, the cameras, and listening devices, and I knew they were monitoring from a nearby apartment. Mark didn't come home and blab, but I had held a top-secret clearance, after all, and it wasn't hard for me to figure out what was going on."

One of Kirkland's first moves was to try to place informants close to the PALMETTOS. The Kirklands had become friendly with a family that lived in the neighborhood, and Mark recruited the woman as an FBI source. At his request, she enrolled in one of Lopez's courses.

"I just knew him as a student," said the woman, who asked not to be named. "I talked to him a couple of times after class and at student-teacher conferences. It was a course in Chicano studies, and he definitely felt Chicanos were mistreated. He talked about the plight of the Mexican peasants and the ones that came as migrant workers. He was focusing on low wages, poor housing. I wrote reports to Mark on Lopez once a week or more. Mark had wanted me to arrange to baby-sit for Lopez, who had both children with him. I was planning to tell him I was in dire straits in the hopes he would say 'We need a baby-sitter.' "

The bureau's other undercover source was a man also enrolled as a student. Both were designated "134s," which in the jargon of the FBI means informants. Kirkland himself mixed with students on the campus to gather intelligence on Lopez. Despite the blanket coverage, however, including the wiretaps and physical surveillance, the FBI never detected Lopez servicing any dead drops in Minnesota or contacting the Soviets.

As the months slipped by, Julie Kirkland became increasingly concerned about her husband's assignment. This was a spy case, and it very likely involved the Russians. She worried about Mark's safety.

"I remember confronting him and saying, 'You obviously are trying to unravel something.' He said, 'For your own good, Julie, let's not talk too much about it.' He said, 'If anything ever happens to me, it's better if you don't know anything.'

"Mark had gone to Washington for the case, and he told me that the information had gone to Attorney General Griffin Bell.

"Right before he died I'd gotten pretty insistent. I didn't think it was good for our relationship for Mark to be so deep in a secret life that I wasn't part of. How long would he stay in espionage work? It gave him the thrill he liked, but it wasn't good for family life.

"On the day he left, he thought the Lopezes were going over the border into Canada. He didn't say what the bureau suspected the Lopezes were planning to do in Canada. I had two babies and I really didn't want to know.

"I was concerned about his flying all the time. He flew a lot with Tren Basford, but Mark was not trained as a copilot. Mark talked Tren into delaying his retirement so the plane would be available. It was Tren's private plane."

And then it was Tuesday, August 23, and Mark Kirkland kissed Julie good-bye on the forehead and told her not to worry.

Two decades after the Cessna went down in Dewey Lake, Julie Kirkland still felt the pain of her husband's death. She had remarried and her two sons were grown men now. But the shadow was always there, even when the days were bright.

"We have a very nice life," she said. "But we can never replace what Mark was to us. You don't forget."

Soon after her husband's death, Julie Kirkland sat down to write a private account of all that had happened. As if entered in a diary, she recalled her feelings in the days before Mark's death, and afterward. "Ever since Ron Williams, Mark's best friend, was killed last year I've taken to worrying and being fearful for Mark," she wrote. "He has been working undercover and I know so little about his daily activities any more. I'm insecure about it.

"We had an argument the morning he left. . . . I feel bad about it now, I wish I hadn't been upset. We smoothed it over though and I hugged him a lot. Kenny was so sweet—hugged Daddy a lot, too. I still worried— mostly I think because I don't understand the case—Top Secret. I hated us not sharing. . . .

"The days were sweet with the babies. I'm used to being on my own with them. Mark is gone a lot and me and the little boys are great buddies.

"I planted flowers around the front of the house. Just took care of the boys and home. Mark called every night."

Then came the entry for August 25. She wrote of her growing fear that night, and her call to the FBI operator, who sounded odd and obviously knew more than she was saying. "The minutes ticked by like hours. I was cold and nervous. I began praying, but nothing helped. . . . Mark *always* called me from the field."

"Sometime between 11–12 I heard cars in the drive, not one, but several. I was panicky. My heart sank. I pleaded with God to stop this from happening, to please, please not take my husband from me. But I knew it was happening."

Then came the knock on the door that, at first, she could not bring herself to answer. She sat on the top step of the stairs, knowing what it was, and finally forced herself to go down and answer the door.

When she received the horrific news from John Shimota and the other FBI men, she wrote, "I kept saying over and over 'It can't be true, it can't be true.' 'What about our boys? Won't they ever know their father?' . . . I was shaking all over. Very cold still. My teeth chattered.

"Then John said Tren was gone, too."

The next few days were a blur. Her father, neighbors, people from church came to comfort her. A close friend, Barbara Olsen, took care of the boys. She slept little.

Alone at the funeral home by Mark's coffin, she looked at her husband for the last time. "By the side of his casket I promised him I would raise good men he would be proud of. And I will."

Then she kissed him good-bye.

The next day she took Mark Kirkland home to Utah. At the graveside, "I thought Mark would have loved this day. It was a breathtaking day, blue skies, wispy clouds, pleasant temperature, breezy." They buried him next to his father, below the mountain in Centerville where he had spent his childhood.

Back in Minnetonka, Julie finished writing.

We are alone now—me and Kenny and Chris. In a big old antique house in Minnesota. What happened to the dream we started only five and a half years ago? I don't know why this happened. I do know we will be OK. And Kenny and Chris will be good men someday. They are such perfect little boys already.

I had the FBI insignia carved on Mark's gravestone. I want anyone who sees it to know how much he loved America and believed in what he was doing.

He died being an FBI agent—what he always wanted to be. He died serving others. I wanted him to be remembered as a husband, father, and an FBI agent.

—Sept. 1977
Julie Kirkland

CHAPTER

17

SHOW TIME

For Phil Parker, the tragic death of the two agents was a severe emotional blow. He felt a personal responsibility, asking himself over and over whether he might have been able to act sooner and do more to bring about an arrest. Had he done so, he thought, the accident might never have happened.

Parker had flown to Minneapolis several times to confer with Kirkland. The two had become good friends, a bond strengthened by their shared determination to roll up the PALMETTOS.

But the plane crash was more than a torment for Parker, it was also a catalyst. He had been importuning the Justice Department for more than a year to act on the case, and now he intensified his efforts. The time had come to move, he argued, to close out the operation that had begun almost two decades earlier when Joe Cassidy was first dangled to the Russians on the volleyball court.

Moreover, the fatal accident itself posed a potential danger to the operation. Parker and others were alarmed that the crash of the Cessna might tip off the PALMETTOS to the fact that they were under surveillance. The remote lake in northern Minnesota where the plane had gone down was near where the Lopezes were camping. If the couple heard reports or read news stories about the crash and the loss of the two FBI agents, they might connect it to their presence in the area and try to flee.

Aware of this new danger, Parker made certain that the bureau continued to keep a close watch on the Lopezes. In Minnesota, Dennis Conway took over the PALMETTO case. He and Kirkland had been good friends; Conway had been one of the agents who came to break the news to Julie the night of the plane crash. Conway, who grew up in Sioux City, Iowa, had played football for Notre Dame. "We called him 'No-Neck' because he was built like a fireplug," Phil Parker said. "He was an outstanding agent."

Parker still hoped, as did Conway, that Lopez would lead the FBI to a spy or spies in the GRU's network in North America. But it never happened, and the FBI was increasingly frustrated.

"They took some funny trips," Parker said. "There were some suspicious activities. Their actions on some of the trips they took to northern Minnesota indicated they were watching for surveillance. But we never saw them clear a drop or meet anyone. We don't know why they were driving to Canada when Mark was killed."

To move the case forward Parker needed approval at a higher level. Although most Americans probably view the FBI as an all-powerful agency that can arrest spies when it wants to, in fact, in sensitive cases involving national security, the bureau takes its marching orders from the Justice Department.

And in 1977, that meant John L. Martin.

For twenty-four years, until he retired in 1997, Martin was the official who decided which spies to arrest and prosecute. He also orchestrated a number of East-West spy swaps during the cold war. Working in the shadows and unknown outside the closed world of intelligence,

Martin chose which espionage cases would be prosecuted and make the front pages and the nightly news. The rest never became public. As head of the internal-security section of the department's criminal division, he was the official who determined, in effect, whether the spies came in from the cold.

On the couch of his office at the Justice Department, Martin kept a stuffed wolf in sheep's clothing, a gift from fellow prosecutors. Its meaning was unmistakable; secured to the wolf's forehead was a red star.

Within the FBI, some officials regarded Martin as overly cautious; they felt he allowed the prosecution only of cases he was sure the government could win. Over his career, however, Martin had cleared the way for some big wins: John A. Walker, Jr., who headed the notorious family ring of navy spies that sold codes to the KGB, convicted and sentenced to life in prison; Jonathan Jay Pollard, convicted of spying for Israel and sentenced to life; Ronald Pelton, a former National Security Agency official who sold secrets to the KGB, sentenced to life; Richard Miller, the first FBI agent to be convicted of espionage, sentenced to life; Aldrich H. Ames, the CIA supermole, sentenced to life for betraying the CIA's Soviet agents, causing ten to be executed; and Christopher Boyce and Andrew Lee, who sold satellite secrets to the Russians and whose story was told in the book and movie *The Falcon and the Snowman*—Lee was sentenced to life, Boyce to forty years.

Some got away. Edward Lee Howard, an ex-CIA officer who revealed the secrets of the agency's Moscow operations to the KGB, escaped to the Soviet Union. And Felix Bloch, a State Department official suspected of spying for the KGB, was subjected to a media circus after a news leak identified him; he was dismissed from his job but never indicted.

Martin, raised in upstate New York, joined the FBI after he graduated from Syracuse University Law School in 1962. He investigated the mob in New Orleans, then was sent to Mississippi to assist in the probe of the 1964 murder of three civil-rights workers. He left the FBI in 1968 to join a Washington law firm, but three years later went back into the government as an attorney in the Justice Department. When he took over the internal-security section, few spies had been prosecuted; government intelligence agencies feared too many secrets might be revealed. Then, in 1980, Congress passed the Classified Information Procedures Act, which provided for ways to protect secrets in federal trials; under the law, judges can prohibit or limit the introduction of classified information in open court. The law had an impact. Seventy-six spies were prosecuted under Martin, all but one convicted.

"I'm a firm believer in giving them their full constitutional rights and then sending them to jail for a lifetime," Martin said when he retired.[1]

But the tough-guy stance, as Phil Parker was to discover, did not apply in every instance; if Martin chose not to prosecute an espionage suspect, the public never got to know about the case.

Pushing hard for action against the PALMETTOS, Parker walked across the street from FBI headquarters in the J. Edgar Hoover Building to see Martin, whose office was not in the headquarters of the Justice Department but on Ninth Street. Martin turned the case over to Joseph Tafe, one of his staff attorneys.

A short, chubby man with sandy hair and glasses, Tafe at first seemed receptive to Parker's entreaties. The FBI man became a frequent visitor to the Ninth Street building. To Parker's dismay, however, the department seemed to be moving at a glacial pace.

In the spring of 1977, FBI headquarters had asked the Tampa office to find out if Joe Cassidy would be willing to testify in open court and to travel to Washington to confer with Justice Department attorneys. Cassidy agreed to both requests.

If there were any signs that the PALMETTOS were planning to escape, the bureau wanted authority to arrest them. Tafe began drafting a twelve-page criminal complaint to have ready in case the Lopezes tried to bolt. The complaint called on a federal magistrate to issue warrants for their arrests.

---

[1] *The Washington Post,* July 31, 1997, p. A13.

On the face of it, the government already had a strong case against the PALMETTOS. There were photographs of Lopez and his wife retrieving films of the documents, many marked TOP SECRET, that Cassidy had placed at the dead drops. And Danilin had assured Cassidy that he had received that material.

But the department was waffling on whether to prosecute on the basis of the copious evidence already in the hands of the government. In the course of the investigation, the FBI had wiretapped and videotaped the PALMETTOS and entered their apartments to place bugs. The Justice Department lawyers could foresee trouble in the courtroom over the bureau's counterintelligence techniques. The entries, taps, and bugs would surely be challenged on Fourth Amendment grounds by the defense.

John Martin, Parker said, raised additional objections. "John argued there is nothing illegal in picking up a package per se. He said it was just an unusual form of communication; you don't have to use the post office, you can leave things in rocks. And Martin said the information in the package had been cleared for transmission to the Soviets and therefore was not classified."

James E. Nolan, Jr., a former high-ranking FBI counterintelligence official, said Martin's view was that clearing material to pass it to the Soviets "constituted a de facto declassification. He felt that made it unusable for prosecution."

Legally, however, the question of whether the feed had technically been declassified or not fell into an arcane, gray area. Nobody really knew. An equally strong argument could be made that a document stamped TOP SECRET was exactly that.[2]

"The documents were approved for passage to a hostile government,"

---

[2] There was reason to believe that the material passed to the Soviets by Joe Cassidy was not legally declassified. "If we did declassify a document passed to the Soviets," said one former counterintelligence official, "we would have to declassify every copy and every other document like it. If the Soviets ever managed to obtain a second copy stamped 'declassified,' they'd know we were playing games."

Parker pointed out, regardless of whether the feed was classified. "You have the conspiracy charge—it had classified markings on it so you would have to assume the person who picked it up would know he was not authorized to have it."

The real reason for the Justice Department's caution, however, was the backstage debate over the wiretaps and entries. The issue was further complicated by the fact that some of the techniques used by the FBI in the PALMETTO investigation had been approved by the attorney general, but some had not.

Despite the legal hurdles, at first Parker was encouraged by the apparent support he received from Martin and Tafe. "At the outset, Tafe said, 'I think we can do a prosecution on this case,' " Parker asserted. "John Martin said face-to-face to me in his office in the Ninth Street building, 'Yes, I think we have a case.' "[3]

As the months slipped by, however, it soon became apparent to Parker that nothing was happening. "What we wanted was prosecution. All we got was talk." Days and weeks went by with little action. "I'm an easy-going guy," Parker said, "but I was kicking over trash cans."

The FBI man had run into a bureaucratic brick wall. "I had been fighting with Joe Tafe for eighteen months to give me an answer," Parker said. "I even spoke to the U.S. attorney in Minnesota, Thor Anderson." Whenever Parker approached Tafe, he said, the Justice Department attorney would say, " 'I'm busy.' I could never pin him down.

"We'd been talking for months. . . . I go into his office, and I said, 'We're ready to go, are you going to make a decision on it?' He said, 'Damn, I just haven't been able to get to it.' That's when I kicked over the trash can rather than hit him in the head. Tafe said, 'Calm down!' and I yelled a little bit."

Parker decided on the spot it was time to confront the Lopezes. As the

---

[3] Even two decades later, with the cold war over, the two Justice Department attorneys were not eager to talk about the PALMETTO case. Martin refused to comment. Tafe, still a lawyer in the internal-security section, declined to speak on the record.

case supervisor, he had the authority to do that much, with or without the Justice Department's approval. Once he did so, he knew, the case would be over, one way or another. Either he would get a confession and win permission from the department to make an arrest, or he would at least have the satisfaction of knowing he had done all he could. Parker had a few parting words for Tafe. "I said, the hell with it, I'm going out to Minneapolis to do an interview. Probably we should have done it before."

It was late May 1978. The Justice Department officials led Parker to believe that if Lopez confessed, there could be a prosecution after all. "Talking to Tafe and Martin, it was, like, 'If we get an admission, you'll authorize an arrest?' And they said, 'Yes.' "

Tafe had concluded there might be a way to pick his way through the legal minefield. With a confession, the government would have a clean case—it would not have to rely on electronic evidence. There was a great deal of other evidence, such as the photographs of the Lopezes clearing drops in Florida, that was not obtained through wiretaps or similar means. And Cassidy was willing to testify in open court.

Parker's decision to fly to Minnesota meant that the criminal complaint would have to be at the ready. On May 24, a teletype went out from FBI headquarters to Tampa and Minneapolis advising those offices that Tafe would fly to Tampa with the complaint, which was to be filed in court if the subjects attempted to flee. Tampa was instructed to warn Joe Cassidy that his name might be about to be made public and to make arrangements to protect him.

The next day, the text of the complaint was teletyped to the FBI office in Tampa for its information. Headquarters advised that if the Justice Department filed the complaint, it would do so in the United States District Court in Tampa before Magistrate Paul Game, Jr., since the alleged criminal acts had been committed in that part of Florida. The complaint was entitled *United States of America* v. *Gilberto M. Lopez and Alicia C. Lopez*, and charged them with violation of Section 794(c) of Title 18 of the U.S. criminal code, the key espionage statute that prohibits the transmittal of defense information to a foreign power. The law provides the same punishment for conspiracy to violate the statute.[4]

The criminal complaint named Mikhail I. Danilin and Oleg I. Likhachev as "co-conspirators but not defendants." Since the two Soviets had diplomatic immunity, they could not be arrested. The complaint charged that the four "did conspire to communicate, deliver and transmit to a foreign government, to wit, the Union of Soviet Socialist Republics . . . information relating to the national defense of the United States, with intent and reason to believe that the said information would be used to the advantage of said foreign government."[5]

The complaint then said that Joseph Cassidy "was acting as a double agent for the FBI. . . . The FBI has been aware of and has supervised Mr. Cassidy's activities as an apparent agent of the USSR during the course of the events stated herein." The complaint listed the details of all of Cassidy's meetings with Danilin and Likhachev, as well as the clearing of the drop sites in Florida by Lopez, sometimes accompanied by his wife. It ended by asking the magistrate to issue "a warrant for the arrest of defendants Gilberto M. Lopez and Alicia C. Lopez."

To all appearances, the espionage complaint and Parker's flight to Minneapolis were being carefully coordinated for the likely arrest of the PALMETTOS. According to Jack O'Flaherty, Cassidy's case agent in Tampa,

---

[4] Under the 1972 Supreme Court ruling outlawing capital punishment, there was no death penalty for espionage from that year until 1994, when Congress, in the wake of the Aldrich Ames spy case, restored the penalty if certain criteria were met. (The Supreme Court restored capital punishment in the states in 1976.) Had the Lopezes been convicted of espionage in 1978, they could have been sentenced to a prison term of any number of years or life, but they would not have faced the death penalty.

[5] The espionage statutes generally bar disclosure not of "classified information" but of "information relating to the national defense." Since 1951, documents have been classified by presidential executive orders, not by law. In practice, since the 1960s, the Justice Department has generally taken the position that data must be classified at the level of secret or above to fall within the definition of "national defense" information. But the statute does not require that the documents be classified. Under the language of the espionage laws, therefore, even if the material left in the rocks had technically been "declassified," that would not necessarily bar the prosecution of a person who retrieved it and passed it to a foreign power.

the FBI office there was instructed to make a hotel reservation for Tafe. "I personally went over on lunch one day and made the reservation at the Sheraton, one block from the FBI office in Tampa." All the ducks were in a row.

But the bureaucratic wheels slowly turning in Washington mysteriously ground to a halt. With no explanation, O'Flaherty was told to cancel Tafe's hotel reservation. "I canceled it on Memorial Day weekend," he said.

Despite the about-face in Washington, Parker flew to Minnesota as scheduled, still determined to get a confession. At the same time, he arranged for Aurelio Flores to meet him in Minneapolis. "The undercover agent was there for a couple of reasons," Parker recounted, "mainly because of the shock value, and because he spoke Spanish."

Carmen Espinoza, an FBI agent from New York who was also fluent in Spanish, flew out to Minnesota to interview Alicia Lopez. Both Lopez and his wife spoke good English, but Parker was covering all bases.

When there are two suspects in a case, police and FBI agents normally try to interview them separately. One might break even if the other does not, and separate interviews make it more difficult for suspects to coordinate their answers to questions.

Espinoza, later an assistant U.S. attorney in Connecticut and a Superior Court judge in Hartford, was bilingual, born in Puerto Rico, and a graduate of Brown University and George Washington University Law School. "They needed a Spanish-speaking female agent," she recalled. "My name popped out of the computer." Espinoza had joined the bureau only two years earlier, and she was intrigued at the prospect of participating in her first espionage case.

In Minneapolis on June 3, Flores checked into the Sheraton Ritz and called the professor. Parker had scripted the scenario.

Flores sounded casual on the telephone. "I said, 'Hey I'm in town, come on over.' So he said, 'I will.' He came over to the room. He was glad to see me."

"What are you doing here?" Lopez asked.

"I'm on a business trip, just passing through town."

Parker and Dennis Conway were waiting in an adjoining room. After a minute, they knocked on the door. Flores let them in.

"Gilberto," Flores said, "this is Phillip Parker and Dennis Conway, and we are all FBI agents."

Lopez looked stunned.

"We showed him our credentials," Flores said. "He turned pale. He looked like he was going to faint. We told him someone was talking to Alicia at this moment."

Agent Conway read Lopez his rights. He was told he would be interviewed about his and his wife's espionage activities.

Lopez stared at Flores. "He said, 'How long have you been an agent? You just got a job with them?' He may have thought the bureau somehow found out about him and approached me to help them. 'No, Gilberto,' I said, 'I've been an agent since the first day I met you.' That's when he sat down.

"He said, 'From the very first day that I met you, you were an agent?' I said, 'Yes. We knew you were a Soviet agent, and we made an effort to get close to you, and that was me.' He kind of went into shock."

Parker picked up the story: "He didn't say anything at first. He was sweating. We said, 'We know you've been working for the Soviets.' He didn't respond.

"We continued talking. Most of the talking was done by Flores, in English and Spanish. We used all the interview techniques—good guy, bad guy. Flores was being sympathetic, we want to get your side of the story. I was the bad guy. Aurelio was expressing sympathy for the plight of Hispanics in Mexico and in the U.S."

Parker had come armed with FBI surveillance photos of Lopez and his wife clearing dead drops. He spread them out on the table. "We showed him the photographs after about twenty minutes. We wanted him to know we knew everything he'd been doing over the past seven years. We showed him surveillance logs, to persuade Lopez we'd been watching him for a long time." The agents also showed Lopez three-by-five-inch bureau index cards listing the radio transmissions he had received from the Soviets. But it was the photos that seemed to do the trick.

"Soon after that he said, 'Yes, I have worked for the Russians, I am working for the Russians, and I will.' "[6]

According to Flores, Lopez admitted he had been active in three countries. "He said he had been working for the Soviets, that he had worked for them in Mexico, the United States, and Calgary, Canada."

Parker pressed Lopez for a motive. "He said, 'It's not that I love the Russians, it's that I hate the United States.' " Lopez, Parker said, explained he had spied for the Russians "because of how the United States has treated Mexico, throughout history. And because of the way Chicanos are treated in the U.S." Mexico, Lopez said, was a puppet of the United States; he had spied for the Russians because any enemy of the United States was his friend.

"He admitted it was him in the pictures," Parker said. "He never admitted meeting Danilin in Washington. We talked to him about three hours. Some of it was, how do you like Minnesota, the weather. We would change the subject."

Conway said the bureau hoped to turn the PALMETTOS. Once Lopez confessed, instead of being arrested, he might agree to work for the FBI against the Russians, becoming a double agent for the United States. Or as Conway put it: "Our main purpose was to try to flip the guy. We were trying to give him a break. We gotcha: You can go to jail, or you can work with us. It was a little more sophisticated than that, but that was the bottom line."

It is a classic maneuver in spy cases and has often worked. In questioning an espionage target, the FBI will attempt—without making any actual promises—to lead a suspect to think he might be able to avoid prison by confessing or acting as a double agent. And sometimes such

---

[6] The official report that Parker filed afterward, known as a 302 report, summarized the interview: "RIVAS was shown photographs of both he and his wife engaged in espionage activities. . . . Upon viewing the photographs he stated, 'You have all of the evidence.' RIVAS further admitted that he was a Soviet agent. . . . RIVAS said he decided to work actively against the United States at a very young age. He explained that he could have become a terrorist or do nothing to help his country. But he decided to work for the Soviets in order to make a positive effort."

cooperation does get the suspects off the hook. In this case, Parker encouraged Lopez to talk but offered no guarantees.

"We would not say if he became a double for the bureau he would not be prosecuted. It would depend on the extent of his cooperation. If he turned over to us half a dozen recruitments by the GRU, there was a good possibility he'd walk.

"We're not after you, we're after the people who are running you. If you'll cooperate with us, things will go easier for you. We didn't promise him he would walk. We did not say we were going to arrest him."

The FBI agents, Parker said, asked Lopez "when and how he was recruited and by whom. He would not say. He seemed on the verge of cooperation at various points, and we did what we could to make him roll over."

While the FBI men were questioning Lopez at the hotel, Alicia Lopez was simultaneously being interviewed by Carmen Espinoza and an agent from the Minneapolis office. The two agents had moved in as soon as Lopez had left for the hotel.

"They lived in a town house," Espinoza said. "We rang the bell, she answered. I went in, and we spoke in Spanish. We told her they were caught. We showed her surveillance photos of them making the drops, some with their child. She was hard as a rock. She was a tough cookie. She said we had fabricated the photographs. She didn't believe it. She wasn't going to say anything, and we're making all this up."

When Espinoza reported that Alicia Lopez was stonewalling, Parker decided to bring the PALMETTOS together. "We had told Lopez his wife was also being interviewed," Parker related. "At that point, we suggested he call his wife. We were at an impasse. He agreed to call his wife and ask her to come to the hotel.

"She showed up about half an hour later. She and her two kids were brought over by Carmen Espinoza and the other agent." Now there were nine people in the room, five agents and four Lopezes. "When Alicia walked in, her husband said, 'They know everything.' "

"Don't say anything," Alicia shot back.

Recognizing Flores, she embraced him. "She gave me a hug and a kiss," he recalled. "She said, '¿*Qué pasa?* What is this all about?' "

The PALMETTOS, of course, knew what it was all about. It was Parker's move. "We decided to leave them alone in the hotel room, and we went to eat," he said.

Parker wanted the Lopezes to have time together to talk over their predicament. But Parker was apprehensive; he had checked the windows in the room, which was on the fourteenth floor, and knew that they could be opened. "I was worried about a suicide pact," he said. "They're in the room, and they're saying, 'Oh shit, what are we going to do?' and they go out the window. That is not a nice thing to happen."

As soon as Parker had left the hotel, he went across the street to the FBI office and called Gene Peterson at FBI headquarters to report that Lopez had confessed. "I briefed him on what Lopez had said. . . . He said, 'OK, get it into a 302,' which is an interview report. I said, 'When do we get the authorization to arrest?' He said 'We'll get back to you.' "

In less than an hour, Peterson called back, having talked to the Justice Department. Parker shook his head at the memory of that moment. "Pete said they wouldn't authorize it."

Parker was crushed and furious. His disappointment was shared by Peterson, who had supervised the case for so long. The bureau had by then worked the overall operation for twenty years—the longest espionage case of its kind in the history of the cold war. Two FBI men had died. The Justice Department had refused to move unless Parker got a confession, and he had just gotten it. But still the answer was no.

The FBI agents returned to the hotel, but the Lopezes declined to say more. "Lopez said, 'What are you going to do to me?' We said we don't know yet, or words to that effect." Parker then told the Lopezes they could go.

Aurelio Flores said the news seemed almost disappointing to the couple. "They wanted to be martyrs, to go on trial. He [Lopez] said, 'We want our kids sent back to Mexico, and we want to stand trial.' They wanted the publicity.

"Alicia said, 'Why are you letting us go, we could have a trial.' She said, 'Is this like a spy swap? The Soviets have somebody they are going to exchange for us?' She said to Gilberto in Spanish, 'Ask Aurelio, why are they letting us go?' " There may have been another reason why the Lopezes were scared, Flores said. "I think she was worried about what might happen when they got back to Mexico and had to explain to their handlers what had happened. She didn't say that, but I felt that."

Espinoza, too, remembered that the Lopezes were reluctant to leave, though for another reason. "They thought they were going to be killed if they walked out the door," she said. "They didn't want to leave. I had to convince them it was OK. Finally, they walked out and left."

Parker knew the spies were slipping out of his grasp, but he was not ready to give up just yet.

The FBI continued to watch the couple. "The Lopezes were under surveillance from the time they left the hotel," Parker said. Two days later, Parker got word that the Lopezes were leaving for the Minneapolis–St. Paul airport.

Lopez may have thought there was safety in numbers. Arturo Madrid, the chairman of the Spanish department, got a frantic call from Manuel Guerrero, Lopez's colleague and friend. "He said, 'Arturo, I need you to meet me at the airport.' " With another professor from the Spanish department, Madrid sped to the airport, where he met Guerrero. "Manuel said, 'I can't explain right now. I need you to come to the gate with me. Gilberto is leaving on a plane for Mexico City right now."

The FBI agents conducting the surveillance had followed the Lopezes to the airport. With several other agents, Parker also drove to the terminal.

He found a telephone and called William O. Cregar, the assistant director of the FBI in charge of the intelligence division.

"They're in the terminal," Parker said. He pleaded with his superior in Washington to try to reverse the decision. "I'll call back later," Parker said.

"No, they're not going to authorize," Cregar replied.

Parker watched the Lopezes get on the plane.

As the airliner taxied toward the runway, he called Cregar again.

"We've got one chance," Parker said. "They're going to land in San Antonio. It's not too late."

"Forget it," Cregar said.

It was clear that the conversation was over. Parker added, "I was not in a position to question Bill Cregar."

Totally frustrated, Parker watched until the plane carrying the Lopezes was only a speck in the distant sky.

He alerted the FBI's San Antonio office, where Edward J. O'Malley was the assistant special agent in charge. "O'Malley had two of his biggest, toughest guys board the plane. One of the agents leaned over and said, 'Have a good trip, Mr. Lopez.' As the agents got off the plane, Lopez threw up."

Professor Rolando Hinojosa-Smith, the new chairman of the Chicano studies department at the University of Minnesota, was startled to get word that day that Professor Lopez had vanished. "I went to work one day, and all of a sudden I was confronted with a missing professor," he said.

No accurate explanation was given to Lopez's students for his mysterious departure. Another faculty member took over his classes.

Among the faculty, there was a good deal of buzzing over the unexpected, fast exit of Lopez and his family. Hinojosa-Smith reported Lopez's abrupt departure to Frank J. Sorauf, an eminent political scientist then serving as dean of the College of Liberal Arts. But Sorauf had apparently already learned something about what had happened, according to Arturo Madrid. Along with a few other colleagues, Madrid knew that Lopez had been confronted by the FBI. Madrid recalled speaking with Hinojosa-Smith at the time.

"I remember saying to Rolando we really must protest this, this is outrageous," Madrid said. "And Rolando said, 'Well, I've already taken it up with the dean, who has informed me that Gilberto was operating as an agent of a foreign power.' "

In the days that followed, word spread among Lopez's closer associates on the faculty that he had somehow been involved with Cubans. It was a cover story encouraged by Lopez himself.

Arturo Madrid remembered running into Lopez a year later in Mexico. "I was in Guadalajara, and I saw Gilberto Lopez at a conference I was at," Madrid said. "He came up and thanked me profusely for having come to the airport that day. I kept Gilberto at a distance. I remember talking to my friend Jorge Bustamente. . . . I said, 'Be careful, he [Lopez] was acting as an agent of a foreign power.' Years later, Jorge told me what happened" the day Lopez and his wife fled to Mexico. "He said he had got a call from Lopez from San Antonio saying, 'It's a life-or-death situation, meet me at the airport in Mexico City.' He came off the plane white as a sheet, scared to death, looking all around, and they drove him to his father-in-law's house. He told Jorge he had been a courier for the Cubans and the FBI had shown him incriminating photos in which he was giving or receiving something from somebody from the Cuban mission to the UN, or the Cuban office in Washington."

When Gene Peterson had relayed the disappointing word from headquarters on June 3, Parker recalled, he said the Justice Department attorneys, in refusing to authorize the arrest, "had alluded to the entries in Austin." Yet the department's internal-security lawyers had known of the taps, bugs, and videos of the PALMETTOS before Parker ever went to Minneapolis to confront the Lopezes.

The decision to let the spies go was due in part to the complex legal issues involved but also to a confluence of external political factors. The PALMETTO case came at a time when the law governing electronic eavesdropping in espionage cases was evolving, and the government's power to intrude in the life of the individual for purposes of national security was being reexamined by Congress and the courts.

Probably no murkier area of law existed at the time than that surrounding wiretaps, bugs, and surreptitious entries in foreign-intelligence cases. The FBI's use of these methods reflected the long and continuing tension in America between liberty and security. The Constitution was designed to protect against government intrusions and viola-tions of the rights of the individual. The FBI, with responsibility for catching spies and terrorists, focused primarily on its mission. And the courts tended to give the bureau more latitude in counterintelligence in-vestigations against foreign targets than in ordinary criminal cases.

In 1936, President Franklin D. Roosevelt authorized J. Edgar Hoover to collect intelligence on domestic "subversive activities." In 1940, Roo-sevelt approved warrantless wiretaps in such cases, as well as against spies. Wiretaps can be installed from outside a building, but installing bugs to pick up room conversations normally requires entry into the premises. Hoover, a bureaucratic master at protecting himself, pressed the Justice Department for permission to plant bugs in national-security cases, authority he finally won in 1954. In 1965, however, Lyndon Johnson's attorney general, Nicholas Katzenbach, changed the rules; from then on, the attorney general would have to give written approval in order for the FBI to plant bugs.

Under Hoover, the FBI had carried out literally hundreds of "black bag" jobs—illicit entries—many to install bugs. Hoover ostensibly banned the practice in 1966 after a subordinate pointed out that bur-glaries were "clearly illegal," but the break-ins continued. In any event, the prohibition did not apply to break-ins to plant bugs against or search premises of foreign targets.

Two years later, Congress passed the Omnibus Crime Control Act of 1968, which required court warrants for wiretaps and bugs in criminal cases. Congress said nothing, however, about national-security targets, a loophole that allowed such practices without a warrant in spy cases. The law also contained a disclaimer that said the statute did not limit the powers of the president to authorize whatever was necessary to collect foreign intelligence or to protect against foreign spies.

In 1972, the Supreme Court in *United States v. United States District Court for the Eastern District of Michigan*, known as the Keith case, barred warrantless wiretaps for domestic-intelligence purposes, but it was and has remained silent on the use of taps in foreign-intelligence cases. Be-tween 1971 and 1976, when the various techniques were used against the PALMETTOS in Salt Lake City, Austin, and Minneapolis, the law was unclear on the status of warrantless wiretaps, bugs, and entries in espionage cases. During the early 1970s, the approval of the attorney general was required by Justice Department policy but not by law or presidential executive order.

In 1976, President Ford issued an executive order on foreign counterintelligence requiring the attorney general, then Edward H. Levi, to issue guidelines allowing warrantless taps and bugs in espionage cases with the approval of the attorney general. The guidelines were classified. In 1978, President Carter issued a similar executive order.

Finally, in 1978, Congress attempted to dispel some of the legal fog by passing the Foreign Intelligence Surveillance Act (FISA) and creating new machinery to govern eavesdropping and entries by the government in espionage cases. Since October 1978, when FISA was signed into law, wiretaps or break-ins to place bugs to eavesdrop on agents of foreign powers must be authorized by a special court.[7] This judicial machinery did not exist, however, when the PALMETTOS and IXORA were subject to electronic surveillance.

In the PALMETTO case, it was not entirely clear why the Justice Department raised questions about the FBI's entries at the eleventh hour, after Lopez had confessed. "The Justice Department knew everything about the case all along," Parker said. "I talked to Tafe about the entries."

Because some of the FBI's actions in the case had not been approved by the attorney general, Parker said, "we all knew it might be a problem. We knew that from the beginning, but we were willing to go to court with it. If DOJ [the Department of Justice] wasn't, why didn't they say

[7] The requirement that the FISA court approve break-ins to conduct physical searches in foreign-intelligence cases, except in places such as embassies, was added to the law by Congress in 1994, following the arrest of CIA mole Aldrich Ames. Beginning in June 1993, the FBI wiretapped Ames's home with a FISA court warrant. On October 9, again with a FISA warrant, bureau agents entered his house to bug the rooms while the Ameses were out of town attending a wedding in Pensacola, Florida. During the same entry, the FBI also searched the premises and downloaded his computer without a warrant, acting on the authority of Attorney General Janet Reno. Had the case gone to trial, Ames's lawyer, Plato Cacheris, was prepared to test the warrantless search. Ames, however, pleaded guilty to conspiracy to commit espionage, and there was no court case.

that at the start?" Given the fuzzy state of the law at the time, Parker felt the department might well have prevailed had it chosen to prosecute.

In meetings with the Justice Department lawyers, FBI officials insisted that there had not even been any unauthorized entry in Austin. Some weeks before the confrontation in Minneapolis, Peterson recalled, he and Parker met with John Martin. "We told Martin unequivocally that nothing was acquired from any unauthorized techniques. There was no trespass."

Peterson's argument rested on the unusual physical circumstances in Austin, where a camera had been installed in a crawl space that was above but not part of the PALMETTOS' duplex. But the camera's pinhole in the ceiling, however minute, could be regarded as an "entry."[8] And the bureau's agents had gone into the Lopezes' house when they were away. On the other hand, since Lopez had freely sent a key to Aurelio Flores, it could also be argued that the entry was consensual. But a defense attorney would certainly maintain that the key had not been given to Flores so that his associates could copy Lopez's code pads and remove his short-wave radio.

Peterson said Martin was noncommittal in response to his arguments and indicated he would take the matter under advisement. On June 3, Peterson said, after receiving word from Parker that Lopez had confessed, he went to see Martin again. "Martin said he could not approve prosecution because of the entry in Austin. Martin said something about the political climate not being right to prosecute where the use of the techniques is going to come out. John Martin had never lost an espionage case. That was a factor."

Bureaucratic confusion also played a part in the department's refusal to authorize the arrest of the PALMETTOS. In 1971, a message went out from FBI headquarters to Tampa and Salt Lake City informing both offices that President Nixon's attorney general, John N. Mitchell, had authorized an entry into the Lopezes' apartment at the University of Utah

---

[8] Robert L. Keuch, a deputy assistant attorney general in the criminal division during the PALMETTO investigation, says he would take that view. "Once you've made a pinhole, I think you've entered."

to install a microphone. Mitchell, Nixon, and the president's national security adviser, Henry A. Kissinger, were all briefed regularly on the progress of the PALMETTO case.

As a result of this message, the FBI agents who tapped and bugged the Lopezes in Salt Lake City believed they were acting under the authority of the attorney general. The message, however, was in error. There is no record in the FBI's files that the request for approval by the attorney general ever left the bureau.

In retrospect, it is clear that several external events, and politics, played at least as great a role in the department's decision as any points of law. It was the post-Watergate era; six years before, Richard Nixon had tried to use the CIA and the FBI to cover up a burglary at Democratic National Committee headquarters. Then, in 1975, the Senate intelligence committee headed by Idaho Democrat Frank Church had revealed abuses by the nation's intelligence agencies—drug testing on unsuspecting subjects, assassination plots, and mail opening by the CIA, and "black bag" jobs by the FBI. The intelligence agencies were on the defensive.

In April 1978, less than two months before Parker flew to Minneapolis to interview the Lopezes, a federal grand jury had indicted two senior FBI officials, Mark Felt and Edward Miller, for authorizing break-ins to search the homes of relatives and acquaintances of fugitive members of the Weather Underground.[9] "The government has to speak with one voice," said a Justice Department attorney who worked on the PALMETTO case. "We're prosecuting somebody at a high level in the FBI for illegal activities, then we're going to go prosecute a case where the bureau was doing the same thing?" The searches in the Felt-Miller case did not take place as part of a foreign counterintelligence investigation, however. But from a political viewpoint, prosecution of the PALMETTOS might have appeared inconsistent.

Finally, the espionage convictions in May of Ronald L. Humphrey, an employee of the United States Information Agency, and David Truong,

---

[9] Both were convicted and fined for violating the civil rights of the persons whose homes were searched; they were pardoned by President Reagan in April 1981.

an anti–Vietnam War activist, also influenced the department's response. Attorney General Griffin Bell had authorized the use of a video camera in Humphrey's office and a bug in Truong's apartment in Washington, both without warrants, but the attorney general had not approved the camera in Austin.[10]

Some weeks after the PALMETTOS had fled to Mexico, the Justice Department sent formal notice to the FBI of its decision not to prosecute the Lopezes, citing the wiretaps and entries as the chief reasons. The case had been reviewed by the deputy attorney general, Benjamin R. Civiletti. By that time, however, the horse was long since out of the barn.

There remained several unexplained aspects to the way the Justice Department handled the case at the end, allowing the two spies to escape. Phil Parker never found any of the department's explanations either satisfactory or clear. Nor was he told why the criminal complaint was never filed in Tampa. The bottom line was that the government permitted two Soviet spies to escape. For Parker, it was particularly galling.

Even two decades later, the Justice Department's decision to let the Lopezes go still rankled inside the FBI's National Security Division, which has responsibility for counterintelligence. John F. Lewis, Jr., who retired in 1998 as assistant director of the FBI in charge of the division, was blunt in his assessment. "Despite the years of intense investigation, a confession from the male PALMETTO, photographs of both subjects receiving classified information, and the loss of two special agents' lives, the PALMETTOS were allowed to board a plane in Minneapolis bound for Mexico on June 5, 1978."

After watching the PALMETTOS' plane disappear into the Minnesota sky, a gloomy Phil Parker drove back to town. There was one more chance to

---

[10] Humphrey and Truong were convicted of spying for Vietnam. They were each sentenced to fifteen years.

gather additional evidence against Lopez. "We wanted a search warrant for his apartment," Parker recalled. "The owner of the apartment said the commode was stopped up. We immediately thought Lopez had been getting rid of stuff."

But Parker and the other FBI agents were spared the indignity of delving into the Soviet agent's toilet. It was catch-22: "DOJ wouldn't authorize a search warrant," Parker said, "because there was no plan for prosecution."

CHAPTER

18

ENDGAME

In the wilderness of mirrors that is counterintelligence, both sides now studied the shadows and reflections and engaged in intricate probability analyses of each other's stratagems. When an espionage operation goes bad, the intelligence agency responsible for the case conducts a damage assessment that normally explores multiple possibilities: The operation may have been betrayed by a mole or by a double agent; a spy may have practiced sloppy "tradecraft," such as neglecting to evade surveillance; or the opposition may have penetrated the agency's codes and communications.[1]

---

[1] When the CIA began losing agents inside the Soviet Union in 1985, for example, the agency first grasped at the possibility that poor tradecraft by the agents or a code break explained the losses. Only much later did the CIA face up to the probability that there was a mole within, a Russian spy who turned out to be Aldrich Ames. Partly because of the institutional reluctance to think the unthinkable, it took nine years to catch him.

Back in FBI headquarters in Washington, Phil Parker decided to try to turn the flight of the Lopezes to the bureau's advantage. Perhaps their departure could still be used to sow confusion inside the GRU. "In their damage assessment, they would have to figure out where it went wrong," Parker said.

It had been more than five years since Lopez had appeared at Cassidy's last drop in Florida; the GRU, Parker reasoned, might trace the trouble back to Cassidy, but it might also logically assume that Lopez had been detected in more recent espionage activity. The FBI had followed Lopez north toward the Canadian border a year earlier because it thought he might be picking up material from real Soviet spies, not just from Joe Cassidy. "We had a strong suspicion Lopez was servicing others," Parker said.

The intelligence division believed, therefore, that the FBI's questioning of the Lopezes would not automatically lead the GRU to conclude that Cassidy was a double agent. For that reason, the FBI decided to try to keep Cassidy in play. Jack O'Flaherty recalled, "We had Joe try to continue to contact the Soviets and follow his instructions. And he did get some more messages."

Parker agreed that Cassidy should continue to try to maintain contact with the Russians. "There were so many potential scenarios as to how we got onto Lopez. We certainly didn't know what Lopez told them. Did he tell them he'd been approached by the FBI? . . . They [the GRU] could have thought it was tradecraft lapses," he said. "They might figure the FBI saw Cassidy meeting with someone from their embassy. The FBI could have followed Cassidy to Tampa and then picked up Lopez's trail."

And Lopez himself, Parker reasoned, would have fallen under suspicion in Moscow, since the Russians would not have known about the battle over the case between the FBI and the Justice Department. "The Soviets would have to wonder, Why did we let him go? We wanted to make them leery of why Lopez was allowed to leave the United States. We were hoping they would think Lopez had been turned."

Keeping Cassidy in play with the Russians presented other hurdles, aside from the possibility that the operation had been compromised once the FBI had confronted the PALMETTOS. In April 1977, six months after his last meeting with the GRU, Cassidy received an envelope through the mail with a fictitious New York City return address. The one-page letter in secret writing canceled the 1977 drops and meets with no explanation. It instructed him to wait for a postcard that would give the dates of future meets and told him to check for radio messages as well. In November, however, he received another letter terminating radio transmissions until further notice. In February 1978, the FBI passed word to its counterintelligence agents that it had learned that the GRU was freezing its agent operations in the United States pending a reevaluation. Cassidy might have been caught up in an across-the-board suspension of activities.

By late summer, however, Cassidy's link to the Russians seemed even more tenuous. On August 2, two months after the Lopezes had flown the coop, Cassidy received a plaintext greeting card from the Russians: "Departing for Europe, I'll get in touch next summer. Mike." The Soviets appeared, for the moment, to be keeping their options open. But the message could also be read as a good-bye note, which is how Cassidy took it.

"I was kind of down in the dumps," he recalled. "I figured this might be the end of it. Somehow my cover was blown. And I really didn't want it to end. It was exciting to me." Despite Cassidy's momentary gloom, the FBI instructed him to not give up and to try to keep in contact with the Soviets. The rock he had received at his last meeting in New York had contained instructions and specific dates for reestablishing contact should it ever be lost. The FBI approved a plan for Cassidy to attempt recontact in New York the following year.

But a month before he left for New York, Cassidy found himself literally thrust into the public spotlight. It was an unnerving experience. Spies like to remain in the shadows, and they normally avoid attracting attention to themselves. Yet in September 1979, Cassidy unexpectedly ended up onstage with Kathie Lee Gifford at Disney World.[2] The son-in-

---

[2] The entertainer, then twenty-six, was billed as Kathie Lee Johnson at the time.

law of Cassidy's old army buddy Woodrow James was appearing on the same bill in Orlando and had arranged a front-row booth at the show for the unsuspecting Cassidy.

At the time, Gifford had gained a measure of fame as the featured singer on the television game show *Name That Tune*. The Cassidys, enjoying the nightclub act from their ringside seats, were in for a surprise. "I didn't know it was a setup," Cassidy said. "She was singing and came and got me and said, 'This is my number-one fan, the president of my fan club.' She was on the TV show where you were supposed to guess the songs. She told me she would sing a little and when we get to the title you hum it." They would do this a couple of times, Gifford indicated, and then she would sing all the words, revealing the title to the audience. Flustered by suddenly finding himself in the glare of the spotlight, Cassidy blew it. The acting skills that had been good enough to fool the Russians for two decades failed him. He recognized the songs. "I sang the title," he said. "I did it each time."

In October, Cassidy drove to New York. On the last Saturday of the month, one of the alternate dates he had been given to reestablish contact with the Soviets, he once again waited in front of the antiques store in Brooklyn, yellow package in hand and pipe in mouth. He brought along a hollow rock containing the film of the emergency planning document and his report, in secret writing, of his trip to the nuclear-weapons depot in Charleston.[3] But no one showed, either that day or the next.

Cassidy made one last attempt. He telephoned the Soviet mission to the United Nations and asked for Mike.

"We don't have any Mike," he was told. "Nobody's here."

"Mike owes me a lot of money," Cassidy protested. "I want my money."

"Nobody's here," the operator said. "They've all gone to the beach."

Cassidy was skeptical of the explanation. "It was October!" he re-

---

[3] This time Cassidy did not conceal the rock at a drop site, since his instructions did not specify one.

called. "So I went back to Florida. That was the end of it." It had been almost twenty-one years since Joe Cassidy had begun his risky career as a
spy on a spring evening in Washington.

Not long afterward, the FBI learned that Mikhail Danilin had been
posted to Canada. The bureau proposed a joint operation with Canadian
intelligence. Under the plan, Cassidy would be sent to Ottawa and accidentally bump into Danilin. The GRU officer would immediately realize
the encounter was no accident, that Cassidy was under American control. That in turn would jeopardize Danilin's own position: His prime
source had turned out to be a double. "The hope was that Danilin, seeing Joe, might be impelled to defect," Jack O'Flaherty said.

The bureau contacted Cassidy, who was ready and willing to take
part. "But the Canadians said no, the political climate was not right,"
O'Flaherty said. "The bureau then proposed that Joe just go on his own,
but Ottawa said no to that, too."

Phil Parker pushed for the Canadian operation, though he did not really expect to turn Danilin. "I don't know that we thought he would actually defect. He seemed a pretty solid Soviet. There was no real hope in
my mind that Danilin was going to roll over and start working for the FBI.

"But if Danilin ran into Joe, he would have to report it, and that
would cause some disruption. The whole idea was to play with their
minds. . . . It would make them wonder—at what point was the case
under control of the FBI? From the beginning? After two years?" In
other words, the GRU would wonder whether Cassidy had been a double
agent from the start or whether he was a genuine spy for Moscow who
had been detected and turned by the FBI.

Soon after the FBI proposed the operation to the Canadian service,
however, Danilin left Ottawa. O'Flaherty wondered whether the Canadians had approached Danilin on their own and tried to "pitch" him to defect. Danilin would have been obliged to report the approach, and he
would automatically have been sent back to Moscow.[4]

---

[4] Both the KGB and the GRU recalled anyone who had been pitched by a Western intelligence service, in order to remove the officer from any temptation. Failure to report a
pitch was regarded as a very serious offense.

On September 16, 1980, Joe and Marie Cassidy journeyed to Washington for another secret award ceremony, this time at FBI headquarters. Cassidy's work was done. Once again, his case officers gathered to honor the man who had, in total anonymity, given so much to his country. Jimmy Morrissey was there, along with Donald Gruentzel, Jack O'Flaherty (resplendent in a three-piece suit), and Charlie Bevels.

Cassidy was presented with a simple certificate with a blue border. Its langauge was cryptic: "The Federal Bureau of Investigation expresses its appreciation to Sergeant Major Joseph Edward Cassidy for service in the public interest." The certificate was signed "William H. Webster, Director."

Webster also wrote a letter to Cassidy thanking him "for your accomplishments in the sensitive area of national security. You have over an extended period of time assisted FBI personnel in achieving our goal whenever called upon and your efforts were absolutely vital to our country's defense."

Marie Cassidy, too, received an award from the FBI, a gold plaque that read simply: "Marie Cassidy, in appreciation 6/68–9/80."

Near the conclusion of the ceremony, someone handed Cassidy his Distinguished Service Medal that General Abrams had taken back more than six years earlier at the Pentagon. With a self-conscious smile, Cassidy, now in mufti, posed for pictures holding a case that displayed the DSM, a gold eagle set against a blue background below a broad red-and-white-striped ribbon.

Now, at last, it was his to keep.

CHAPTER

19

THE TURNING OF IXORA

By late June 1978, the FBI had been watching Edmund Freundlich, code name IXORA, the GRU sleeper agent in New York, for almost seven years.

Now that the PALMETTOS had flown back to Mexico, it was possible that the GRU damage assessment would affect IXORA. Although Moscow could not be sure how its operations had been penetrated, it might well choose to play it safe and cut its losses. IXORA could be pulled out of New York.

If the bureau was to make a move, the time to act might rapidly be running out. The decision was made to approach IXORA and try to turn him into a double agent for the United States. That delicate mission was assigned to Special Agent James Kehoe and two other counterintelligence agents in New York City, Jack Lowe and Dan LeSaffre.

In attempting to turn IXORA, however, the bureau was taking a risk. If

Freundlich chose to tell his Soviet handlers of the approach, his information would point to Joe Cassidy, who had been told to call Freundlich in case of war. It was possible, of course, that real Russian spies inside the U.S. government had also been instructed to call Freundlich if they detected military preparations for an attack, and in that case the GRU would not be sure that Cassidy was the problem. But, combined with the bureau's approach to the PALMETTOS, any tip by IXORA to the GRU would certainly have removed any lingering doubt about Cassidy's real allegiance.

James Kehoe, the case agent for the IXORA operation, was a tall, bespectacled New Yorker, gray haired and balding, and considerably older than the other two agents assigned to make the approach. A Fordham graduate, Kehoe was a veteran counterintelligence agent who had participated in the capture of Rudolf Abel, a KGB colonel who had slipped into the United States as an illegal. Abel, who had posed as a struggling artist in Brooklyn, had been convicted and sent to prison but had been traded in 1962 for the CIA's U-2 pilot Francis Gary Powers.

Kehoe's partner, Jack Lowe, had known Powers. Lowe, a big man, blond and heavyset, had grown up in Norton, Virginia, where the U-2 pilot's father was a cobbler. Lowe had joined the bureau in 1972 and had been assigned to foreign counterintelligence in New York. As it turned out, one of the first drops Lowe covered was Joe Cassidy putting down a hollow rock.

Dan LeSaffre, the third agent, was six foot three and 210 pounds, an athlete and college baseball player from Methuen, Massachusetts. He graduated from Bridgewater State College, south of Boston, joined the bureau in 1972, and had been working in foreign counterintelligence in New York for two years. With LeSaffre at the wheel, the three agents drove to Broadway near West 230th Street, where Freundlich's car pool usually dropped him off, a few blocks from his apartment.

The three agents, all fairly big men, got out and surrounded IXORA at 5:30 P.M. They flashed their credentials.

"We want to talk to you," Kehoe said. "We need you to come to our office so we can talk privately."

Freundlich looked scared to death. "He volunteered to come with us," Lowe said, "but we were helping him volunteer. We had hold of his arm and were moving him toward the car. In the car, he was visibly shaken. Taking deep breaths, swallowing, hands shaking. He had that 'Oh shit' look. A lot of this was fear of the unknown—what's going to happen to me? When you are doing something over the years, you know it's wrong and that one day the knock may come on the door." For IXORA, it had come.

"He thought it was like what he had experienced in Europe. It took us a while to explain to him that we weren't going to kill him. We weren't going to harm him. We just wanted his cooperation."

The FBI men drove Freundlich to the bureau's office in Manhattan at 201 East Sixty-ninth Street. For maximum psychological effect, they took him upstairs to the offices of the special agent in charge. "We took him to the executive conference room outside the SAC's office, a very official-looking place. We began to talk to him. There was no video, no tape running."

The counterintelligence men knew this game very well. IXORA was trapped and fearful. "He is wondering was he caught because of something he did?" The agents painted a grim picture for Freundlich: The Soviets would never trust him now; they might even assassinate him.

Then the agents offered IXORA a lifeline. "Part of the conversation was to put him at ease, to show him there was a way out," Lowe said. "We'll protect you. There is a way out. We need to know the details."

As the evening wore on, gradually IXORA began to cooperate. "He said he had done some things for the Soviets, but not bad things. The turning took several months. It was a slow process over time—he did not tell us everything all at once."

Freundlich revealed astonishing details. If he received a warning that a nuclear attack was imminent, he was to flash the word to the Russians from a vantage point in the very heart of New York City.

"He was given a radio that worked and played music," Lowe said. But it was no ordinary radio. "When he got a call warning of military prepa-rations, then he was to go to Sixty-eighth Street and Fifth Avenue. Just inside the wall of Central Park, there was this huge rock. He was to climb up on the rock, take out the radio, and open the back."[1]

Under the rear panel of the special radio were buttons that activated a tiny transmitter concealed inside. It broadcast to the Soviet mission to the United Nations a few blocks away on East Sixty-seventh Street be-tween Third and Lexington avenues. "He had a choice of one of five but-tons. He would push the button that matched the number in the parol."

The radio buttons were in sequence, numbered 11, 22, 33, 44, and 55. If, for example, Joe Cassidy placed an order for twenty-two books, as he did early in May 1972, Freundlich would push the 22 button on the radio. Since the double-digit numbers signified single digits, his call warned of a military action in two days.[2]

IXORA was instructed to back up the signal he transmitted by placing a message in a dead drop. He could not show the radio to the FBI, be-cause he no longer had it; he had returned it to the Soviets at their re-quest.

The radio and the signal procedure posed some intriguing questions for the FBI's counterintelligence analysts. Was there an unknown num-ber of real Russian spies out there? Or were there other sentinels in the United States like IXORA, with the identical mission, each outfitted with the same type of radio?

"We think IXORA was set up just for Joe," said one FBI man. The bu-

---

[1] The rock, as big as a house, is located to the north of a playground in an area of the park known as "The Dene," a British term for a dune or sandy area near the seashore. The rus-tic shelter that sits atop the rock formation now was not there at the time that IXORA was active.

[2] IXORA told the FBI that he had once sent a signal from the Central Park rock, but that he could not remember the date or the circumstances. Oddly, and for reasons IXORA never ex-plained, he did not transmit from the rock after he received the warning call from Cassidy in May 1972; the watching FBI agents saw him go straight to a dead drop. After Freund-lich began cooperating with the FBI in 1978, he was not asked why he had failed to go to the rock; the bureau did not want to compromise Operation SHOCKER by revealing to IXORA that it knew about the call.

reau's experts speculated that the Soviets would not have risked having other agents telephone IXORA, for fear that if Freundlich or one of the other agents was detected, the entire network of spies would be jeopardized. Yet IXORA had received a cryptic call in December 1971 that might have been some sort of warning, though IXORA never knew the identity of the person who telephoned him.

Former agent Robert Loughney believed there had to be other IXORAS as well. "Our theory is IXORA was one of several people," he said. "You have to assume they were not putting all their money on one horse."

Jack Lowe agreed. "There might be other IXORAS. We did not know of any others, but based on our knowledge of their operations we had to think there would be."

While it might seem incredible that there was a spy with IXORA's singular mission, living inconspicuously in New York City during the cold war and simply waiting for the telephone to ring, it was not really surprising in retrospect. "It was at a time," Lowe noted, "when the Soviet Union was deathly afraid of attack by the U.S."

The initial questioning of Edmund Freundlich at the FBI office in Manhattan lasted for almost four hours. "We took him back home around eleven P.M.," Lowe recalled.

Now that IXORA had begun to talk, the FBI met with him almost continuously. "There were three and a half months of very intensive discussions," Lowe said. "We were trying to see him every other day." Little by little, Freundlich's motivation for becoming a spy, and the details of his recruitment, emerged. It was in Switzerland that he had first come to the attention of Russian intelligence.

"In the Swiss camps," Jack Lowe said, "one person he met gave his name to the Russians and said, 'This man might be of help to you.' He [IXORA] was easily manipulated, and found it hard to say no to people who asked him for favors.

"When he returned to Vienna at the end of the war, the Soviets came to him and said, 'We'd like you to deliver some letters, little things we can't do for ourselves.' He was receptive because the Communists had been kind to him. They paid him. And a big point in their favor—they weren't Nazis."

Freundlich was given espionage training before he came to America in 1968, and he also told the FBI he received additional training in the United States. He was shown how to leave signals, such as chalk marks on telephone poles, and how to fill and empty dead drops. He also had some minimal training in photography.

Before he left Vienna, he was given a tie by his Soviet handler in Austria. "He was to show up here wearing the tie, at one of the meeting sites," Dan LeSaffre said. "That was the parol."

Freundlich was not taken again to FBI headquarters in Manhattan, Lowe said. "We went to restaurants to meet him. . . . We went up to West Point one summer day and walked through the museum. We found a German restaurant nearby.

"We took a long weekend trip to Boston and toured Boston with him, solidifying the relationship." All the while, IXORA was revealing more. "He identified to us close to fifty dead drops, locations, and meeting sites. Mostly in the Bronx, some in Brooklyn. He showed us the signal sites."

In addition to waiting for a warning telephone call, IXORA also acted as a cutout, a conduit for letters. He told the FBI that when letters arrived at his apartment with a certain return address or other indicator, he delivered them to dead drops. In the jargon of Soviet intelligence, he was serving as a "dead letter box."

One meeting site in front of a theater in Brooklyn was what the Soviets called IXORA's "constant condition site"—a location where a spy was instructed to show up, usually once a year, to indicate he was still alive and well.[3] The FBI encouraged Freundlich to continue to go to the site, though now the bureau would be watching. "In his case, he was to go to the site on Thanksgiving Day and simply stand there for about ten minutes," Lowe said. "A GRU guy would drive by and recognize him. To verify he was OK." The bureau assumed that the Russians had chosen

---

[3] The procedure is also known within Soviet intelligence as giving "a sign of life."

Thanksgiving Day on the theory that the FBI's counterintelligence agents would be home eating turkey.

It fell to Dan LeSaffre, as one of the younger agents, to work on the holiday. "I covered the constant-condition site on several Thanksgivings because I was single at the time. We used a fixed location site, a Port Authority police office, catty-corner from the theater. A Jewish deli was open, and I went for corned beef or a hot dog. That was my Thanksgiving dinner."

In late July or early August 1978, about two months after the first approach to IXORA, the FBI was able, with his help, to establish the identity of Freundlich's GRU control. His name was Nikolai I. Alenochkin, and he was a Soviet intelligence officer undercover as first secretary and later counselor of the Soviet mission to the United Nations.

Alenochkin was identified through a photo lineup, Lowe said. The FBI agents met with IXORA in an Old Europe–style restaurant near his apartment and showed him a series of photographs. The bureau knew who the likely GRU illegal-support officers in the UN mission were.

Freundlich pointed to Alenochkin's photo. He had, as it turned out, met him twice. "Alenochkin came to his house one night, and they went into the bathroom to talk and sat on the side of the tub with the water running in the tub and the sink."

IXORA said he had also met Alenochkin at the constant-condition site in 1975 or 1976. Freundlich said he had not been active for two years and that it was at Alenochkin's request that he had returned the radio to the Russians. His only assignment now was to appear in front of the theater every Thanksgiving Day.

Sheila W. Horan, then a young counterintelligence agent in New York, worked on the IXORA case and got to know Freundlich. "Jim, Dan, and I took him to dinner several times. Not interviewing him, just talking about his past. We wanted to maintain the relationship. He, Freundlich, liked Jim very much.

"He was the ultimate Caspar Milquetoast. He had no friends, just his brother and his nephew. He had no outside interests whatsoever. Work and home, that was it. The perfect spy. He was not vulnerable to anything. Nobody would look at him twice." She paused and added, "He was a nice guy."[4]

Within a few months, after giving Freundlich a polygraph test, the FBI was satisfied that IXORA had been turned. He did not ask to be paid in his new role as an American agent. "He lived very frugally," Lowe said. "We'd slip him small amounts of money for expenses."

By early fall, the agents offered no objections when IXORA said he planned to visit London. When he returned, he proudly presented two souvenir nail clippers to Lowe and LeSaffre. "On the handle of the nail clipper there is the insignia of the Queen's Guards. He brought one to me and one to Dan. By which time he had told us a great deal."

Unknown to his family and to the Russians, "Uncle Eddie," the nondescript loner who commuted each workday to his low-level job at Pergamon Press, and who seemed to have no friends and no life, had just switched sides in the cold war. It was a triumph of quiet counterintelligence work by Kehoe, Lowe, and LeSaffre.

Without Joe Cassidy, of course, IXORA would never have surfaced. IXORA was an almost invisible man, an unremarkable man who would never be noticed in a crowd, who had escaped the Nazis, and whose mission in life was to climb up on a rock in Central Park and, if that dreadful day ever came, signal the start of World War III.

The GRU had all but dropped him, but the FBI had one more mission in mind for IXORA.

---

[4] Twenty years later, Sheila Horan, in Nairobi and wearing a white hard hat, became a familiar face to television viewers all over the world as head of the FBI team that investigated the August 7, 1998, terrorist bombings of the U.S. embassies in Kenya and Tanzania.

MOSCOW: A DEADLY SECRET

They came for Vil Mirzayanov early on the morning of October 22, 1992.

At 7:30 A.M., the agents from the successor to the KGB's internal-security arm closed in on his fourth-floor apartment at 14 Ulitsa Stalevarov in Moscow. The two-room flat was not far from the nerve-gas laboratory where he had worked, at the State Scientific Research Institute on the Shosse Entuziastov.

Mirzayanov let the men in only after they threatened to break down the door. His sons, Iskandar, twelve, and Sultan, four, were too young really to understand, but his wife, Nuria, a thin, dark-haired poetess, understood all too well. The Soviet Union had collapsed almost ten months before, but some things, including the dreaded knock on the door by the secret police, did not appear to have changed.

They arrested Mirzayanov and took him to Moscow's infamous

Lefortovo Prison, where the interrogations began. A short, bespectacled man, whose mild exterior masked a tough, inner strength, Mirzayanov was a fifty-seven-year-old physical chemist who had worked in the top-secret Soviet nerve-gas program for almost three decades. As a senior researcher, he had been involved directly in the development in Moscow of the nerve gases that were tested and produced in the plants and military sites along the Volga basin. His specialty was mass spectrometry.

In October 1993, Mirzayanov, although no longer in prison, was awaiting trial on charges of having revealed state secrets. If convicted, he faced a sentence of up to eight years. He was taking an additional risk by agreeing to a series of interviews with the author, in which he talked in detail about Russia's chemical weapons and the history of its nerve-gas program.

In the late 1970s, Mirzayanov said, he began to have pangs of conscience. "It occurred to me I was engaged in a criminal enterprise. I had participated in the development of weapons of mass destruction. When I came to this conclusion, my work in the research institute became a struggle with myself." Although he had harbored these misgivings for years, it was not until Mikhail Gorbachev came to power in 1985 and relaxed some of the authoritarian controls of the Soviet state that he felt he could speak out.

"It was only during perestroika that I could share my views with other people. My wife knew, of course, but if I spoke to anyone else, the KGB might hear. So it was inside myself. I felt I was a member of a criminal gang and I didn't want to do this." Then in October 1991, Mirzayanov boldly went public in *Kuranty*, a Moscow daily.

In his brief but extraordinary article, Mirzayanov said not much had really changed; the KGB still controlled people in defense installations, telephones were bugged, dissenters destroyed or fired. "My own secret research institute in the center of Moscow has been poisoning people for decades by its harmful emissions," he wrote.

Even as the nations of the world were completing work on a treaty banning chemical weapons, the article continued, Viktor Petronin, the institute's chief, told his staff that "capitalism did not change, we have the same potential enemy, and that our civic duty is to consolidate the country's defense power."

Then, obliquely, and with no details, Mirzayanov dropped his bombshell: "The development of a novel chemical weapon was in full swing, the agent was tested on an open range in the most environmentally dangerous area." He added, "So the question is, why are they trying to deceive the West?"

Amazingly, there was no public reaction by the Soviet government. But in January 1992, only days after the collapse of the Communist state, Mirzayanov was fired by the research institute. His older son, not understanding, taunted him. Why didn't he go to work like other people? Their income cut off, the family was barely able to scrape by. Mirzayanov had a small pension, and his wife earned a little from writing. A Norwegian humanitarian organization contributed forty dollars a month, and the Carvallo Foundation in Cambridge, Massachusetts, gave him a modest grant in recognition of his moral courage.

Perhaps his background explains Mirzayanov's willingness to take on the establishment at the cost of his career. He was a Tatar, a Turkic-speaking, mostly Muslim minority that historically has had troubled relations with Russia. In the thirteenth century, the Tatars mixed with the Mongol forces of Genghis Khan, and their very name became synonymous with the invading hordes. Mirzayanov grew up on the European side of the Ural Mountains and moved to Moscow as a young man. He studied chemistry and began work in the nerve gas program when he was thirty.

A month before his arrest, Mirzayanov and Lev Fedorov, a physical chemist, courageously coauthored a revealing article in *Moscow News* that elaborated on what Mirzayanov had hinted at a year earlier. As far back as 1987, the Soviet Union claimed to have halted all production of nerve gas, they wrote. But Soviet scientists, they continued, had developed in binary form the world's most powerful nerve gas, which Mirzayanov later identified as Novichok, or "newcomer."

Mirzayanov knew a great deal about the super nerve gas; his last job had been to measure air and soil samples around the research laboratory to see whether enough chemicals had escaped to enable the CIA or other foreign intelligence services to detect the presence of the new gas.

In the Moscow interviews with the author, Mirzayanov said that Novichok was "eight, maybe ten times more toxic" than any nerve gas in the U.S. arsenal. Russia's total stockpile of nerve gases, which the government had officially declared at forty thousand metric tons—the world's largest—could cause devastation equal to that of a major nuclear attack. "Tens of millions could be killed by the entire inventory," he said.

Although he estimated that "probably less than a thousand tons" of Novichok had been produced, "theoretically several hundred thousand people could be killed" by even that amount of the deadly new gas, "if people have no protection and are out in the open. Even if they only breathe fumes they may not die but there could be terrible consequences. Nerve gas can cause mutations in the next generation and in future generations after that."

According to Mirzayanov, the super nerve gas was developed in 1973 by Pyotr Petrovich Kirpichev, a Soviet scientist at the research institute's branch at Shikhany, near Volsk. "The binary form was developed in Moscow, the substance itself was done in Shikhany," he said. Two years later, Kirpichev was joined in his research by Vladimir Uglev, who helped to perfect Novichok.

"Uglev claims the binary form of the gas can be produced in a garage," Mirzayanov said. "He exaggerates a little, but it is basically true."

Some of Novichok's properties cannot be measured, Mirzayanov said, at least by anyone who wants to live to tell about it. "In pure form the binary gas is colorless, and since it is lethal you would not want to taste or smell it." Was Novichok odorless? Mirzayanov was asked. "If you smell it you're dead," he replied, "so no one knows if it smells. It is basically invisible."

The effect of Novichok on humans was described chillingly by one victim, Andrei Zheleznyakov, a Soviet scientist exposed to only a residue of the gas in an accident in the spring of 1987 in the same Moscow laboratory where Mirzayanov worked. The two scientists were friends.

Zheleznyakov was a member of a select and secret group that tested Novichok at the institute. His job was to blend two components of the nerve gas and measure the temperature of the end product. The higher the temperature during the blending process, the more toxic the nerve gas. The test equipment was housed inside a fume cabinet to protect the scientists working outside it.

One morning in May, Zheleznyakov switched on the fume cabinet as usual, and something went wrong. He later described what happened in an interview with *New Times*, a Moscow magazine. "I saw rings before my eyes—red, orange. Bells were ringing inside my head, I choked." Gripped by fear, "I sat down, and told the guys: I think it has got me." His chief told him to go home and lie down, he would feel better. "They assigned me an escort, and we walked past a few bus stops. We were passing the church near Ilich Square when suddenly I saw the church lighting up and falling apart. I remember nothing else."

Mirzayanov provided additional details. When the accident occurred, he said, Zheleznyakov's chief "told him he was drunk and to go home and did not call an ambulance. They took him to the square and dropped him there. He fell on the street, a friend brought him back, and then they called an ambulance."

Zheleznyakov was taken to the hospital by KGB agents, who told physicians that he had been poisoned by eating bad sausage. The KGB agents made the doctors sign a pledge never to talk about the case. Zheleznyakov was kept in strict isolation. His heart was barely beating, and the level of cholinesterase in his bloodstream was close to zero.

After he had spent eighteen days in intensive care, the doctors managed to save his life. But he was left totally disabled, diagnosed with, among other illnesses, cirrhosis of the liver, toxic hepatitis, and epilepsy. In July 1992, he died.

Unlike his doomed colleague, Vil Mirzayanov did not work on the final, binary form of Novichok, but he participated in the development of A-230, one of the precursor chemicals of the powerful new nerve gas. The initial tests of Novichok, he said, were carried out at Shikhany and in Nukus, Uzbekistan, eighty miles south of the Aral Sea. The final military tests were conducted between 1986 and 1989 in Nukus, he added.

Without access to the top-secret archives of the Soviet nerve-gas program, it is not possible to know whether the nerve-gas formulas passed to the Russians by Operation SHOCKER led, directly or indirectly, to the development of Novichok. But there is evidence that information obtained by Soviet intelligence about the American nerve-gas program did influence Moscow's own decisions and efforts.

Vil Mirzayanov said that both the Soviet version of VX, known as Agent 33, and binary weapons, such as Novichok, "were developed in response to American programs and Soviet intelligence. I sometimes saw intelligence information, sourced to American sources but not to individuals. No other country had nerve-gas research. We even knew what chemicals were developed in what laboratories.

"In 1965, when I started at the research institute, there was no talk of binary weapons. In the early seventies, work began here on binary. I think we saw some intelligence information." Some of that information could have come from the Joint Chiefs via Operation SHOCKER. Data about GJ—the nerve gas pursued but never attained as a weapon by American scientists—was passed to the GRU between 1966 and 1969; the formula supposedly would have produced a result in binary form.

Mirzayanov said that in the early 1960s, the Soviets obtained VX from the United States through intelligence and had synthesized it in Volgograd by 1963. "The people who did it got the Lenin Prize. Leonid Zaharovich Soborovsky was one, and a woman named Ia Danilovna Shilakova. She was the first to synthesize Agent 33. We know the formula for VX, but the Americans don't know our Agent 33 formula. Agent 33 is a binary weapon, a combination of two chemicals."

One reason that Mirzayanov risked all by going public, he said, was that the Soviets had concealed Novichok from the world. In September 1992, negotiations were completed in Geneva on the Chemical Weapons Convention, which requires participating countries to declare and then destroy all chemical-warfare stocks. The United States and Russia have signed and ratified the treaty. But as Mirzayanov noted,

Novichok was not listed by Russia among the types of nerve gas it possessed.

Five years after signing the treaty, Moscow had still not acknowledged Novichok in its inventory of nerve gases. In 1998, however, a senior U.S. arms-control official, who spoke on condition of anonymity, confirmed the existence of Novichok. Although both sides have pledged to dispose of their chemical weapons, and began to do so after signing the Chemical Weapons Convention, the Russians still possess the unacknowledged super nerve gas—a weapon that, if ever produced in sufficient quantities, could be used to instantly kill millions of Americans.

Until Vil Mirzayanov spoke out, however, no one knew that the Soviets had developed Novichok. He was convinced that the reason the Russian government wanted to keep the existence of the powerful nerve gas secret was to avoid having to destroy it under the Chemical Weapons Convention.

On January 24, 1994, the closed trial of Mirzayanov began in Moscow City Court. He was charged with revealing state secrets. At the time that Mirzayanov went public, however, the laws dealing with chemical weapons were themselves secret. Mirzayanov and his lawyer argued that under Russia's new constitution, a person could not be convicted on the basis of secret laws.

Mirzayanov told the author that he was charged with violating part 1, the state secrets section, of article 75 of Russia's criminal code. "There is a top-secret list of what constitutes state secrets," Mirzayanov related. "As soon as you are put in prison, you are told there is such a list. I was shown the list once, so was my lawyer, but we were only allowed to keep it for one day and not copy it." It was, he said, "just like Kafka."

The scientist refused to participate in or testify at a secret trial. Predictably, three days later, Mirzayanov was arrested again and held for almost a month, this time at Matrosskaya Tishina, a maximum-security prison in Moscow.

U.S. Ambassador Thomas Pickering issued a statement in support of Mirzayanov, protesting that "someone could be either prosecuted or persecuted for telling the truth about an activity which is contrary to a treaty obligation of a foreign government."

Around the world, human-rights activists rallied to Mirzayanov's cause. Their efforts were spurred in the United States by two determined women in Princeton, New Jersey, environmental activists Gale M. Colby and Irene Goldman, who bombarded opinion leaders, journalists, members of Congress and others with faxes and updates on the Mirzayanov case.

Then in February, a month after the trial began, Mirzayanov was among the first persons to be freed from prison under a new habeas corpus law. He went home to Nuria and his sons, but the charges were not dropped. Finally, on March 11, Russia's chief prosecutor closed the case for what a spokesperson said was lack of evidence.

Mirzayanov was free. But the Russians still had Novichok.

CHAPTER

21

CASSIDY'S RUN

In many ways, Operation SHOCKER was a microcosm of the cold war. Like so much that happened during that unique and dangerous period, it was conducted in secret. It ran for twenty-three years, which made it the longest espionage operation of its kind in the history of the cold war. It was marked by success, failure, triumph, and tragedy.

SHOCKER was a classic illustration of how the cold war was fought by the intelligence agencies of the two sides, largely unseen by the public. For more than four decades, the often dangerous games of espionage were played in the shadows. The opposing armies clashed in a silent war known only to the combatants.

Operation SHOCKER and the two cases it spawned, PALMETTO and IXORA, demonstrated both the lengths to which Soviet intelligence went to seek to penetrate America's defenses and the efforts of the FBI's counterintelligence agents to contain the threat and protect the nation's security. In the process, both sides experienced gains and losses.

SHOCKER, as this book has revealed, cost the lives of two FBI agents. It may arguably have placed the lives of many more Americans at risk by providing Soviet scientists with the formula for a secret, albeit unstable, nerve gas—information that might have proved useful or spurred the Russians to accomplish a breakthrough in that deadly field.

At the same time, SHOCKER achieved many of its intelligence goals. Ten Soviet spies were identified, including three illegals: the PALMETTOS and IXORA.[1] The surfacing of the illegals, rare in the annals of espionage, alone justified the lengthy counterintelligence operation, at least in the view of the FBI agents who ran it.

By the questions the Soviets put to WALLFLOWER, the FBI and the Pentagon discovered a good deal about what the Russians knew and did not know about American military strength and secrets. The United States also learned more about how the Soviets recruited and ran American agents and more about their tradecraft techniques as well, from hollow rocks, new chemicals for secret writing, and rollover cameras, to codes and communications.

In addition, the six Soviets sent to handle Joe Cassidy were kept busy running a controlled source, which left them less time to recruit and run real spies. From defectors and Soviet scientists now in America, the FBI obtained fragmentary feedback indicating that the Russians had wasted time and money trying to replicate or counter GJ, the nerve-gas formula fed to them by Joe Cassidy. But as Vil Mirzayanov disclosed, they also developed Novichok.

Operation SHOCKER was only one skirmish in a much larger war.

---

[1] The ten spies were the six Soviets who handled Joe Cassidy, IXORA's control, and the three illegals. The six Soviet handlers were Boris M. Polikarpov, Gennady Dimitrievich Fursa, Boris G. Kolodjazhnyi, Mikhail I. Danilin, Oleg Ivanovich Likhachev, and Vladimir Vybornov. The seventh Soviet spy was Nikolai I. Alenochkin, IXORA's handler. The three illegals were Gilberto Lopez y Rivas, and his wife, Alicia Lopez, the PALMETTOS; and Edmund Freundlich, IXORA.

Both superpowers were secretly working at full tilt to develop hideous nerve-gas weapons. If the sarin and VX brewed in the labs of Edgewood or the soman and Novichok produced in the plants along the Volga had ever been unleashed in war, millions of people might have perished. Few Americans or Russians knew about the secret research conducted and the nerve-gas weapons produced in their respective countries.

During the cold war, the world lived with the constant threat of nuclear annihilation. The essential insanity of the period was captured by a single, familiar acronym: The nuclear strategy of the United States, mirrored by that of the Soviets, was officially called Mutual Assured Destruction (MAD).

As the cold war has receded into history, the nuclear danger has diminished but by no means disappeared. Today, there is increased concern over the threat of biological and chemical warfare. The 1995 sarin attack in the Tokyo subways and the emergence of terrorism at home— including the bombings of the World Trade Center in New York and the federal building in Oklahoma City—have led to greater public awareness that the new peril might come not from the atom but from weapons of all kinds, including a droplet of nerve gas or a microscopic anthrax spore.

The vulnerability of American civilians and the nation's military forces to chemical and biological warfare has become a politically volatile issue. Gulf War syndrome, the unexplained illness that has struck thousands of U.S. troops who served in the 1991 war against Iraq, is blamed by many veterans and at least some experts on exposure to nerve gas. After years of denials, the Pentagon admitted in 1996 that American troops might have been exposed to nerve gas when combat engineers blew up an ammunition dump at Khamisiyah in southern Iraq in March 1991.[2]

The political sensitivity of anything to do with nerve gas might explain why the Pentagon has refused to make any information available

---

[2] A CIA report released in 1997 provided further details; the munitions stored at the site included 122 mm "binary sarin" rockets "filled with a mixture of GB and GF."

about Operation SHOCKER. The Defense Department, it can be assumed safely, does not want to explain why it approved passing *any* data about nerve gas to the Russians, especially information about a nerve gas for which there is no known antidote, even though the gas was never perfected and put into production.

One of the army intelligence agents who worked on Operation SHOCKER for many years had a son who served in the Gulf War. He spoke about the risks of the deception phase of Operation SHOCKER but would not allow his name to be used. Even so, he was extremely reticent and guarded in his comments, until suddenly he blurted out, "Wouldn't it be a shame if you killed your kid because of something stupid you did twenty years ago?"

Behind his comment were presumptions that the information passed from Edgewood to Moscow in some way enhanced the Soviet nerve-gas program and that the Russians in turn helped Saddam Hussein to acquire chemical weapons. But the extent of such aid is uncertain. Vil Mirzayanov has asserted that the Soviets gave Iraq Agent 33 and perhaps other chemical weapons, although he also said he was sure that Novichok was not sent to Iraq.

Some of the people involved in the Iraqi chemical-weapons program did study in the Soviet Union. For example, Dr. Emad el-Ani, a leading Iraqi chemical-weapons expert, studied at the Timoshenko Defense Academy, the Soviet chemical-warfare school in Moscow. And in 1995, Russia's Federal Security Service (FSB) said it had blocked an attempt by Lieutenant General Anatoly Kuntsevich, former deputy chief of Soviet chemical-weapons forces, to sell five tons of nerve-gas components to Syria. The FSB reportedly concluded that the chemicals were really destined for Iraq.

According to American officials, there is little evidence that Iraq received significant assistance from the Soviets in procuring or producing its supplies of nerve gas. One high-level U.S. arms-control official said that Saddam Hussein obtained the equipment he needed to manufacture nerve gas mostly from Western European companies. The chemicals themselves, such as ordinary alcohol and organophosphate compounds, are easily available. "It is probably not beyond the ability of a reasonable Ph.D. in organic chemistry to mix the stuff together," the official said. "It's not clear they would need help from the Soviets."

A CIA official cautioned that the agency had only fragmentary information on possible Soviet help to Iraq's nerve-gas production and added, "By the mid–nineteen eighties, they [the Iraqis] had pretty much indigenous capability. They did not have to go outside."

Charles A. Duelfer, the deputy chairman of the United Nations Special Commission (UNSCOM), which was created after the Gulf War to search for Iraqi weapons of mass destruction, said, "We have no firm evidence that there was direct Soviet involvement in the Iraqi chemical program. . . . Which is not to say it didn't happen, but we haven't seen any direct evidence."

Few of the scientists on either side seemed to have many regrets about their role in developing nerve gas; Vil Mirzayanov and Saul Hormats were the exception, not the rule. "Millions of civilians will die if nerve gas is used," Hormats, the former director of development at Edgewood, said in an interview with the author. "We would kill a whole generation of babies." Hormats worked at Edgewood for thirty-seven years, and his views changed only gradually. "Had we gone to war with the Soviets in the nineteen fifties, CW would have been a decisive weapon," he said. "We would have won more battles, and less of our soldiers would have become casualties. My responsibility was to help our army fight the war with minimum casualties and the greatest chance of success. As for morality, is it more moral to kill a soldier, to disembowel him and leave him to die, or to have him take a whiff of gas and die in five minutes? Which is more moral? The immorality—and half a dozen generals would say same thing—is the sons of bitches who get us into war, not how the war is fought."

By the early 1980s, however, Hormats's opinion of nerve gas had changed sharply. "Because by then it was a war against civilians, the Soviet army would not be harmed. They had masks and protective gear.

CW would not contribute to our winning the war. A chemical war in the fifties was moral; a chemical war in the eighties would have had no effect on winning the war and would only have harmed civilians."

Hormats, white haired and in his mid-eighties when interviewed, had lost none of his intellectual vigor. "War is a failure of democracy and of government," he said. "We ought to worry more about getting into wars, not how we fight them."

It is easy and even fashionable to say with the benefit of hindsight that the cold war was a useless conflict or that intelligence operations such as SHOCKER ultimately had no impact on the outcome. But those arguments overlook an essential truth. One does not have to resort to Reaganesque rhetoric about evil empires to understand that there is a critical difference between democratic institutions and totalitarian governments.

Indeed, the history of the twentieth century is the history of the battle between democracy and dictatorship, between governments, however imperfect, where the people rule and governments of the right or left whose rulers crush freedom to maintain their power. The cold war was a part of that larger conflict. It was fought, to a considerable extent, by the intelligence agencies on both sides. The men and women who carried out these operations believed they were doing what was right in that time and place.

Looking back, few regret the effort. Colin T. Thompson participated in the hidden war for several decades, mostly in Asia, as a clandestine officer of the CIA. He is a thoughtful man, far from a gung-ho defender of all of the agency's schemes and operations. But, reflecting on the cold war years, he asked: "What were we supposed to do? Let the Soviets take over the world?"

That same conviction—that somehow the battle needed to be fought, even if the victories were few and limited—motivated men such as Phil Parker, Jack O'Flaherty, Gene Peterson, Charlie Bevels, Jimmy Morrissey, Mark Kirkland, Tren Basford, and the other FBI agents who participated over the years in Operation SHOCKER.

But the central figure, upon whom the entire operation depended, was Joseph Edward Cassidy, a plain American soldier, who saw his duty and performed it without question even as it took over, and at times could have endangered, his life. None of the frustrations of the operation—the escape of the PALMETTOS, or the risky decision to pass information about nerve gas to the Russians—in any way detracts from his own service.

For twenty-one years, Cassidy successfully pretended to be a traitor to his country, an Aldrich Ames inside the United States Army. He played his extraordinary role to perfection and never once slipped up to betray his true loyalty. In an age of few heroes, Joe Cassidy was a genuine American hero.

"Cassidy," Phil Parker said, "had a good run."

During the life of the operation, more than 4,500 pages of classified documents, all cleared by the Joint Chiefs of Staff, were passed to the Soviets in exchange for hundreds of thousands of dollars. One former bureau official with knowledge of the case said the Russians paid their "agent" more than $200,000. The FBI would not divulge the overall cost of the operation.

Gilberto Lopez y Rivas and his wife resumed their academic careers after their precipitous return to Mexico in 1978. Their past remained a secret. But some of Lopez's former colleagues at the University of Minnesota later heard additional shards of information about the pair.

The story that Lopez was only helping the Cubans circulated after he left the campus, but Professor Rolando Hinojosa-Smith learned something more when he ran into Lopez at a conference in Mexico. "I went to teach creative writing at the University of the Americas in Puebla in the late seventies. He came down to see me because I was chairman of department, and he had left all of a sudden, and he apologized. But he said he can't come back to us. I said, 'Well, you broke a contract but that's not irreparable, it was only a summer course.' He said it was impossible for him to come back. He said, 'I'm a member of the Communist Party.' "

In the 1980s, Lopez gained media attention in Mexico as a firebrand anti-American activist. In May 1983, for example, after the murder of navy Lieutenant Commander Albert Schaufelberger, an American military official, in El Salvador, Lopez led a street demonstration of four thousand people that blocked rush-hour traffic in Mexico City for hours.

"The death of the North American is the natural result of U.S. intervention in the country," Lopez declared. "Latin American nations have the right to assassinate those people who meddle in internal affairs in a direct manner." The marchers outside the American embassy chanted: "If you don't want to die, leave Salvador."[3]

By the 1990s, Lopez had become prominent in Mexican politics as a leading member of the Party of the Democratic Revolution (PRD), the main opposition party of the left in Mexico.

In late March 1991, Lopez was in Moscow again, this time as a participant in a three-day conference on "Lenin and the 20th Century." Although the Soviet Union was only nine months away from collapse, *Pravda*, the Communist Party newspaper, reported the event in familiar phrases, referring to Lenin as "our great compatriot."[4]

While researching this book, the author discovered that Lopez was working at the Instituto Nacional de Antropología e Historia in San Angel, a section of Mexico City. At the time, his wife, Alicia, was teaching in the anthropology department of the Universidad Autónoma Metropolitana in nearby Ixtapalapa.

In a telephone conversation, Lopez was asked whether he would be willing to be interviewed. From his reaction, it was clear that the call came as a big surprise. "Well," he said carefully, "I have to consider my position here and that of my wife."[5]

It was pointed out that Lopez was safely in Mexico and could talk about whatever he had done if he wished. Besides, the cold war was

---

[3] "Leader of Protest March Calls U.S. Adviser's Death 'Logical,' " United Press International, May 27, 1983. Schaufelberger, thirty-three, of San Diego, was one of six members of a group assigned to El Salvador to coordinate military aid. He was shot in the head four times while waiting in a car for a friend on a college campus in San Salvador.

[4] The newspaper's account mentioned Lopez as one of four notable foreign speakers.

[5] More recently, word filtered back to FBI headquarters in Washington that Gilberto and Alicia Lopez had divorced.

over. Lopez said he would meet with the author if he came to Mexico, but he was not promising an interview. Soon afterward, Manuel Guerrero called the author from Minnesota. Lopez, he said, had thought about the request and definitely would not agree to an interview.

In 1997, Lopez was elected to the Mexican Chamber of Deputies, the lower house of the Mexican Congress. As a PRD congressman, Lopez became the spokesperson, and for a time the head, of the congressional commission attempting to mediate the conflict in Chiapas, where Zapatista rebels took up arms in 1994, calling for more democracy and Indian rights.

In the summer of 1998, Lopez accused President Ernesto Zedillo of escalating the Chiapas conflict and preparing to crush the rebels militarily. The federal and state governments, he said, "displace the Chiapas indigenous people from their communities, they massacre them; they pursue them; they torture them, and they jail them."[6] In July, when two U.S. diplomats were detained by suspicious villagers in Chiapas, Lopez called their presence "open meddling" in Mexican affairs.[7]

Until the publication of this book, Lopez's previous secret life as a Soviet spy was undisclosed. His term as a member of the Chamber of Deputies is up in 2000.

Early in May 1981, Freundlich, having cooperated with the FBI for three years, was asked by the bureau to approach his Soviet control, Nikolai Alenochkin. From the unexpected contact by the illegal, Alenochkin would immediately surmise that IXORA had been compromised.

Dan LeSaffre was IXORA's case agent when the bureau orchestrated the approach. "Our objective was to get rid of Alenochkin," he said. "Once he's been approached by IXORA, he has to report it." And once he reported the contact, he might be sent back to Moscow.

---

[6] Associated Press, June 11, 1998.
[7] The *Houston Chronicle*, July 31, 1998, p. A28.

"We did not expect to turn Alenochkin, a heavy-duty GRU man," said the FBI's Jack Lowe. "But it might cast a shadow on Alenochkin with his own people. It makes them rethink all the cases and freeze other operations."

Alenochkin was serving his third tour in the United States. He had handled IXORA in the 1970s and had returned to New York a little over a year earlier. The FBI believed he was the deputy resident of the GRU station inside the Soviet mission.

When an approach of this sort took place, LeSaffre said, the Soviet officer "would often go under 'house arrest.' . . . He would never be alone. There would always be someone with him, even to drive to the office."

From the bureau's point of view, there was a logical reason to disrupt the GRU's operations and attempt to force Alenochkin's departure from New York. True, he would simply be replaced. "But when you start replacing officers they are usually not as good," LeSaffre explained. "When you get rid of a top-grade officer like Alenochkin, you may get a lesser one in his place."

For the encounter with Alenochkin, Edmund Freundlich wore a tiny recorder for two reasons: so that the FBI's counterintelligence agents could gauge Alenochkin's reaction and to make sure that IXORA followed instructions and did not try to deceive the bureau.

The ploy succeeded. Alenochkin, who normally could have been expected to remain in Manhattan another two or three years, was abruptly recalled to Moscow on August 7, a little more than a month after IXORA approached him.[8]

Edmund Freundlich died in New York at age seventy-one on the day after Christmas 1990. His nephew, Robert, lived in a New York City sub-

---

[8] The approach to Alenochkin was one of the last moves in Operation SHOCKER, which ran from its beginnings in 1958 until 1981, when Alenochkin was contacted by IXORA and Danilin left Canada. Within that time frame, Cassidy's own role extended almost twenty-one years, from the day he was dangled to the GRU in March 1959 at the YMCA in Washington until his final telephone call to the Soviet mission in New York in October 1979.

urb with his wife, Jill. They were flabbergasted to learn from the author that Uncle Edmund had been a Russian spy.

"I had a sense he had in some way been active pursuing his communist leanings," Robert said. "But I didn't know it involved doing anything that remotely approached espionage."

Jill Freundlich could scarcely believe that this kindly, avuncular man had a secret life. "Everybody loved Uncle Eddie," she said. "I have two children and there are several others in the family. He loved children."

When Jill and Robert Freundlich cleaned out Edmund's apartment, they kept few of his possessions. "There were many letters signed 'Amigo,' Edmund's unknown friend, that Robert found . . . ," Jill said, "but he threw them away."

There was one keepsake she recalled, however, that perhaps, in retrospect, revealed something of the inner life of the man who had survived the Nazis, then toiled at a nondescript job for Robert Maxwell while living a double life as a spy for Moscow, waiting for the telephone call that might signal nuclear Armageddon.

"He had his mother's notebook," Jill remembered, "with a four-leaf clover in it."

Mikhail Danilin was still working for the GRU in Moscow as late as 1993. According to a friend, he had broken a leg and then was hospitalized with a heart attack late that year. In 1994, he died in Moscow.

Boris Libman, who ran the soman plant for the Soviets after he was let out of prison, emigrated to the United States in 1990 and eight years later was living quietly in an East Coast city.[9]

Vil Mirzayanov, too, came to the United States in 1995, after all charges against him were dropped. He was admitted under a law that assists Soviet scientists in emigrating. His wife and sons joined him, but

---

[9] His son, Michael, had preceded him. Because the family is Jewish, Michael, who is also a chemist, received permission to leave the Soviet Union for Israel. From there, he made his way to the United States. Libman then came to visit his son and received permission from the immigration authorities to stay.

the marriage broke up. In December 1997, Mirzayanov married Gale Colby, the activist from Princeton who had rallied to his cause.

Robert Schamay, the FBI man who was pulled off the mountain to go to Minnesota in 1976, was shot during a bank robbery in Salt Lake City in 1982.[10] Schamay recovered from his wound and retired to the Sun Belt seven years later.

Charles Elmore, the young FBI agent who had translated the PAL-METTO wiretaps in Minneapolis, won his desired transfer to California after the Lopezes fled to Mexico. On August 9, 1979, he had just begun work for the day in the small resident agency in El Centro, California, 110 miles east of San Diego, when James Maloney, an employee of the federal job-training program, walked into the office with a shotgun and killed Elmore and a second FBI agent, Robert Porter, then shot and killed himself. Maloney had been arrested and questioned by the FBI seven years earlier after an anti–Vietnam War protest in San Francisco.[11]

Jack Lowe, one of the FBI agents who had helped to turn IXORA, was working at bureau headquarters in the 1990s. On his desk he kept a small gift, a memento to which no one paid any particular attention, a nail clipper bearing the insignia of the Queen's Guards.

Phil Parker retired to his native Virginia, where he worked as a security consultant. Joe Cassidy's case agents, Jack O'Flaherty, Charlie Bevels, Jimmy Morrissey, and Donald Gruentzel, have all retired. O'Flaherty lived not far from the Cassidys, and their families remained close over the years.

Joe and Marie Cassidy retired anonymously to the Sun Belt, revealing to no one their double lives. They did not tell their friends and family;

---

[10] Schamay and another FBI agent were depositing some evidence money in the bank, when the bank robber made the mistake of getting in line behind them. Schamay was shot in the shoulder but helped to subdue the man, Robert James Anderson, who was convicted and sentenced to twenty-five years for attempted bank robbery and ten years for assault on a federal officer with a deadly weapon.

[11] Elmore thus became the third FBI agent to be killed, at least indirectly, in Operation SHOCKER; he had volunteered to go to Minnesota to work on the PALMETTO case as a way to get back to the West Coast.

even Cassidy's own son and daughter knew nothing of his years as a spy. To their neighbors, the Cassidys seemed a typical older couple. Marie remained active in dancing and theatrics in the pleasant community where they lived, and Joe, to those who knew him, appeared to be a genial, retired army sergeant, just another ordinary American content to live out his golden years peacefully in the sunshine.

Julie Kirkland remarried and built a new life for herself in the far West. But she has never forgotten her years with Mark. Their sons are grown men now.

The government never formally acknowledged to her that Mark Kirkland died while working on an espionage case for the FBI. In April 1991, however, the bureau held a ceremony at its new Minneapolis field office at which both Kirkland and Tren Basford were given official recognition for their service. Julie and her children were there, along with Tish Basford and her son and granddaughter.

At the ceremony, a wall was unveiled in which the names of the two agents, and other FBI agents who had died in the line of duty, are inscribed. On behalf of Mark, Julie Kirkland received the FBI's purple cross, which the bureau gives to the families of fallen agents, and a citation. The citation did not say anything about national security or espionage, but she was told the truth informally. That day, Julie Kirkland said, "was the first I got the name of the case—PALMETTO. Dennis Conway told me."

The purple cross rests in a walnut box. The medal is a five-pointed gold cross that surrounds a medallion with a purple star at its center. It hangs below a white ribbon with a purple center stripe. Officially, the medal is known as the FBI Memorial Star.

A brass plate on the box bears these engraved words: "In memory of Mark A. Kirkland, Special Agent, Federal Bureau of Investigation, United States Department of Justice. In honor of Special Agent Kirkland who lost his life in a plane crash in Dewey Lake, Minnesota, on August 25, 1977, while conducting an aerial surveillance for the FBI in connection with a highly sensitive matter. Mr. Kirkland's performance in this case was in the highest traditions of the Bureau and this special acknowledgment is presented in his memory. William S. Sessions, Director, April 26, 1991."

Julie Kirkland treasures the purple cross. She keeps it in a place of honor, on a shelf in the dining room of her home.

"I think I'll give it to my son Kenny," she said. "It means a lot to him. He was only three, but he remembers his father."

It was in 1991, a few months before the collapse of the Soviet Union, that I first heard fragmentary reports of an extraordinary espionage case that had lasted for more than two decades during the height of the cold war.

In the course of the operation, I was told, two FBI agents had been killed while engaged in aerial surveillance. Secret nerve-gas formulas had been passed to the Soviets as part of a massive but potentially dangerous deception operation. A Mexican couple was involved, but the Justice Department had allowed them to escape at the last moment.

Not one word of the dramatic case had ever been made public. It remained locked in the government's classified files. Researching the story would be, to say the least, a challenge.

I began to try. At the heart of the operation, I learned, was an American double agent. I found out that he was a noncommissioned army officer, but for five years, for perhaps understandable reasons, no one would tell me his name or where he was.

I did discover the identity of Mikhail Danilin, his principal Soviet control, however. With the support and encouragement of Mike Sullivan, the executive producer of television's *Frontline*, I went to Moscow in 1993 to try to find and interview him and to see if I could learn more about the case from Russian officials or files. Where to begin? There are no telephone books in Moscow, but through my contacts I was fortunate enough to find someone who knew Danilin and got in touch with him at my request. Word came back that Danilin was close to retirement but still worked for the GRU and could not speak with me. Still playing his role as a spy, Danilin claimed through my intermediary that "he had nothing to do with the case. It belonged to someone else."

I knew better, but the Danilin route was blocked. The Soviet Ministry of Defense refused to answer any questions about the case. Soon after I left Moscow, Danilin died. I later spoke with his widow, Margarita, but she declined to provide any information about him or his career.

The Pentagon was no more forthcoming than the Soviets. My requests for files under the Freedom of Information Act brought the misleading reply that the army had "no record" of the case. In 1996, I approached Kenneth H. Bacon, the assistant secretary of defense for public affairs, who was responsive and asked the then secretary of the army, Togo D. West, Jr., to review the matter. Secretary West agreed. After many months I was told that yes, the files existed after all, but, no, nothing would be released, for reasons of national security.

Around the same time, however, I learned the identity of the American double agent and gained his cooperation and that of his wife, who had shared his secret life. It was a major breakthrough in my knowledge of what the Joint Chiefs of Staff had called Operation SHOCKER. Over time, I was able to interview many former FBI agents, who gradually began to provide details of the case and its two offshoots, PALMETTO and IXORA. A number of Pentagon sources cautiously talked to me as well. The more I learned, the more I realized that SHOCKER was emblematic of how the cold war had been fought in secret by the intelligence agencies of the two superpowers.

All the while, I appealed to the FBI to open its case files and assist me in telling the story. Although some of the bureau's senior counterintelligence officials felt that with the end of the cold war the story could now be told, they were unwilling to help unless the army also agreed to make information available, and it refused. There the matter remained until finally, late in 1997, John F. Lewis, Jr., FBI assistant director in charge of the national-security division, broke the logjam. Beginning in the summer of 1998, Lewis and James T. "Tim" Caruso, head of the FBI section concerned with Russian intelligence, provided limited but valuable assistance that helped greatly in my understanding of the history of the PALMETTO and IXORA cases. They also made it possible for me to interview several current and former agents who might not otherwise have talked with me.

To research this book, I conducted some 450 interviews with almost 200 persons. I am indebted first and foremost to Joe and Marie Cassidy, who spoke to me at length and answered all of my questions with abiding patience and good humor. I shall always value their friendship and generous assistance.

Julie Kirkland, the widow of Special Agent Mark A. Kirkland, was enormously helpful and also earned my enduring gratitude. I am greatly indebted as well to Letitia Basford, whose husband, Special Agent Trenwith S. Basford, perished in the same plane crash.

Many present and former FBI agents helped me to tell this story, even though they understood that the operation, like any human endeavor, was not without risk, flaws, and problems, along with its considerable successes. Among the retired agents to whom I am especially indebted are Phillip A. Parker, John J. O'Flaherty, Eugene C. Peterson, and Charles Bevels. Many others helped, including James E. Nolan, Jr., James F. Morrissey, Robert J. Schamay, Charles T. Weis, James E. Lancaster, Edgar Dade, Douglas MacDougall, Donald F. Lord, Richard McCarthy, Robert C. Loughney, John W. McKinnon, William O. Cregar, Carmen Espinoza, and Courtland J. Jones. Others preferred not to be identified, but I am equally appreciative of their help.

I am grateful as well to several officials and agents who were still working for the FBI as I researched the book. In addition to John Lewis and Tim Caruso, I am indebted to Bill Carter of the FBI's national press office; A. Jackson Lowe and Dan LeSaffre, who provided many details of the fascinating IXORA case; as well as Aurelio Flores, Leslie G. Wiser, Jr., Sheila Horan, Dennis Conway, Ronald J. Van Vranken, and William M. Clifford. Before he retired in 1994, R. Patrick Watson, then deputy director of the FBI's intelligence division, also helped.

Robert and Jill Freundlich were generous in sharing their recollections and photographs of Edmund Freundlich, IXORA. I very much appreciate the confidence they placed in me. Two former executives of Pergamon Press, Laszlo Straka and Robert Miranda, as well as Lori Miranda, filled in details about Edmund Freundlich's work at the publishing house.

Because the deception over nerve gas was central to the early stages of the operation, I needed to know much more about the secret research in chemical weapons conducted in this country and the former Soviet Union. I was able to find and speak to many scientists who had worked at Edgewood Arsenal, as well as Soviet scientists who had participated in their country's counterpart nerve-gas program.

My thanks in particular go to Saul Hormats, Benjamin L. Harris, William J. Weber, Jefferson C. Davis, Jr., Bernard Zeffert, and Edmund H. Schwanke. I was helped as well by some current officials at Edgewood, including Jim Allingham; Jeff Smart, the base historian; and William C. Dee, former manager of the binary nerve-gas program. Professor Matthew Meselson of Harvard provided an overview of this country's nerve-gas research and history. Other data was made available by Charles A. Duelfer of the United Nations Special Commission on Iraq.

I am especially indebted to Vil Mirzayanov, who provided detailed information about the Soviet nerve-gas program at considerable personal risk, and to his former wife, Nuria, as well as to Gale M. Colby and Irene Goldman. In Moscow, Lev Fedorov also shared his knowledge about Soviet nerve-gas weapons.

My research in Moscow also benefited from interviews with General Georgy Aleksandrovich Mikhailov, deputy director of the GRU for ten years in the 1980s; Georgi Arbatov, director of the USA-Canada Institute; Yuri G. Kobaladze and Oleg Tsarev of the SVR, the Russian intelligence service; and Mikhail P. Lyubimov and Boris A. Solomatin, former senior officers of the foreign-intelligence directorate of the KGB. I had generous help as well from Joseph Albright and Marcia Kunstel, then the Cox Newspapers' correspondents in Moscow. Yuri H. Totrov, a former KGB counterintelligence specialist, was interviewed in Washington, and Victor Gundarev, a former KGB officer now living in the United States, provided additional data.

My special thanks also go to Taro Yoshihashi, the former double-agent specialist for the army chief of staff for intelligence, who patiently walked me through the complex web of secret boards that created and approved deception operations for the Pentagon. Brigadier General Charles F. Scanlon, former head of INSCOM, the army intelligence command, provided valuable guidance in the early stages of my research. Henry A. Strecker, another former army intelligence official, was also helpful, as were Harold F. St. Aubin, a former chemical- and biological-warfare specialist for the Defense Intelligence Agency, and several former officers of army intelligence. I also appreciate the efforts of Kenneth Bacon on my behalf.

Several colleagues of Gilberto Lopez y Rivas at the University of Minnesota were kind enough to share their recollections of him. They included Arturo Madrid, Frank Miller, Manuel Guerrero, Alfredo Gonzales, and Rolando Hinojosa-Smith.

Several friends and former colleagues helped generously, and I am particularly grateful to them. They include Thomas B. Ross, my coauthor on three books; Andrew J. Glass, senior correspondent of the Cox Newspapers Washington bureau; and Joel Seidman.

Morton H. Halperin, Kenneth C. Bass III, Mark Lynch, Kate Martin, Robert L. Keuch, and Jonathan R. Turley all helped me to understand the rapidly changing laws, Supreme Court decisions, and presidential orders governing the FBI's warrantless investigative techniques during the period covered by this book. I am grateful for their advice on this complex subject.

Kristin Kenney Williams assisted in some of the early research, particularly in tracking down sources at the University of Minnesota who helped me to conclude that PALMETTO, whose identity I did not then know, was Professor Gilberto Lopez y Rivas. My thanks go to her, as well as to my brother, William A. Wise, who located the former executives of Pergamon Press and assisted with other research.

This is the eighth book on which I have been fortunate enough to have Robert D. Loomis, vice president and executive editor at Random House, as my editor. His talent is legendary, and deservedly so. I am grateful for his steadfast support on this book, which is dedicated to him, and for his friendship of more than three decades.

Finally, I am indebted, as always, to my wife, Joan, and to my two sons, Christopher and Jonathan, all of whom provided valuable advice and counsel along the way.

—David Wise
Washington, D.C.
June 16, 1999

INDEX

ABOUT THE AUTHOR

DAVID WISE is America's leading writer on intelligence and espionage. He is coauthor of *The Invisible Government*, a number one bestseller that has been widely credited with bringing about a reappraisal of the role of the CIA in a democratic society. He is the author of *Nightmover: How Aldrich Ames Sold the CIA to the KGB for $4.6 Million; Molehunt; The Spy Who Got Away; The American Police State*; and *The Politics of Lying* and coauthor with Thomas B. Ross of *The Espionage Establishment; The Invisible Government;* and *The U-2 Affair*. Mr. Wise has also written three espionage novels, *The Samarkand Dimension; The Children's Game;* and *Spectrum*. A native New Yorker and graduate of Columbia College, he is the former chief of the Washington bureau of the *New York Herald Tribune* and has contributed articles on government and politics to many national magazines. He is married and has two sons.

ABOUT THE TYPE

This book was set in Photina, a typeface designed by José Mendoza in 1971. It is a very elegant design with high legibility, and its close character fit has made it a popular choice for use in quality magazines and art gallery publications.